Defoe's Politics

This study of Defoe's politics aims to challenge the critical demand that we see Defoe as a "modern" and to counter misrepresentations of his political writings by restoring them to their seventeenth-century contexts. It recovers his traditional, conservative, and anti-Lockean ideas on contemporary issues: the origins of society, the role of the people in the establishment of a political community, and how monarchies are created and maintained as the means of achieving a beneficent political order. A full contextual examination of Defoe's years as a political reporter and journalist (1689–1715) reveals his dissatisfaction with the intrusive demands of parliaments, his inherent royalism, and his awareness of the military revolution in his time. At the heart of Defoe's political imagination Manuel Schonhorn finds the vision of a warrior-king, derived from sources in the Bible and in ancient and English history. This model illuminates his original reading of Defoe's greatest political fiction, *Robinson Crusoe*, which emerges less in terms of a family romance, a tract for the rising bourgeoisie or a Lockean parable of government, than as a dramatic re-enactment of Defoe's lifelong political pre-occupations concerning society, government, and kingship.

CAMBRIDGE STUDIES IN EIGHTEENTH-CENTURY
ENGLISH LITERATURE AND THOUGHT 9

Defoe's Politics

The growth in recent years of eighteenth-century studies has prompted the establishment of this series of books devoted to the period. The series is designed to accommodate monographs and critical studies on authors, works, genres and other aspects of literary culture from the later part of the seventeenth century to the end of the eighteenth. Since academic engagement with this field has become an increasingly interdisciplinary enterprise, books will be especially encouraged which in some way stress the cultural context of the literature, or examine it in relation to contemporary art, music, philosophy, historiography, religion, politics, social affairs, and so on.

Titles Published

Defoe's Politics
Parliament, Power, Kingship, and Robinson Crusoe

MANUEL SCHONHORN

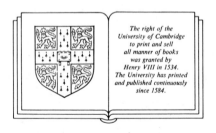

The right of the
University of Cambridge
to print and sell
all manner of books
was granted by
Henry VIII in 1534.
The University has printed
and published continuously
since 1584.

CAMBRIDGE UNIVERSITY PRESS

CAMBRIDGE
NEW YORK PORT CHESTER
MELBOURNE SYDNEY

Published by the Press Syndicate of the University of Cambridge
The Pitt Building, Trumpington Street, Cambridge CB2 1RP
40 West 20th Street, New York, NY 10011, USA
10 Stamford Road, Oakleigh, Melbourne 3166, Australia

First published 1991

Printed in Great Britain at the University Press, Cambridge

British Library cataloguing in publication data
Schonhorn, Manuel
Defoe's Politics : Parliament, Power, Kingship, and Robinson Crusoe – (Cambridge
studies in eighteenth-century English literature and thought: 9).
1. Fiction in English. Defoe, Daniel, 1661?–1731
I. Title
823'.5

Library of Congress cataloguing in publication data
Schonhorn, Manuel.
Defoe's Politics : Parliament, Power, Kingship and Robinson Crusoe / Manuel Schonhorn.
p.   cm. – (Cambridge studies in eighteenth-century English literature and thought: 9)
Includes bibliographical references
Includes index.
ISBN 0-521-38452-4
1. Defoe, Daniel, 1661?–1731 – Political and social views.
2. Defoe, Daniel, 1661?–1731. Robinson Crusoe.
3. Politics and literature – Great Britain – History – 18th century.
4. Political fiction. English – History and criticism.
5. Great Britain – Politics and government – 1660–1714.
I. Title. II. Series.
PR3408. P6S36   1991
823'.5 – dc20   90–2067   CIP

ISBN 0 521 38452 4 hardback

GG

Contents

For Bonnie

Even now
I know that I have savored the hot taste of life
Lifting green cups and gold at the great feast.
Just for a small and forgotten time
I have had full in my eyes from off my girl
The whitest pouring of eternal light.

(From the *Caurapañcāsikā*, the Sanskrit freely translated as
Black Marigolds by E. Powys Mathers)

Preface and acknowledgments

With Defoe we have all too often read the present into the past and judged and commended him because he anticipated *our* future rather than because he mirrored *his* present and *his* past. The following study presents a Defoe whose political ideas, while they were developed in the ideologically dense post-Revolution decade following the Allegiance controversy, rested on a firm Old Testament foundation. De-mythologizing the "Lockean" Defoe, this study returns him at the same time to the centrality of seventeenth-century political thought, with its rich biblical and constitutional contexts. Defoe has also been misinterpreted because we have failed to see his works as both propaganda and political theory. To understand Defoe rightly, he must be viewed as a writer concerned not only with this or that particular point of political policy, to paraphrase G. H. D. Cole, but also with the origins of government, the reasons for the successes and failures of political society, the ultimate principles of political obligation, and the nature of leadership at a historical crisis in western culture.

In this challenge to the traditional understanding of the "radical" Defoe, the "populist" Defoe, and his greatest political fiction, *Robinson Crusoe*, I hope that I will be considered as *more* than a certain meddlesome spirit, which, as Washington Irving wrote in his *Life and Voyages of Christopher Columbus*, "goes prying about the traces of history, casting down its monuments, and marring and mutilating its fairest trophies."

Years ago, writing on Defoe's maritime and pirate history, I incurred many debts as a result of my excursions in unfamiliar waters actual and metaphorical. Trying to make sense of some of the most turbulent decades in English politics, again I have many to thank, this time for helping me master the disciplines of history and political theory. Frank Bastian, Alan Downie, Frank Ellis, Howard Nenner, Henry Snyder and Martyn Thompson read, advised, and corrected much, always generously. I could have listened more and better. Richard Ashcraft, Stephen Baxter, Laura Curtis, Robert Eccleshall, P. N. Furbank, Mark Goldie, Henry Horwitz, Maximillian Novak, W. R. Owens, Spiro Peterson, J. G. A. Pocock, Clayton Roberts, Pat Rogers, W. A. Speck, Brian Tierney, and John Wallace helped. Howard Erskine-Hill and John Richetti guided me well to publication.

Permission to use previously published material was given by the editors of the University of California Press, the University of Wisconsin Press, and

Studies in the Literary Imagination. The Newberry Library had great faith in my project from its inception. The British Library, The New York Public Library and the William Andrews Clark Memorial Library always assisted with texts. Alan Martin Cohn, Humanities Librarian, Southern Illinois University-Carbondale, my colleague and friend, lived long enough to hold the finished text in his hands. His stylistic integrity breathes from every page. Without him and his superlative staff this book would have been impossible.

Mardi and Morris, though they did not do this Index, helped by just being around; I hope they did not suffer too much neglect.

My wife Bonnie endured. This, then, as she well knows, is truly her book.

A note on attributions

The recent publication of P. N. Furbank and W. R. Owens, *The Canonisation of Daniel Defoe* (New Haven: Yale University Press, 1988), has cast in doubt some of the works attributed to Defoe by bibliographers in the past two centuries. The following can be said about the "largely destructive" (p. 125) consequences of their study: rather than an attack on the canon, it is primarily a debunking of the methods of the canonizers. And the doubts exhibited extend primarily to the attributions of the post-Queen Anne years, from 1714 and beyond, during Defoe's Hanoverian tenure, when he was writing, in every possible and conflicting style and voice, tracts which supported, questioned, challenged, and humored the political and ideological confusions of the time; for example, the Walpole/Townsend faction's defection to the Tories, or the Bangorian controversy of 1717–18.

The authors' extended examination of what is, at least, "two Defoes" (p. 146), accommodates a portrait of an artist who was "contrary" (p. 142), "perverse" (p. 143), who revealed a "love of paradox" (p. 144), and had "no compunction about lying" (p. 148) – a compulsively complex personality with superior dramatic and impersonating abilities, who was capable of "working off secretive jokes on the public" (p. 148). In a word, in spite of their healthy and invigorating skepticism about the ascriptive procedures of their predecessors, the authors do not seriously undermine an eighteenth-century anecdotal tradition of a Daniel Defoe at a double desk, "whereon one (sic) he placed his *own Pamphlet*, & on the other he wrote *his own Answer to it*" (p. 11).

The following study of Defoe's political ideas rests on a secure foundation of works indisputably by Defoe. They are a part of the Defoe canon because Defoe himself put them there, by signing his initials to them or by claiming them in his collective works. Others we admit because of the preponderance of opinion and the consensus which has emerged from the historical record. And it should be remarked that the most intimate and revealing exposition of Defoe's political imagination, the most coherent definition of his psychology of leadership and his principles of political organization, is reaffirmed in his lengthy memorandum to his patron, Robert Harley, unsigned but in his own hand, preserved in the British Library. When there have been significant doubts about authorship I have indicated those doubts in the text and the notes.

Like Furbank and Owens, I suspect attributions based upon the recognition of favorite phrases. But also like them I have accepted Defoe's authorship of disputed texts because of certain idiomatic ''tics'' of style, but ''tics'' that, rather than being syntactical or grammatical, reveal themselves as weighty ideological counters in the transmission of his political ideas.

Abbreviations

Bastian, *Defoe's Early Life*	Frank Bastian, *Defoe's Early Life* (London: Macmillan, 1981)
Downie, *Robert Harley*	J. A. Downie, *Robert Harley and the Press: Propaganda and Public Opinion in the Age of Swift and Defoe* (Cambridge: Cambridge University Press, 1979)
Locke, *Two Treatises*	John Locke, *Two Treatises of Government*, ed. Peter Laslett (London: Cambridge University Press, 1967)
Moore, *Daniel Defoe*	John Robert Moore, *Daniel Defoe, Citizen of the Modern World* (Chicago: University of Chicago Press, 1958)
POAS	*Poems on Affairs of State: Augustan Satirical Verse, 1660–1714*, vol. VI, ed. F. H. Ellis (New Haven: Yale University Press, 1970)
Review	*Defoe's "Review," Reproduced from the Original Editions with an Introduction and Bibliographical Notes by Arthur Wellesley Secord*, 22 vols. (New York: Columbia University Press, 1938)
Somers Tracts	*A Collection of Scarce and Valuable Tracts on the Most Interesting and Entertaining Subjects*, 13 vols., ed. Walter Scott, 2nd ed. (London: T. Cadell, 1809–15)

Introduction

"Defoe war ein grosser Politiker." Such is the unequivocal conclusion of Hans-Dietrich Kuckuk's 1962 examination of Daniel Defoe's political ideas.[1] Though it would come as a surprise to Defoe's twentieth-century readers, it echoes the judgments of his eighteenth- and nineteenth-century ones. In the years following his death in 1731, nearly all of those commentators have responded to his political insights, which he derived from his supreme knowledge of the English people, their institutions, and their laws. Smollett admitted him to the ranks of "the most remarkable political writers of his age",[2] and a century later, in 1869, J. S. Keltie deemed him the heir of the political Milton, who, though he "arose at a different crisis of the nation's history, when all was confusion and turmoil, . . . saw the safety of the State rested as much upon the power of the pen as upon the power of the sword. The weapon that he could use, with more permanent effect than kings and parliaments could bring to bear, he used with unequalled persistency and success."[3]

But in the twentieth century, democracy and transformations in the genre of the novel have not served the political Defoe well. Writing always from the protagonist's point of view, Defoe came to be identified with the orphans and waifs, the put-upon females and the possessive individualists, of his fictions. Able to elicit the dominant "'liberal'" sympathies of our time, imbued with an emerging capitalist vigor that celebrated middle-class values, and consumed with the passion of a social reformer, Defoe struck the dominant chords of the present century. He became our contemporary. Tracts that had remained anonymous for years were attributed to him because they were "modern" in their propositions or because they seemed to champion the right causes or classes. In his handling of time, space, and tempo, he was pictured as a present-

---

[1] "Die Politischen Ideen Daniel Defoes," Diss., Christian-Albrechts-Universität (Kiel, 1962), p. 1.

[2] In his *History of England* (1757–58), cited in *Defoe: The Critical Heritage*, ed. Pat Rogers (London: Routledge & Kegan Paul, 1972), p. 13.

[3] *British Quarterly Review*, 50 (1869), cited in Rogers, p. 193. The essay is assigned to Keltie in the fourth volume of the *Wellesley Index to Victorian Periodicals, 1824–1900* (Toronto: University of Toronto Press, 1987), IV, 160, item 1045. It might be informative to note the reasons for attribution: 'The preface to Keltie's edition of *Defoe's Works; with Chalmers' Life of the Author*. Edinburgh, 1869, raises many points found here with similar phrases and verbatim passages.'

1

day cinematographer.[4] He was "like Norman Mailer" in his journalism;[5] he could claim "Conrad, Twain, Bellow" as his progeny.[6]

But politically Defoe has been given short shrift by the twentieth century. He was recognized correctly as a great political reporter and journalist, possessing heaps of information, but he was found unable to contain all that he knew within any conceptual framework. He has been perceived as chameleon-like, contradicting himself, becoming all things to all men in order to promote, pragmatist that he was, any aspect of government policy that he was paid to promote. Thus, what had once been seen as an astute political imagination is now revealed as only that of a polemicist and party writer. If Defoe had any fundamental political ideas, like his economic ones they challenged outworn orthodoxies. Defoe "is a modern, writing to defend the Junto Whigs, the Bank of England, and the standing army."[7] Or he is seen as diametrically opposed to Aphra Behn's Royalist stance: 'Robinson . . . might even be described as a sort of counter-*Oroonoko*.'[8] Jeffrey Hart's 1964 anthology, *Political Writers of Eighteenth-Century England*, omitted any mention of Defoe. It included, among others, Swift's *Modest Proposal*, some *Spectator* essays, and an excerpt from Goldsmith's *Vicar of Wakefield*.[9] And when Defoe's political ideas were seriously examined, they were only the reflected ideas of the philosopher who seemingly provided the dominant political ideology of our time: John Locke. In his poetry and prose, Defoe did nothing more but paraphrase the familiar ideas – rather crudely and superficially – of the *Two Treatises of Government*. In 1986 Richard Ashcraft published his meticulous and comprehensive study of Locke's revolutionary ideas. Examining a single Defoe essay written in one of the most volatile years of William's reign when partisan passions were excessively high and an extraordinary quantity of propaganda was published, his judgment echoed that of every political commentator in the twentieth century: Defoe's "principles are distinctly Lockean and radical."[10] One part of the following study contends that Defoe did more than proselytize for Locke in mediocre verse, and to monotonously proclaim Defoe as Lockean is an unfair and oversimplified perspective.

[4] Paul K. Alkon, *Defoe and Fictional Time* (Athens: University of Georgia Press, 1979), chapter 5.

[5] Maximillian E. Novak, *Realism, Myth, and History in Defoe's Fiction* (Lincoln: University of Nebraska Press, 1983), p. 25; cf. pp. 44, 46, 95, 112.

[6] Paula Backscheider, *Daniel Defoe: Ambition & Innovation* (Lexington: University Press of Kentucky, 1986), p. 122; cf. pp. 91–92, 93, 238.

[7] J. G. A. Pocock, *The Machiavellian Moment: Florentine Political Thought and the Atlantic Republican Tradition* (Princeton: Princeton University Press, 1975), pp. 433–34. It should be noted that Professor Pocock very infrequently goes beyond citations from the *Review* for his "modern" reading of Defoe.

[8] Eve Tavor, *Scepticism, Society and the Eighteenth-Century Novel* (New York: St Martin's Press, 1987), p. 245; cf. her rare judgment that the society on Crusoe's island is "an egalitarian society" (p. 23).

[9] New York: Alfred A. Knopf.

[10] *Revolutionary Politics and Locke's "Two Treatises of Government"* (Princeton: Princeton University Press, 1986), p. 565.

Defoe appears rarely to have disguised his sources. James Sutherland noted that "Defoe's reader is usually presented with most of the information he needs," that is, information that generally contains both the assumed ideas and their authorship.[11] Perhaps some credence, then, could be given to Defoe when he wrote, during a long-running political debate with Rev. Charles Leslie, Mr. Rehearsal, on the subject of government:

> I know, what Mr. *Lock, Sidney* and others have said on this Head, and I must confess, I never thought their Systems fully answer'd - - - - But I am arguing by my own Light, not other Mens; and therefore my Notions may be new, yet I beg the Favour to be heard, and if confuted, no Man shall be sooner silenc'd than I.[12]

It is a truism that genius makes its breakthrough by compounding the traditional and the original. Much of the content of Defoe's political writings, reviewed in their immediate context, has resulted in evaluations that concentrate on its novelty. Rhetorical analysis taken over from the study of his fictions has narrowed the measure of Defoe's political intelligence, for it has removed his polemical writings from the historical moment that, at the very least, birthed them.[13] Brian Tierney has wisely cautioned us that "two contexts at least must always be taken into account when we consider any sophisticated work of political theory – the actual world of experience which the author was trying to explain, and the inherited world of ideas which helped to shape his attitudes toward that experience."[14] Defoe's modern critics have stressed the former: the following chapters explore the latter. Though I have explored the insistently topical nature of his writings, I have also sought abiding themes and metaphoric and allusionary strains that move beyond the actual world of experience. They present a Defoe who did not yet believe that God had removed himself from the world of politics, and a Defoe who did not share a Whig and Lockean preoccupation with the evils of executive power, but a Defoe who was a vigorous defender of monarchical control.

There is no denying Defoe's radical and Lockean language, but the Defoe of the following chapters is not the radical or the Lockean we have come to accept. Paradoxically, the Defoe discovered in my examination of the larger cultural and historical contexts has important correspondences with Locke, not the Locke of the twentieth century, but the Locke of the seventeenth, whose primary commitment was to the principles of Christianity.[15] For Defoe, as for Locke, theological determinants were the basis of his political arguments, and a Protestant-Calvinist heritage serves as the foundation of his political thought. Studying the constituent elements of Defoe's vocabulary

---

[11] *Daniel Defoe: A Critical Study* (Cambridge, MA: Harvard University Press, 1971), p. 22.

[12] *Review*, III, 108 (10 Sept. 1706). Citations are to volume and issue, not page.

[13] See the useful summary in John J. Richetti, *Daniel Defoe* (Boston: G. K. Hall, 1987), pp. 15–33.

[14] *Religion, Law, and the Growth of Constitutional Thought, 1150–1650* (New York: Cambridge University Press, 1982), p. 81.

[15] See John Dunn, *The Political Thought of John Locke: An Historical Account of the Argument of the "Two Treatises of Government"* (Cambridge: University Press, 1966). But Defoe's militarism separates him from Locke as it does from virtually all of his contemporaries; see Richard H. Cox, *Locke on War and Peace* (Oxford: Clarendon Press, 1960), chapter 4.

that remained constant beyond the polemical occasions that called them forth, we discover an antiquated rhetoric of politics and kingship that is anchored in Old Testament story and admits the immediate hand of the Israelite God in the nomination of kings.

Technological developments evolve from the simple to the refined; what is sophisticated is anticipated in the rudimentary. We have come to understand how Defoe the novelist evolved out of Defoe the journalist. Thus in the following chapters I have ordered by chronology rather than by theme, for I see Defoe's major political ideas evolving over the course of his life. Controversy and current events refined his political myth; his early and instinctual ideas were not significantly altered. In his first political essays following the Revolution of 1688, Defoe discloses his distinctive political stance that was definitively elaborated in *Jure Divino* (1706) and characterized his mindset to the end of his career. It is a myth of communal origins and monarchy, educed by a mind susceptible to experience. In an age during which the rhetoric, symbols, and even the locale of traditional authority were being forsaken, Defoe sustained the ideal of the warrior-king, whose beginnings lay both in sacred and human time. The sword-bearing sovereign was made necessary by England's variegated society. His importance was reinforced by the tendencies of Defoe's mind, which harbored no illusions about the sociability of mankind. Perhaps this vision is the upside, so to speak, of Defoe's potentially self-destructive and socially dangerous rootlessness and individualism. Skeptical about the idea of a secular social contract and unconvinced that legislative sovereignty could contain the tensions of a changing world, Defoe fixated on the more traditional theme of the soldier-redeemer who, like the warrior-prophets of the Old Testament, rescues his people from tyranny. In his day, he would provide heroic leadership to the international Protestant crusade that energized the reign of every English prince from the time of the Reformation. Confronting a nation that seemed on the verge of a parliamentary constitutionalism, Defoe turned to traditional royalism. It is a royalism in which the king was the indispensable keystone in the arch of society, but yet a royalism that retained its scriptural, medieval, and English antecedents and never forgot that the people shared in the activating power of government. Defoe's mind, imbued with the romance and reward of trade, both personal and imperial, remained possessed with the heroics of the campaign. Defoe's tendency was to have it both ways, for, as Stephen Baxter has written, "no one is less popular in a trading nation than an army man – when there is no fighting to do."[16]

---

[16] *William III and the Defense of European Liberty, 1650–1702* (New York: Harcourt, Brace, and World, 1966), p. 177. For the tendency in Defoe's critics to see him having it both ways, see Alkon, *Defoe and Fictional Time*, p. 35; Novak, *Realism, Myth, and History in Defoe's Fiction*, p. 65; and C. Hill, "Robinson Crusoe," *History Workshop: A Journal of Socialist Historians*, 10 (1980), 18.

Defoe's concept of the prince, who creates harmonies in the social order, frees the imprisoned and disenfranchised, and leads his people step by step to liberty, as he poetized in *Mock-Mourners* (1702), connects Defoe to the central tradition of the west. Though I have not chosen to explore the continual occurrences of the hero-prince theme, from its obscurity in folklore to its mythological elaboration in classical literature and its revival in the Renaissance, some passing observations are in order. Defoe's Old Testament God, who sanctifies the origins and morality of the martial monarch, distinguishes Defoe's creation from its emblematic counterparts in its past. Plato, for example, divorces arms from leadership as he develops his ideal of the philosopher-king, one whose temperament and duties are different from those of his warrior-guardians. The lawgiver will be structured on educational foundations provided for and developed in the warrior-guardian, but bravery and courage, attributes of the latter, are the necessary but not sufficient conditions for leadership. Arms, in fact, are not the ingredients of ultimate authority. It is the tyrant in Plato's myth who is associated with wars.[17] But it is Defoe's guardian-king who reigns supreme, not by his intelligence, but by virtue of his weapons. He maintains order and discipline in his state because he wields, not "the sword of the spirit," but the more earthly and visible sword of the campaign.[18]

And, unlike Erasmus's Christian prince of peace, Defoe's monarch is tainted with blood, modeled after conquering kings like Saul and Solomon.[19] For Erasmus, the soldier was the height of evil; those who lived by the sword were agents of social misrule. The last chapter of his *Education of a Christian Prince* denounces *in toto* what the earlier pages had noted in passing: war, its pretexts, agents, and aftermath. The Erasmian ideal, a summary of sources from the ancient to the medieval period, is judged good and great by the distance between himself and the actions and ethos of the warrior. But Defoe's myth establishes an equation between bravery and princeliness, between the quest for martial honor and the good of mankind.

Both God and the sword, the Gospel and the camp, are also absent from the universe of Bolingbroke's Patriot King. Bolingbroke has no interest in origins. Thus he may chant phrases like "the monarchy of the Supreme Being" or "the Author" of Nature, but God is disjoined from what can only loosely be called his political theory.[20] *The Idea of a Patriot King* is an Opposition manifesto and, like all manifestoes, is long on emotion and short on substance. It projects a "mystical" monarch who will eradicate parties; Defoe, who took faction and opposition as universal givens, remained with a prince of power who dominated and controlled party by virtue of his control

[17] *The Republic*, trans. Paul Shorey, 2 vols. (Cambridge, MA: Harvard University Press, 1953), I, 295–307; 163–75.

[18] I take the phrase from John R. Knott, Jr., *The Sword of the Spirit: Puritan Responses to the Bible* (Chicago: University of Chicago Press, 1980).

[19] *The Education of a Christian Prince.* trans. Lester K. Born (1936; rpt., New York: Octagon Books, 1965), p. 134.

[20] *The Idea of a Patriot King*, ed. Sydney K. Jackman (Indianapolis: Bobbs-Merrill, 1965), pp. 19, 13.

of the power of the sword. If Bolingbroke beamed his monarch down to his
English and earthly community via Horace, Seneca, Tacitus, and Terence,
Defoe beamed his down via Saul and David. Bolingbroke's Patriot King may
be "the common father of his people" and dominate the "patriarchal family,
where the head and all the members are united by one common interest,"[21]
but his Tudor imagery denies the polemical import of the tract. His ideal is
less a portrait of a Renaissance prince and more a chapter in his Opposition
history to the Walpole ministry, less a myth of kings and community, as
Defoe's is, and more, as Simon Varey concludes, "a punitive satire on King
George, the would-be tyrant who destroys the value of British life."[22]

Some years ago, Maximillian Novak intimated that Defoe could have
found justification for his doctrine of necessity in Machiavelli, but he concluded that Grotius and Pufendorf, whom Defoe clearly read and often cited,
were more significant influences on his ideas.[23] If Defoe's ideology of kingship and rule also calls to mind a Machiavellian inheritance, two things must
be remembered. The first is that an affinity is not an influence. Detailing the
necessary properties of his monarch-prince, Defoe, at times, in public – and,
as we shall see, in private in his memorandums to Harley – naturally echoed
the proverbial content of the advices-to-princes genre of secular tradition.
Bracton, for example, enjoined that "to rule well a king requires two things,
arms and laws," a maxim that fixed itself in the English imagination two and
one-half centuries before it was repeated in *The Prince*.[24] The inherited tags
of political discourse, such as "vox populi vox dei," or "salus populi suprema
lex," that are found in both Machiavelli and Defoe, are unavoidable
similarities of thought that show, in these obvious cases at least, no signs of
indebtedness. The second thing to note is that Defoe very rarely turns to
Machiavelli, despite the fact that, as Felix Raab proved, the Italian's name
had disappeared as a term of abuse and his work could be mined to support
almost any ideological fashion.[25] Defoe's very few quotations from
Machiavelli – he calls them "Maxims" – are really distillations of policy
and procedure, usually from the *Discourses*, and are concentrated in his later
years. Between 1715 and 1717 Defoe cited Machiavelli three times. One
"Machiavillian Maxim . . . whenever it has been practiced, we shall always
find it had been fatal." Another is put in the mouth of a "certain Lord" who

---

21 *The Idea of a Patriot King*, pp. 45, 53, 46.

22 *Henry St. John, Viscount Bolingbroke* (Boston: G. K. Hall, 1985), p. 101."As political philosophy
   the *Idea* is disappointingly superficial" (p. 98). For Bolingbroke, it might be noted, the trinity
   of monarchical authority is the crown, scepter, and throne, or the crown, scepter and miter.
   A warrior-monarch carrying the sword is totally absent from his imagination.

23 *Defoe and the Nature of Man* (London: Oxford University Press, 1963), p. 58, and chapter 3.

24 *Bracton on the Laws and Customs of England*, trans. Samuel E. Thorne, 2 vols. (Cambridge, MA:
   Harvard University Press, 1968), II, 19; *The Prince*, trans. and ed. Robert M. Adams (New
   York: W. W. Norton, 1977), p. 35.

25 *The English Face of Machiavelli: A Changing Interpretation, 1500–1700* (London: Routledge &
   Kegan Paul, 1965), pp. 238–63.

is a member of a group of treasonous malcontents who design to bring in the Pretender. The third bends, perhaps, a theme from the *Discourses* to indict the High Church faction for its unrelenting adherence to principles of persecution and tyranny.[26] Defoe surely read Machiavelli but the evidence suggests that he found little substance in his secular program for rule to influence his Sauline myth of kingship.

Defoe's concept of the social contract in his *Reflections Upon the Late Great Revolution*, in print six months before the *Two Treatises of Government*, is insistently theological. Just as he did not need Locke for his theory of mutual agreements between God, king, and community, having learned from the Old Testament of the Israelite monarchs who were heavenly appointed mediators between God and the people,[27] Defoe did not need Machiavelli to educate him about the malignity of men, nor of the martial ingredient of princely leadership. Machiavelli went to the Old Testament parable of Saul and David to educe support for his conviction that one is victorious in one's own armor; that is, that the prince must eschew mercenaries and fight with his own native armies.[28] Defoe turned to Saul and David to assert the necessity for a warrior-statesman in the origins of the commonwealth. Like Machiavelli, Defoe was greatly attracted to the idea of "fortune's first gift," the unique lawgiver-founder of the state.[29] But unlike Machiavelli, who rejects the strongest and the bravest for the wisest and most just, Defoe cannot dislodge political wisdom from martial prowess. Writing as a British soldier in 1715 to counter mounting propaganda attacks on the army, Defoe claimed fortitude, or bravery, as pre-eminent among the moral virtues:

I know of none that dare vye or enter into Comparison with it but *Justice*; under which Head I particularly comprehend, and have regard to, the truly *venerable Art* of *framing Laws*, and governing with *Equity*, and restraining *Vice*. But surely, among *Virtues*, the Precedence is mostly due to that, without which the others cannot subsist. *Solon* and *Lycurgus* had ranged Mankind under admirable Regulations in vain, had there been no *Themistocles*, no *Agesilaus*, no *Epaminondas*, to protect *Constitutions* formed with the utmost *Foresight* and *Wisdom*.[30]

26 *His Majesty's Obligations to the Whigs* (London, 1715), pp. 17–18 ("fatal"); *Secret Memoirs of a Treasonable Conference at Somerset House, For Deposing the Present Ministry, and Making a New Turn at Court* (London, 1717), p. 60 ("a certain Lord"); *Faction in Power* (London, 1717), p. 32. See also "*Machiavel*, a Politician of the first Reputation," preferring Rome to Greece, in *The Ballance* (London, 1705), pp. 34–35. For the Machiavellian maxims see *The Discourses of Niccolo Machiavelli*, trans. Leslie J. Walker, 2 vols. (New Haven: Yale University Press, 1950), I, 253, 272, 295, 395, 214.

27 For covenant-contract language in Jewish and Protestant thought see Klaus Baltzer, *The Covenant Formulary In Old Testament, Jewish, and the Early Christian Writings*, trans. David E. Green (Philadelphia: Fortress Press, 1971): Kenneth Hagen, "From Testament to Covenant in the Early Sixteenth Century," *Sixteenth-Century Journal*, 3 (1972), 1–24; Richard L. Greaves, "The Origins and Early Development of English Covenant Thought," *The Historian*, 31 (1968), 21–35; and Leonard J. Trinterud, "The Origins of Puritanism," *Church History*, 20 (1951), 37–57.

28 *The Prince*, pp. 40–41.

29 *Discourses*, I, 215, For Solon and Lycurgus see I, 215, 235, 211. For them "having recourse to God" see I, 242.

30 *An Apology for the Army. In A Short Essay on Fortitude, Etc. Written by an Officer* (London, 1715), p. 10.

Finally, it should be noted that Machiavelli does not appear in the annotations to *Jure Divino*, where Defoe not only threw the book at his readers but a sizable portion of his library as well.[31] The author of *Il Principe* would not have been out of place, for example, in Book I, in which Defoe cites, among others, Virgil, Horace, Plautus, Livy, Varro, Sir Walter Raleigh, Bishop Richard Cumberland, John Ogilby, Charles Cotton, Jeremy Collier, Pufendorf, and the old song, "Vulcan heat an iron bar."

The fortitude of the soldier was that "*Ray* of the *Divinity*, imprinted for the Good of *Mankind* in those whose Souls are wound up to a higher Pitch than ordinary, and influenced so, as to grow enamour'd of *glorious Danger*, while it despises ignoble Ease, and *Safety* basely bought.[32] To the very end of his life, in his latest writings, unlike all of his contemporaries, Defoe continued to discern those rays "shin[ing] with a particular glory" in Scripture, in Saul and those armed prophets following him, both "kings and leaders of armyes," who were "design'd and determin'd for great employment and glorious accions," sanctioned by God as captain-princes in what appears to have been Defoe's paradigmatic commonwealth.[33]

Defoe's anachronistic piety is a quintessential ingredient of his politics. The following pages offer a Defoe for whom, then, a secular Lockean paradigm has been unduly constricting in evaluating his political thought. This Defoe is not intended to replace the "modern" Defoe; it only hopes to reveal the conservative-royalist thread in the complex weave of his political imagination. To see that thread spun in the constitutional battles of his day that pitted the heavenly appointed monarch against the encroachments of parliaments, and to discover that component in the political drama that is *Robinson Crusoe*, is to claim finally for Defoe an uncertain and insecure modernity.

[31] Though the volume is of limited usefulness note Defoe's "ownership" of Machiavelli's works in *The Libraries of Daniel Defoe and Phillips Farewell*, ed. Helmut Heidenreich (Berlin, 1970), pp. 34, 54.

[32] *An Apology for the Army*, pp. 8–9.

[33] *Of Royall Educacion*, ed. Karl D. Bülbring (London: David Nutt, 1895), pp. 3–4.

1

Defoe, dissent, and monarchy

On 11 June 1685, James Scott, Duke of Monmouth, landed on England's west country shore proclaiming liberty and inveighing against the arbitrary rule of his uncle, King James II, who had ascended the throne scarcely four months earlier. On 13 June the invasion was officially known in London and the King's proclamation of that day declared Monmouth and Lord Grey traitors to the nation. Though the government immediately began to contain the rebellion, and the army stopped many from travelling to the west to enlist in the rebel cause, as early as 13 June a small body of recruits arrived from the capital, perhaps in time to hear the dashing, martial, but illegitimate son of Charles II proclaimed "our lawful and rightful sovereign and king by the name of James II."[1]

Whether Daniel Defoe rode westward with that first contingent of London volunteers, or whether he slipped into Monmouth's camp later that eventful summer, any examination of Defoe's political thought would be rendered less uncertain if we could answer the question that John Robert Moore posed and left unanswered after a half-century's study of his subject's life and writings: "Why had a merchant not quite twenty-five years old left his young wife to follow an adventurer in battle more than a hundred miles away?"[2] Why had this Presbyterian dissenter jeopardized his marriage, career, even life, to enlist under the banner of a self-proclaimed deliverer of parliament, "pro religione et libertate?"[3]

Twentieth-century scholarship has illuminated Defoe's life and career, his early satires, and his courageous attacks on a stultifying urban power elite. And it has examined his novels' sympathetic portrayal of frail, ordinary, but

---

[1] Charles C. Trench, *The Western Rising* (London: Longman, 1969), p. 154. See also William R. Emerson, *Monmouth's Rebellion* (New Haven: Yale University Press, 1951); and Peter Earle, *Monmouth's Rebels* (London: Weidenfeld and Nicolson, 1977).

[2] Moore, *Daniel Defoe*, pp. 54–55.

[3] George Roberts, *The Life, Progresses, and Rebellion of James, Duke of Monmouth* (London, 1844), I, 235. For Defoe's sympathetic yet ambiguous judgments on Monmouth see *Review*, IV, 168 (9 March 1708); V, 49 (20 July 1708); I [IX], 14 (16 Sept. 1712); I [IX], 77 (31 March 1713). Also his *Tour Through the Whole Island of Great Britain* (London: Dent, 1962), II, 14, 148.

redeemable, common people. Stressing the modernity of Defoe, it has tended
to overlook, even to obscure and misread, a conservative – or traditional –
heritage that provided a foundation for his political thought. If, as we now
realize, "he was no impassioned preacher of a new social [and economic]
evangel,"[4] perhaps a new consideration of Defoe's formative years and influences might cast doubt on the political radicalism that has been implicitly
claimed for him in the writings of so many of his modern admirers. Defoe's
response to Monmouth's banner at Taunton does not necessarily present us
with an upstart republican with a leveller disregard for monarchy and a
hatred for extravagant royalism. He grew up in an age when, as Bulstrode
Whitelocke's biographer reminds us, "men were born with the idea of king
in their heads as camels with indurations on their knees."[5]

Defoe was "*a great Admirer and constant Hearer*"[6] of Samuel Annesley,
minister of St. Giles Cripplegate, in whose parish Defoe had been born in
1660 and at whose meeting house at Little St. Helen's Bishopsgate the Defoe
family worshipped after Annesley's ejection in 1662. In 1648, at twenty-six,
together with Stephen Marshall, one of the most radical puritan preachers of
the time, Annesley had preached the monthly fast-day sermon before the
House of Commons.[7] While the ideological persuasion of parliament's in-
vitees was usually liberal, and the Commons was careful of its choices, there
is nothing to suggest that Annesley was anything more than a pious and gentle
man with little political awareness. In December 1681, after the dissolution
of the Oxford Parliament, he was denominationally suspect, one of a group
of twenty-two dissenting ministers of London upon whom fines were imposed.[8] Defoe's elegy on Annesley in 1697 recites the virtues of a Christian
minister of no exceptional intellectual attainments, a man of sweetness, piety,
and manners, "the Best of Ministers, and Best of Men."[9]

The dissenting academy that Defoe attended from his sixteenth to his nine-
teenth years was far from the breeding ground of "Atheism, Deism, Tritheism,
Socianism with all the hellish Principles of Fanaticism, Regicide, and Anarchy"
that the rabid Henry Sacheverell no doubt wished it to be.[10] The academy at
Newington Green was presided over by Charles Morton, a university graduate
of some intellectual attainments, but also one who was singled out by Rev.
Samuel Wesley, in his diatribe against academies and their incitement to
rebellion and assertive non-conformity, as a safe and conservative mentor:

[4] David W. Rannie, *Daniel Defoe, The Stanhope Essay* (Oxford, 1890), p. 3. For Defoe's economic
conservatism see Peter Earle, *The World of Defoe* (London: Weidenfeld and Nicolson, 1976).
[5] R. H. Whitelocke, *Memoirs, Biographical and Historical, of Bulstrode Whitelocke* (London, 1860), p. 430.
[6] John Dunton, *The Impeachment* (London, 1714), p. 13.
[7] John F. Wilson, *Pulpit in Parliament: Puritanism During the English Civil Wars, 1640–1648*
(Princeton: Princeton University Press, 1969), pp. 37, 128.
[8] Michael R. Watts, *The Dissenters* (Oxford: Clarendon, 1978), I, 254.
[9] *The Character of the late Dr. Samuel Annesley* (London, 1697), p. 10.
[10] Henry Sacheverell, *The Perils of False Brethren* (London, 1709), p. 25.

For my Tutor himself, I must and ever will do him that Justice to assert, that whenever the Young Men had any discourse of the Government, and talk'd disaffectedly or disloyally, he never fail'd to rebuke and admonish 'em to the Contrary, telling us, I remember, Expressly, more then once, That 'twas none of our business to Censure such as God had placed above us. That small miscarriages ought not to be magnified, nor severely reflected on, (Especially by those who had other busines to mind) there never having been a Government so exact, or perfect, but had some of those *Naeri* in it: And further, he particularly Caution'd us against Lampoons, or Scandalous Libels against Superiours, and that from the Immorality, as well as Danger of being the Authors or Dispensers of them.[11]

But Wesley was far from complimentary about the general tendency of the political education of young dissenters; thus Defoe attacked the "Reverend Dr. Renegado" – Wesley had conformed to the Church of England in 1688 – for suggesting that the academies were preparatories for republicanism and regicide. Referring to what appears to be a study guide and a political exercise, Defoe wrote: "I find a Declamation relating to the benefit of a single Person in a Commonwealth, wherein it is declar'd and prov'd from History and Reason, that Monarchy is the best Government, and the best suited to the Nature of Government, and the Defence of Property . . ."[12]

Samuel Palmer, like Defoe educated for the dissenting ministry, came to the defense of his dissenting academies in general and Charles Morton in particular. Morton, he wrote, had drawn up a 'System of Politics" which "is exactly corresponding with the *English Monarchy*. It secures the *Rights* and Honour of the Crown and the *Liberties* of the *Subject*. It requires from the Subject Love to the person of the King, a ready and cheerful Obedience to the Laws and a constant Assistance by dutiful Submission to Legal Taxes for the support of the *Crown*, and the *Laws*. It makes the Original of all Government to be the Institution of God, as indeed it is by our *Law*."[13]

If Defoe's formative years of religious and academic education reveal no radical political influences, there is nothing to be found in his Presbyterian heritage that would inculcate a diminished respect for monarchy.[14] Whatever his reasons, in 1704, writing one of his many defenses of his dissenting faith and its followers, Defoe declared that he wore "a mourning ring on

---

[11] *A Letter From A Country Divine To His Friend in London, Concerning the Education of the Dissenters* (London, 1703), p. 6. For Morton see J. W. Ashley Smith, *The Birth of Modern Education* (London: Independent Press, 1954).

[12] *More Short-Ways with the Dissenters*, in *A Second Volume of the Writings of the Author of the True-Born Englishman* (London, 1705), p. 277. See also J. A. Downie, "An Unknown Defoe Broadside on the Regulation of the Press," *The Library*, 5th. ser., 33 (1978), 57.

[13] *A Vindication of the Learning, Loyalty, Morals, and Most Christian Behaviour of the Dissenters* (London, 1705), p. 54.

[14] See George R. Abernathy, Jr., *The English Presbyterians and the Stuart Restoration, 1648–1663*, American Philosophical Society, Transactions, n.s., vol. 55 (1965), part 2; Abernathy, "Clarendon and the Declaration of Indulgence," *Journal of Ecclesiastical History*, 11 (1960), 55–73; Leland H, Carlson, "A History of the Presbyterian Party From Pride's Purge to the Dissolution of the Long Parliament," *Church History*, 11 (1942), 83–122. Also the debate in *Past and Present*, 47 (1970), 116–46; and C. H. Firth, "Cromwell and the Crown," *English Historical Review*, 17 (1902), 429–38.

his finger, given at the funeral of Mr. Christopher Love, a presbyterian minister, beheaded *Anno* 1653, for the horrid fanatic plot for bringing in, as they then called him, Charles Stuart, and restoring the monarchy."[15] Presbyterians were not, then, as Charles II believed, "all republicans at heart."[16] And Calvinism is no longer judged a creed of rebels against autocracy and bigotry, nor as an ideology legitimizing populist disobedience against wicked kings and parliaments.[17] William Lamont's studies of the millenarian impulse in seventeenth-century England reveal the puritans' devotion to king worship, for "England, the Elect Nation, was locked in a momentous struggle with Roman Catholicism. And in that struggle the Royal Supremacy was the Catholic target, the Protestant shield."[18] Throughout the century "it was the abuse of authority they attacked, and not the system of authority itself." Until the English civil wars the moderate dissenters from the Established Church "never faltered in upholding the obedience which subjects owed to kings by the law of God. There was scarcely a breath among them of the doctrine that justified resistance to a tyrant prince . . . On the contrary, they preached the divine right of kings." Defoe's forebears in dissent never did "develop an ideology of revolt in any way comparable to that of the French Huguenots or the Scottish Presbyterians. Towards both monarchy and the social hierarchy they broadly maintained the Tudor tradition."[19] With as much fervour and conviction as their Anglican brethren, Presbyterian ministers could deliver a sermon on 1 Peter 2, Titus 3.1, or Romans 13.1, exhorting the necessity for Christians to obey magistrates and invoking damnation to resisters.[20] Their program of a national, authoritarian, and hierarchical church required the presence of a strong and dynamic monarch as its protector to defend their ecclesiastical monopoly in the state.[21]

Primarily religious in their interests, almost indifferent to pragmatic policy considerations, and intransigent in their attitudes to their English Catholic

[15] *The Dissenters Answer to the High-Church Challenge* (London, 1704), p. 43.

[16] John Miller, *Popery and Politics in England, 1660–1688* (Cambridge: Cambridge University Press, 1973), p. 123.

[17] Quentin Skinner, *The Foundations of Modern Political Thought*, 2 vols. (Cambridge: Cambridge Unversity Press, 1978), II, 232–33; Skinner, "The Origins of the Calvinist Theory of Revolution," in *After the Revolution: Essays in Honor of J. H. Hexter*, ed. Barbara C. Malament (Philadelphia: University of Pennsylvania Press, 1980), pp. 309–30. See also the exchange in *Journal of Ecclesiastical History*, 32 (1981), 65–67, 69–70, 499–501.

[18] *Politics, Religion, and Literature in the Seventeenth Century*, ed. William Lamont and Sybil Oldfield (London: Dent, 1975), p. xix.

[19] Austin Woolrych, "Puritanism, Politics, and Society," in *The English Revolution, 1600–1660*, ed. E. W. Ives (New York: Barnes & Noble, 1969), pp. 91–92.

[20] See, for example, Richard Vines, *Subjection to Magistrates Both Supreme and Subordination* (London, 1654), and *Obedience to Magistrates* (London, 1656); Edward Reynolds, *A Seasonable Exhortation of Sundry Ministers in London to the People of their Respective Congregations* (London, 1660).

[21] Harry Grant Plum, *Restoration Puritanism* (Chapel Hill: University of North Carolina Press, 1943), p. 19.

brethren, the Presbyterians through all their actions sought a strong executive who could guarantee the preservation of church and society. In 1680, an anonymous account of the main opinions of the sect reiterated its basic tenets, that they believed still "in a *Christian Magistrate* (who is to be a nursing Father to the Church)," that "they believe it to be their duty to be obedient to such *Governours* in all places, as the laws in that place have established, and in the exercise of such power as those laws have given them"; they asserted their liberty of conscience and judgment, and "they conceive their own *consciences must be judges*; and as to such things they conceive themselves onely to suffer *the penalties* for such disobedience peacably."[22]

The years of Defoe's birth and early development are the years of vengeance and fear following the return of the Stuarts, the failure of ecclesiastical accommodation, and the enactment of the Clarendon Code. Taking a sympathetic view of English dissenters, it is possible to admit that their response to the persecutions of the Restoration years ran the gamut from passive acquiescence to the repressive actions of the Anglican establishment to deliberate and public contempt for the penalties which they suffered so grievously. Douglas Lacey, in his detailed study of dissent and parliamentary politics from the Restoration to the Revolution, concluded that the dissenters "remained advocates of a monarchy in which the authority of the king would be constitutionally limited and in which his actions would be effectively controlled by a parliament with a broader representative base."[23] Yet twice, in 1662 and 1672, with the promulgation of Charles II's declarations of indulgence, they were given the choice of "accepting or rejecting a religious liberty that was not in accordance with the laws of the realm."[24] Numbers of dissenting clergy accepted licenses that dispensed them from the Act of Uniformity; they were fully aware that they were thus giving sanction to actions that repealed parliamentary enactments. In Lacey's words, "they were willing to justify a royal act which in effect repealed parliamentary statutes; thus they tacitly rejected the essence of a limited monarchy." Defoe's own minister, Samuel Annesley, was the leader of the younger group of Restoration dissenters who wanted toleration outside the Church and thus were inadvertently allies of the Stuart court.[25]

Whatever constraints had been placed on Charles II because of his foreign policy, which necessitated the calling of parliament to secure funds, and whatever the success of the "royalist" or "cavalier" parliament in compelling the king to modify his authoritarian demands, the Popish Plot and its aftermath introduced years of repression against non-conformity that were unparalleled

[22] *English Presbytery : Or, An Account of the Main Opinions . . . of Presbyterians* (London, 1680), pp. 7, 11.
[23] *Dissent and Parliamentary Politics in England, 1661–1689* (New Brunswick: Rutgers University Press, 1969), p. 247.
[24] *Ibid.*, pp. 69–70.
[25] *Ibid.*, p. 64; for other pro-monarchical views of the Presbyterians see pp. 205–09, 226–27.

since the Restoration. For one historian "the secret of Monmouth's temporary success can only be explained by pointing to the persecution of the dissenters that preceded it."[26] In 1705, exhorting his fellow dissenters to be content with the present state of affairs, Defoe recalled the fear and anxiety of his brethren: "How many Honest *but over-Frighted* People, set to Work to Copy the Bible into Short-Hand, lest when Popery came in, We should be Prohibited the use of it, and so might secure it in little Compass? At which Work, I my self then, but a Boy [he was 18 or so years old], Work'd like a Horse, till I Wrote out the whole Pentateuch; and then was so tyr'd, I was willing to run the Risque of the rest."[27] Though skeptical about the excesses of violence attributed to the Catholics, Defoe believed in the fact of the conspiracy to subvert government and bring in popery and slavery. Many times Defoe's retrospective assessments, here and elsewhere, of his nation's experience under Charles II and James II reveal a mind troubled by the divinely absolute powers attributed to the king. More distressing to him were the political and religious tyranny the Stuarts were importing from Rome and the Anglican hierarchy's cowardly and self-serving acquiescence in a policy that justified immediate revolution, the placing of England under the jurisdiction of a foreign power.[28]

During the last four years of Charles II's reign, Defoe witnessed the harsh enforcement of the penal laws. As a prelude, in December 1681, twenty-two of the most respected and influential dissenting ministers in the capital were heavily fined for holding religious services, among them the Rev. Samuel Annesley.[29] Moderation was no longer to be counseled as royal decrees new-modeled local governments to secure control of parliament. Defoe never forgot the human cost of Stuart tyranny; years later he reminded his readers of the imprisonment and death in Newgate of many honorable dissenting clergy.[30]

Thus popery and arbitrary power, Catholicism and executive tyranny, were feared to be the consequence of the accession of a Catholic prince to the throne of Protestant England in February 1685. James II's authoritarian vision of monarchy was no secret; in fact he chose to confront the expectation of a politically repressive reign head-on in his first address to his Privy Council;

I have been Reported to be a Man for Arbitrary Power, but that is not the only Story has been made of Me: And I shall make it my Endeavours to preserve this Government both in Church and State, as it is now by Law Establish'd: I know the Principles of the Church of *England* are for Monarchy, and the Members of it have shewed themselves Good and Loyal Subjects, therefore I shall always take care to Defend and Support it: I know too, That the Laws of *England* are sufficient to make the King as

---

[26] *The Bloody Assizes*, ed. J. G. Muddiman (Edinburgh: William Hodge & Co., Ltd., 1929), p. 16; cf. Watts, *The Dissenters*, I, 254.

[27] *Review*, II, 125 (22 Dec. 1705); II, 51 (30 June 1705).

[28] *Ibid.*; also IV, 130 (18 Dec. 1707); VII, 75 (16 Sept. 1710).

[29] Watts, *The Dissenters*, I,154.

[30] *De Laune's Plea for the Non-Conformists* (London, 1706), p. ii.

Great a Monarch as I can wish; And as I shall never Depart from the Just Rights and Prerogatives of the Crown, so I shall never Invade any mans Property.[31]

Von Ranke observed that "no prince has ever had less thought for the balance of power in Europe than James II."[32] It may also be observed that no prince ever gave less thought to the dread that his accession created in the minds of his subjects.[33] He continued to suppress dissent just as he had as a Royal Commissioner in Scotland in 1681. He rewrote English judicial history when he secured the release of the Catholic judges sent to the Tower as a result of Oates' testimony and had Oates indicted for perjury. Defoe never forgot the "ill omens" at the coronation of a king who, he wrote, "being Popish had no right to rule."[34] But what might have disturbed him even more, and helped to precipitate a flight to Monmouth to defend England from popery and slavery, was the commitment of the Rev. Richard Baxter to the King's Bench Prison in February and his trial the following May on a charge of alleged seditious libel. The king's vindictiveness was directed at a "dissenting minister, a pious and learned man, of exemplary character, always remarkable for his attachment to monarchy, and for leaning to moderate measures in the differences between the church, and those of his persuasion."[35] Bishop Burnet voiced the fears of Defoe and thousands of his co-religionists that "England now seemed lost, unless some happy accident should save it."[36] On 29 June, two weeks after Monmouth's landing in the west, attended by Dr. William Bates – one of the few dissenters of an earlier generation whom Defoe mentions by name – Baxter heard the harsh judgment levied upon him: fined five hundred marks, to lie in prison until he paid it, and to be bound to his good behaviour for seven years.[37] As Macaulay wrote, James's accession "had excited hopes and fears in every Continental court"; and the commencement of his administration was watched as assiduously and with as much interest by his English subjects.[38]

What the young Defoe thought of these events we do not know. But the recently discovered manuscripts of his juvenile readings and transcriptions,

---

[31] *An Account of What His Majesty Said at His First Coming to Council* (London, 1684 [1685]).

[32] Cited in F. C. Turner, *James II* (London: Eyre & Spottiswoode, 1950), p. 345n.

[33] See Maurice Ashley, *James II* (London: Dent, 1977), pp. 137–38; cf. Charles James Fox, *A History of the Early Part of the Reign of James II* (London, 1808), pp. 105–08).

[34] *The Present State of Jacobitism Consider'd* (London, 1701), p. 21. See also *Review*, VII, 78 (23 Sept. 1710).

[35] Fox, *James II*, pp. 96–97.

[36] Gilbert Burnet, *History of His Own Time*, ed. Martin J. Routh, 6 vols. (1833; rpt., Hildesheim: G. Olms, 1969), III, 18.

[37] See T. B. Howell, *A Complete Collection of State Trials* (London, 1811), XI, 493–502. For writing *The Shortest Way with the Dissenters* Defoe's sentence was to be more harsh: he was to pay a fine of 200 marks, he was to stand in the pillory for an hour on three successive days, and he was to find sureties to be of good behaviour for seven years.

[38] Thomas B. Macaulay, *The History of England*, ed. C. H. Firth, 6 vols. (London: Macmillan, 1913), I, 458.

dated 1683, collected from authors such as Plutarch, Thomas Fuller, and Richard Knolles, reveal the present set of his mind and the future interests of the mature journalist – propagandist. There are the expected anecdotes and exemplars of the activity of Providence in the affairs of men and God's judgments on the sinful and the righteous. Others stress the themes of loyalty and gratitude that Defoe sustained in his later fictional and nonfictional publications. But what comes through insistently is a strident anti-Catholicism and an interest in martial kings and the professionalism of soldiers. Two stories, for example, tell how Selymus, the Emperor of the Turks, and Iphicates, the Athenian, punish dereliction from duty, the former punishing a traitor by rolling him about in a barrel with nails lining the inside, the latter killing a sleeping sentinel with his own sword. From Knolles's *General History of the Turks*, Defoe copied almost a dozen narratives about kings who are great in war. Some display the heroism of the camp and the moral and financial rewards that derive from bravery in battle. In short, whether the tale is about a Greek, a Moslem, or a Christian, Defoe exhibits a fascination with the right relations between commanders and the rank-and-file, courage and cowardice in uniform, and the moral and military responses of true kings, be they pagan or Christian.[39]

The conjunction of Catholic James II's accession, the trials of Baxter and Oates, the invasion of the Protestant Duke of Monmouth, and the anti-dissenter vendetta of Judge Jeffries and the courts are events of great moment that have yet to be adequately explored by Defoe's modern-day biographers. They introduce a theme that has been completely ignored by those seeking to divulge Defoe's elusive political sympathies. That is the theme of the "elect nation," the hopes for a godly prince and the millennial expectations that were sustained throughout the seventeenth century, as the writings of William Haller, William Lamont, and other historians have made clear.[40] These millennial visions and redemptive fancies were not the concern of the lunatic fringes of left-wing Protestantism alone; they were also the thoughtful and well-reasoned convictions of responsible Englishmen, like Richard Baxter, John Evelyn, Isaac Newton, and William Lloyd. By too narrowly placing Defoe in a capitalistic culture we have, as I shall argue, missed the residual eschatological element that invigorates greatly Defoe's depiction of his charismatic and scriptural monarch.

In fact, despite the failures of the Cromwellian commonwealth, the return of the Stuarts, and the greater inwardness of analysis on the part of the English Protestants, "in the last forty years of the seventeenth century,

[39] See Maximillian E. Novak, "Lost Defoe Manuscript Discovered," *The Clark Newsletter*, 1 (1981), 1–3. I am extremely indebted to Professor Novak for his transcription of the still-unpublished Clark Library manuscript.

[40] See William Haller, *The Elect Nation* (New York: Harper & Row, 1963); William Lamont, *Godly Rule: Politics and Religion, 1603–60* (London: Macmillan, 1969); Lamont, *Richard Baxter and the Millennium* (London: Croom Helm, 1979).

expectations of the Millennium ran high in England."[41] These expectations seemed well justified by the events of Defoe's early life: the Popish Plot, the prospect of James's accession, the revocation of the Edict of Nantes, the growing Catholic domination and expansion of power of Louis XIV. As Richard McKeon has shown, from 1660, the year of Defoe's birth, to the plague and fire years of 1665 and 1666, prophetic millennial writings by both royalists and revolutionaries exploded from the printing presses of London.[42] Once again, a Protestant prince, a Stuart conqueror – despite Charles II's martial inadequacy – was the central focus of eschatological poems, prayers, and pamphlets. England's internal religious and political tensions fostered apocalyptic hopes until the end of the century. The 1690s "was the very decade when William III's Protestant government was threatened by Catholic wars and incursions from the Continent and when some writers portrayed William as the Messiah and James II as the Antichrist."[43] The heart of this millennial dream, the essential ingredient of the theme of the elect nation, was a crusading and godly prince, who was to usher in Christ's kingdom brandishing the sword of God. From Elizabeth to Charles II, though a monarch might prove inadequate, disillusionment did not bring rejection of the hope; the hope instead was shifted onto the succeeding leader. New events were always benignly interpreted. The century retained its hunger for a Protestant Deliverer who, Richard Baxter believed, would be a sacred leader and would wield the sword for Christian truth.[44]

The political and ideological influences working on the young Defoe can help to explain his later addiction to the image of the charismatic warrior-king, who was to redeem English and European Protestantism. The co-existence of religious radicalism, millennial expectations, and the mediation of a godly Protestant monarch in the history of the young Defoe and his family go far toward explaining his religio-political bent. Defoe's earliest memories were of the parish of St. Stephen, Coleman Street, and of Swan Alley, Coleman Street Ward, where the family not only lived but in whose neighborhood nearly all of the historically accurate narrative of the *Journal of the Plague Year* occurs.[45] It was also in Swan Alley in 1661 that the most serious insurrection

[41] Paul Korshin, "Queuing and Waiting: The Apocalypse in England, 1660–1750," in *The Apocalypse in English Renaissance Thought and Culture*, ed. C. A. Patrides and Joseph Wittreich (Manchester: Manchester University Press, 1984), p. 242.

[42] *Politics and Poetry in Restoration England: The Case of Dryden's "Annus Mirabilis"* (Cambridge: Cambridge University Press, 1975), pp. 190–204, 231–57.

[43] Korshin, "Queuing and Waiting," p. 243.

[44] Bernard Capp, "The Millennium and Eschatology in England," in *Puritans, The Millennium and the Future of Israel*, ed. Peter Toon (Cambridge: Cambridge University Press, 1970), pp. 427–34; William Lamont, "Richard Baxter, The Apocalypse, and the Mad Major," in Toon, pp. 399–426; Lamont, "Christian Magistrate and Romish Wolf," in *Prophecy and Millenarianism: Essays in Honour of Marjorie Reeves*, ed. Ann Williams (London: Longman, 1980), pp. 279–303.

[45] Frank Bastian, "Defoe's *Journal of the Plague Year* Reconsidered," *Review of English Studies*, n.s., 16 (1965), 151–73.

of the Restoration took place, led by the radical Fifth Monarchists, their "millenarian faith shaken but intact."[46] The day in the plague year of 1665 on which another insurrection against the Stuart monarchy was to begin was chosen because it had apocalyptic significance; both the rebels against an ungodly prince and Defoe's narrator in the *Journal of the Plague Year* had their eyes fixed on the skies, seeking justification for their actions of the moment.[47] When Defoe attended a private boarding school in Dorking, Surrey, in the early 1670s, he was in the immediate neighborhood of Christopher Feake. The most important Fifth monarchist leader in London before the Restoration, Feake had also headed a church in Swan Alley, had settled in Dorking at the Restoration, and was holding conventicles there as late as 1682.[48]

Just as the heavens had been read in the reign of Charles II to explain and to foretell portentous political occurrences, they too proclaimed and confirmed the right of Monmouth's rebellion in the west in 1685.[49] As before, the language of the defenders of English liberties fused anti-popery outbursts and hopes for the millennium. It has been recognized that Monmouth's army was a "godly army,"[50] but recent historians, stressing the political and economic motivations of his rank and file, have minimized the army's religious zeal.[51] Once again – as it was to continue to be in 1689 – the struggle was between God and Christ, against Satan and Anti-Christ.[52] And once again, a home-grown Christian savior, the Duke of Monmouth, was in the saddle, a royal conqueror assuming the mantle and sword of the Lord against Satan, popery, and slavery. The fervor of the moment can only be imagined in the paragraph one writer contributed to the "Church Book" of the Axminster Independent Chapel:

Now were the hearts of the people of God gladdened, and their hopes and expectations raised, that this man might be a deliverer for the nation, and the interest of Christ in it, who had been even harassed out with trouble and persecution, and were broken with the weight of oppression under which they had long groaned. Now also they hoped that the day was come in the which the good old cause of God and religion, that had lain as dead and buried for a long time, would revive again.[53]

In 1712 Defoe gave some thought to the political state of Great Britain and the incessantly destructive party warfare that was wracking his nation.

[46] B. S. Capp, *The Fifth Monarchy Men* (Totowa, NJ: Rowman and Littlefield, 1972), p. 198.

[47] Maurice Ashley, *John Wildman, Plotter and Postmaster* (New Haven: Yale University Press, 1947), p. 201; Defoe, *Journal of the Plague Year*, ed. Louis Landa (London: Oxford University Press, 1969), pp. 19–22.

[48] Capp, *Fifth Monarchy Men*, pp. 197, 249; Moore, *Daniel Defoe*, p. 84.

[49] Roberts, *Monmouth*, I, 217–18.

[50] See Emerson, *Monmouth's Rebellion*, pp. 72–73.

[51] Earle, *Monmouth's Rebels* (p. 11) notes the army's religious component; cf. Lacey, *Dissent*, p. 173.

[52] For 1689 see *A Brief Memoir of Mr. Justice Rokeby*, ed. W. Collins (Surtees Society, 1861), vol. 37, pp. 35, 49. Consult Joseph Wittreich's fine bibliography of these years in *The Apocalypse*, pp. 408–10.

[53] Roberts, *Monmouth*, I, 232.

England's present was conditioned by its past. "The Years 1637 to 1641 were all acted over again in the Wicked, but more Politick Reign of *Charles* II, and the Fury of *Civil-War* itself began to revive in the Popish and Tyrannical Government of King *James* II."[54] The reign of Queen Anne, with its Jacobite intrigue, Defoe saw as a recapitulation of the crises of the previous century. At those earlier critical junctures in his country's life, Defoe appears to have sought a man of the Lord – a Monmouth, a William III – a messianic conquerer to save England from Catholic domination. (Following William's death, with changing conditions – the accession of a queen, Marlborough's generalship, and Defoe's duties as the chief propagandist of the government – Defoe was to give his allegiance and devotion to a statesman-politician, Robert Harley.) To the twenty-five-year-old London merchant in 1685, Monmouth was the first, as the Prince of Orange was to be the finest, embodiment of the godly Protestant prince who was to lead his people, Moses-like, to the promised land. To imagine Defoe as a sharer in these millennial visions and possibilities of the late seventeenth century would help to explain his singular admiration for the crusading zeal of Queen Elizabeth and her defenses of European Protestantism. It would also give enriched meaning to his glorification of Gustavus Adolphus and his Protestant campaigns of the seventeenth century, for the Swedish monarch had been claimed by many as the herald of the millennium.[55] The residue of Defoe's earlier apocalyptic excitement might also be behind his rather tolerant and unusually considerate judgments of the French Prophets, when they scandalized London in 1708 with their delusions and millenarian fancies.[56] It would open up the mind of this gentleman-tradesman who, following his arrest for writing *The Shortest Way with the Dissenters*, begged, instead of incarceration, to enter "her Majties Service. If her Majtie Will be pleased to Order me, to Serve her a year, or More at my Own Charges, I will Surrender my Self a Voluntier at the head of her Armyes, in the Netherlands, To any Collonell of horse, her Majtie Shall Direct, and without Doubt my Lord [Daniel Finch, Earl of Nottingham] I shall Dye There Much More To her Service than in a Prison."[57]

And finally, the theme of England as an elect nation under its Deliverer King would provide another level of insight into the mind of Defoe, when, following the march of William's triumphant army into London and enrolling, as much trooper as tradesman, in the newly formed Royal Regiment of Volunteer Horse, consisting of 400 leading citizens, mostly dissenters, under

---

[54] *The Present State of the Parties in Great Britain* (London, 1712), p. 4.

[55] Richard Hayter, *The Meaning of the Revelation* (London, 1675), p. A3r; Capp, *Fifth Monarchy Men*, p. 234.

[56] *Review*, V. 12 (24 April 1708); V, 32 (10 June 1708); V. 33 (12 June 1708); and V. 48 (17 July 1708). See Hillel Schwartz, *The French Prophets: The History of a Millenarian Group in Eighteenth-Century England* (Berkeley: University of California Press, 1980), pp. 37–121.

[57] *The Letters of Daniel Defoe*, ed. George H. Healey (Oxford, Clarendon Press, 1955), p. 3.

the colonelcy of the king himself, he began his insightful examinations of the politics of his time.[58]

[58] Bastian, *Defoe's Early Life*, p. 141; Moore, *Daniel Defoe*, p. 279; William Lee, *Daniel Defoe: His Life and Recently Discovered Writings*, 3 vols. (London, 1869), I, 23–24.

2

Defoe's *Reflections Upon the Late Great Revolution* and the political languages of 1689

On 6 February 1689 Englishmen who had met in the Convention to resolve the remarkable happenings of the previous three months declared

that James the Second, having endeavoured to subvert the constitution of the kingdom by breaking the original contract between king and people, and by the advice of Jesuits and other wicked persons having violated the fundamental laws and having withdrawn himself out of this kingdom, has abdicated the government and that the throne is thereby become vacant.[1]

The Prince and Princess of Orange were then proclaimed King and Queen of England. In awesome ceremony one week later, the coronation of the new monarchs formalized the dramatic and, for many, unexpected consequence of the English Revolution. One aspect of the pamphlet debate that had begun with William's invasion and James II's flight came to an end. The proposals that had appeared during those heady days before the proclamation of the lords and commons of the Convention, of melting down the English constitution and making it anew, or of reconstituting the commonwealth, now gave way to the need to justify the new regime.[2] The Declaration of Rights, which was read to and accepted by the new monarchs on 13 February, stipulated the new oaths of allegiance and supremacy that were to be taken. Thus, before April, when the Convention Parliament passed the Act requiring those oaths of all civil and ecclesiastical office holders on pain of suspension, and after six months of grace, deprivation from office, pamphlets exploded into print elucidating the propriety, or less frequently, the impropriety of transferring allegiance from James to the new regime.[3] It was in the midst of this pamphlet

[1] *Journal of the House of Commons, 1688–89*, p. 115.

[2] For the radical programs of January see Lois G. Schwoerer, *The Declaration of Rights, 1689* (Baltimore: Johns Hopkins University Press, 1981), pp. 153–68; for "melting down" see *The Correspondence of John Locke*, ed. E. S. de Beer, 8 vols. (Oxford: Clarendon Press, 1976), III, 538.

[3] See Mark Goldie, "The Revolution of 1689 and the Structure of Political Argument: An Essay and an Annotated Bibliography on Pamphlets on the Allegiance Controversy," *Bulletin of Research in the Humanities*, 83 (1980), 473–564. I am greatly indebted to Goldie's superb essay and bibliography. It must be noted that his designation of Defoe as a "radical Whig" (pp. 508, 509), in the company of Locke and others, is the view that I will be questioning in the chapters that follow.

war over the Revolution, allegiance, and the nature of political obligation that
on 9 April Defoe's first essay defending the Revolution and William's right
to rule appeared.

As Defoe observed in 1712, the issues of the moment were once again
"founded on the same Questions which were disputed, and Complaints which
were granted by the *Petition of Right* [which] were all acted over again in the
Wicked and more Politick Reign of *Charles* II, and . . . began to revive in the
Popish and Tyrannical Government of King *James* II."[4] The language of
debate in the allegiance controversy was a continuation of the language of the
past; it dwelled on the same distinctions

> between monarchy absolute and limited; limited and mixt; between a power radically
> limited, and not only in the use and exercise of it; between a moral power to resist,
> and an authoritative and civil power; between resistance of the person, and of the
> authority; between resistance of the king himself, and of his agents and officers; between
> resistance positive and active; negative and passive; between Jus Regiminis et Usurpa-
> tionis; and that a King commanding not according to God's law, and man's law also:
> that this resistance in such case, is not a resistance of the king's power, but of his will;
> not fighting against the magistrate, but against the man; and the king not performing
> his duty, the subjects are released from theirs.[5]

The year 1689 saw the reintroduction of issues of resistance, of the origin
of civil power, and of the location and transfer of sovereignty; it re-explored
others, such as contract, conquest, possession, and distinctions between
abdication and desertion.[6]

This plethora of rationalizations for allegiance, with their confusions and
contradictions, led to what Professor Kenyon has labeled the "blunderbuss
technique," in which authors threw "in every argument they thought would
serve."[7] Authority was piled on authority; the Old and New Testaments,
Rome's classical authors, Protestant reformers, Church fathers, Elizabethan
precedents and the canons and homilies of the Church of England, Bracton,
Grotius, Fortescue, Selden, Pufendorf, and Coke were repeatedly cited,
repetitiously summarized, and marginally noted in the eighty tracts published
in 1689 that "were substantially concerned to vindicate or attack the constitutional, philosophical, or moral legitimacy of allegiance to the Revolution."[8]

---

[4] *The Present State of the Parties in Great Britain*, p. 4.

[5] Cited in James Daly, *Sir Robert Filmer and English Political Thought* (Toronto: University of
Toronto Press, 1979), p. 6.

[6] See Goldie's bibliography, pp. 526–27. See also Thomas P. Slaughter, " 'Abdicate' and 'Contract' in the Glorious Revolution," *Historical Journal*, 24 (1981), 323–38, and his " 'Abdicate'
and 'Contract' Restored," *Historical Journal*, 28 (1985), 399–403; Charles D. Tarlton, " 'The
Rulers Now on Earth'; Locke's *Two Treatises* and the Revolution of 1688," *Historical Journal*,
28 (1985), 279–98.

[7] J. P. Kenyon, *Revolution Principles: The Politics of Party, 1689–1720* (Cambridge: Cambridge
University Press, 1977), p. 22.

[8] Goldie, "The Revolution of 1689," p. 524.

Though the bulk of the authors were moderate Whigs and Tories, their ideological range varied greatly. In addition to Defoe the dissenter they included Peter Allix, an exiled Huguenot Whig radical; the Tory Edmund Bohun, Sir Robert Filmer's co-adjutor in the early 1680s; Gilbert Burnet, King William's principal propagandist and now Bishop of Sarum; Thomas Long, once a "hot head" of 1685 who, on the day appointed for thanksgiving for King James's victory over the Monmouth rebels four years earlier, had preached a sermon eulogizing the Stuarts and defaming the dissenters;[9] and the non-juring Jacobite divine, Abednigo Seller.

Before we turn to the arguments of Defoe's *Reflections Upon the Late Great Revolution. Written by a Lay-Hand in the Country, For the Satisfaction of Some Neighbours*, we can profitably look at its putative author and the tone and structure of his pamphlet. "[I]t was widely anticipated that many [incumbent Anglican clergy] would scruple even the appearance of violating their previous oath to James or of repudiating their fervid advocacy in the past of the doctrine of passive obedience to duly constituted authority."[10] That scrupulousness, loyalty, and ideology met the occasion with general silence; few pamphlets were written in defense of the deposed monarch. Pro-allegiance tracts authored by Anglican divines who had subscribed to the new government abounded. They asserted the lawfulness of taking the oaths or vindicated the Church of England clergy for their owning and praying for King William and Queen Mary. Letters were written from city ministers to friends, fellow clergy, and parliament men; clergymen wrote to their neighbors, engaged in friendly debates, or casuistically resolved queries concerning submission to the present regime. Defoe's decision, therefore, to speak as a layman was a deliberate ruse which would allay the imputation of self-interest and timeserving that were argued both by the anti-clericalists and the dedicated Tory-Jacobite.[11] Defoe's pamphlet was one of the first to be published by an "outsider." In addition, his *Reflections* from a "lay-hand" moved arguments for a new loyalty beyond the select but narrow ministerial establishment and pitched them to the electorate at large, who were just as much concerned about the lawfulness of the new regime and the varied foundations of its legitimacy.

Defoe sustained his Church of England *persona* as completely and as capably as he did any of his later fictional personations. Religion, faith, and the sanctity of the Anglican communion invest every page of the tract. This piety is not only signaled by the obvious grounding of his brief in "the Sacred Scriptures,"

[9] Edward Arber, *The Term Catalogues, 1688–1709 A.D.*, 3 vols. (London: 1903–06), II, x.

[10] Henry Horwitz, *Parliament, Policy and Politics in the Reign of William III* (Manchester: Manchester University Press, 1977), p. 21. Cf. F. G. James, "The Bishops in Politics, 1688–1714," in *Conflict in Stuart England: Essays in Honour of Wallace Notestein*, ed. William A. Aiken and Basil D. Henning (Hamden, CN: Archon), p. 231.

[11] From Goldie's extensive bibliography it appears that Defoe's is the first lay voice in the allegiance controversy.

but by more extreme commentary.[12] For example, he forthrightly defends the seven candlesticks of the church – the six bishops and the Archbishop of Canterbury who had been jailed by King James because of their refusal to order the reading of his Declaration of Indulgence in churches (p. 48); he recalls with shame the martyrdom of Charles I, "the best of Kings, and of Men" (p. 22; also p. 65); and he can even assert, opening his tract, that if any order of men are *jure divino*, it is those who consitute the episcopate. In fact, epsicopacy itself is the only true church government that can lawfully be set up for the conversion of heathens in newly discovered lands (p. 5). In his earliest tract, then, we find Defoe, in reasoned polemical discourse able to embrace one of the most despised doctrines ascribed to the episcopate by his dissenting ministers. And yet, his most radical inference, drawn from the Bible, is his justification for regicide, since he is able to enumerate great numbers of kings killed because of their impiety. Defoe has established for his readers a traditionally conservative Anglican voice that is yet able to find support for revolution, usurpation, regicide, and political obligation in the languages and the silences of "God's own Word and Law" (p. 6), and not, surprisingly, given the language of prevailing debate surrounding him, according to doctrines of natural law or readings in secular history.

Yet the audacity of these inferences is remarkably tempered, and their radical impact diluted of shock and dismay, by the hesitant, yielding, and concessive tone of the text; the narrator's deference to the "sacred Writ" is matched by his consideration for the sensibility and good-will of his reader. Defoe avoided the extreme of virulence and banter that characterized most contemporary productions. His is a voice of quiet reasoning, supposing, inferring, thinking, safely averring, hoping, seeming, remarking by the way, and safely concluding.[13] No assaults are made on church sycophants or on hesitant and hypocritical supporters of William's *de facto* rule. The author of the *Reflections*, yielding and polite, is always loath to affirm the worst inferences of the holy text (p. 21). Thus, Defoe has fashioned a writer who, on every page of his defense, reveals himself to be a thoughtful and considerate citizen whose reflections should carry conviction because of their balanced reasonableness and distanced objectivity.

If, as we shall see, Defoe's mix of arguments for allegiance resembled the "blunderbuss technique" noted by Professor Kenyon, that mix was organized so as to avoid the rambling compendiums that characterized its competitors. At his opening Defoe confronts the two "Foundation Stones" of Jacobite ideology: "That Monarchy is *Jure Divino*" and "that if the King Command us any thing contrary to our Laws, we are yet in Conscience obliged to obey, and yield Obedience either Active or Passive" (pp. 5–6). Two issues logically follow: "*First*, From

---

[12] *Reflections*, p. 6. All further citations will be noted in the text.
[13] See, e.g., pp. 30–31 where Defoe "supposes" three times, "thinks", "infer," "collects," and "concludes" once.

whence Kings in general do derive their Authority (which answers to the first Point of Monarchy being *Jure Divino*;) and *Secondly*, What is that particular Authority that is vested in our Kings (from which I hope to clear the second Point)'' (p. 6). The first issue will be confuted from ''the Sacred Scriptures'' by three proofs: ''*First*, That Monarchy was not at the first Instituted by God Almighty; *Secondly*, That after Monarchy was permitted and established among the Jews, the People did make and set up their Kings; and *Thirdly*, That those Kings which were named and appointed by God himself had not an absolute Power, but were under Conditions and Covenants'' (pp. 6–7). When Defoe turned to the second issue, the peculiar authority vested in English monarchs, that is, from the scriptural to the historical mode, the sustained coherence of his essay flounders. His commonplace assertion, that '' 'tis from the Statute-Book, not the Bible, that we must judge of the Power our Kings are invested withal, and also of our own Obligations, and the measures of our Subjection'' (p. 35), is negated both by the general absence of expected documentation and any intelligent appraisal of the available English sources. This silence is notable if, as one historian has written, one of the mandatory inclusions in any pamphlet written to justify allegiance was the argument drawn from English history and ''carefully grounded in the specifics of the English constitution and employ[ing] concrete English political examples.''[14] It could be suggested that Defoe's refutation from Scripture alone was his conscious adaptation of a mode that was absent from the early pamphlet literature in the spring of 1689. Yet his citations from Bracton, which were lifted from a pamphlet published a month earlier, would lead us to believe that not only has there ''been so much writ on this Subject already'' (p. 43), but at this point in time his readings in English constitutional history were sparse.[15] A schoolboy's truism from Horne's *Mirrour of Justices* confirms a medieval precedent; he echoes the commonplace that ''*William* the First was willing to wave his Title of Conquerour, and by confirming the Ancient Rights and Priviledges of the People, be receiv'd as their Legal, not their Conquerour, or Arbitrary Governour'' (p. 41); and he alludes to Henry VII as another ''Prince of the Blood'' who had been a legitimate claimant to the throne though not in the immediate line of succession (p. 50). This was a crucial point, made to reassure his fearful contemporaries who ''made a horrible out-cry, as if both the Constitution of the Government, and

---

[14] Tarlton, '' 'The Rulers Now on Earth','' p. 282. ''So crucial were these historical arguments,'' Tarlton continues, ''that they obviated the need to resort to religious ones'' (p. 284).

[15] Defoe's citation from Bracton (p. 42; mispaged ''24'') appeared a month earlier in *A Friendly Debate Between Dr. Kingsman, a Dissatisfied Clergy-Man, and Gratianus Trimmer, a Neighbour Minister* (London: 1689), p. 22. If there is one pamphlet that Defoe is most indebted to, it is this one. It cites, as Defoe does, Fleta (p. 28) and Sadler (p. 27), and its tone is closest to Defoe's. Significantly, it also cites Hooker (p. 29), the fundamental constitution (pp. 21, 49), and remarks that a king ''holds his Crown and Scepter, by Scripture-Patent, and Divine Right'' (p. 6). For Defoe's silences on these subjects see below.

the Laws of Succession, were all subverted and broken'' and the English crown
made an elective one (p. 50). In his conclusions, ostensibly still historical, Defoe
ends as he began, ranging all over the Testaments, from Exodus to the Epistle of
Peter, harmonizing Romans 13 and 1 Peter 2, sustaining his own ''sober
Sense and plain Reason'' applied to the Scriptures to argue the rightness of
the revolution and the morality of swearing obedience to King William and
Queen Mary.[16]

   All that being said, one has to admit that Defoe's *Reflections* canvassed and combined, as did nearly all of the tracts, almost every prevailing argument for
allegiance. His first publication is a product of the political moment; it reveals little
of the accepted paradoxes that make up his more mature political essays. For
example, the presentation of Nimrod as the archetype of kingship, who began his
reign by ''Force and Violence'' (p. 10), reiterates the exegeses of the fervid
republicans who saw the kingly office founded in despotism and
tyranny.[17] Kingship thus carried a stain from its inception. Perhaps as a consequence, his explication of the First Book of Samuel pays little attention to the
martial character and the military exploits of Saul; that is, Defoe makes no attempt
to enhance the royal office. As we shall see in our examination of *Jure Divino*,
supreme generalship in war, substantiated by Defoe's poetic rendering of the testament of Israel's God, will become the *sine qua non* of Saul's kingship and the
cornerstone for all true monarchy. What Defoe does stress in the *Reflections* is the
more traditional whiggish view that the Israelite nation confirmed the prophecy
of the Lord; thus the approbation of the people was necessary before Saul could
receive the crown (pp. 17, 18, 23, 24). ''So true is sometimes that saying, *Vox Populi
est Vox Dei*'' (p. 15). Yet his introductory remarks about the providential nature
of the Revolution, his repeated observation that the Jewish nation submitted
weakly, and with God's silent consent, to the strongest claimant to the throne (pp.
20, 27), and his inference that ''Usurpers are raised by, and may pretend to reign
by God's Power; and therefore may claim the same Obedience that Lawful Kings
[do]'' (p. 19), prove that God's writ teaches submission and obedience. These were
the doctrines that permitted Tory churchmen to take their oaths without qualms
to the *de facto* government of William and Mary. Not only, then, did the Jews sit
''Neuters, and did not concern themselves of either side, but obeyed him that
proved the strongest'' (p. 20); English law too made it treason to resist a *de facto*
king, ''so that Possession is not only, as we used to say, eleven Points of the Law,
but is in this Case [William's right to the throne] all twelve'' (p. 62).[18]

---

[16] The phrase is Swift's; see his ''Upon Sleeping in Church,'' *Irish Tracts, 1721–1723. And Sermons*,
   ed. Herbert Davis and Louis Landa (Oxford: Basil Blackwell, 1963), p. 217.

[17] For the tradition see Arnold Williams, *The Common Expositor* (Chapel Hill: University of
   North Carolina Press, 1948), pp. 222–23.

[18] In 1691, before the official proscription of the conquest argument by Parliament in 1693,
   Defoe attacked William Sherlock's *de facto* argument for William's legitimacy; see *A New
   Discovery of an Old Intreague*, in *A Second Volume of the Writings of The Author of the True-Born
   Englishman*, p. 11.

What can be called Defoe's toryish voice echoes current conservative defences of the Revolution and the legitimacy of the new oaths. In addition to stressing the *de facto* argument that permitted passive allegiance to the king in possession, Defoe assured those who had qualms about the "revolutionary" occurrence that it was a unique occasion in English history, for while King James had forfeited his right to rule and had freed his subjects of their allegiance to him, no precedent had been set. By stressing the exceptional occurrence of 1688 Defoe forestalled fears that a tradition of revolt by disaffected Englishmen had thus been established.

Defoe's political ideas, we shall see, developed under pressure of personal experience coincident with momentous changes that were to affect dramatically the long-standing relationship between crown and parliament. In 1689 Defoe's political literature embraces a wideranging, confusing, and contradictory eclecticism. It has the tags of *salus populi supreme lex* (pp. 61, 62), the balanced constitution comprising the king-in-parliament (p. 36), and the co-ordination of the three estates, the latter without any suggestion of its revolutionary implication.[19] But he does not suggest that the parliament is sovereign, nor does he conclude that, given the striking situation of 1688, the Convention had the right to nominate any heir to the throne. Nothing in the *Reflections* approximates the radical notion that the people, however one defined them, had the right to transfer their allegiance to *any* leader who could guarantee them peace and safety.[20] Tangentially, it could be noted that Defoe's refusal to justify the legitimacy of the new regime through the Stuart monarch's "Abdication" aligns him with the more toryish voices in and out of Parliament.[21] As one virulent Jacobite wrote, abdication "is a hard word, which I will not pretend to understand, because my dictionary does not."[22] The writer of the *Reflections* insists the late King James has "forefeited the Crown" (p. 48; also pp. 49, 60, 62); did "Unking himself" (p. 51); or has "quitted" or "deserted" the government (pp. 63, 66).

The ringing tenet of philosophical or constitutional radicalism which could be heard throughout the spring of 1689, that it is "the common opinion of all knowing men that all men are born free," or that upon the dissolution

---

[19] For the co-ordination controversy see Corinne C. Weston and Janelle R. Greenberg, *Subjects and Sovereigns: The Grand Controversy over Legal Sovereignty in Stuart England* (Cambridge: Cambridge University Press, 1981).

[20] See, e.g., Edward Stephens, *Important Questions of State, Law, Justice and Prudence*, reprinted in *The True English Government* (London, 1689), p. 11.

[21] See Schwoerer, *Declaration of Rights*, pp. 217–18. But cf. Julian H. Franklin, *John Locke and the Theory of Sovereignty* (Cambridge: Cambridge University Press, 1978), for the Tory argument for "constructive abdication" (p. 101). To the end of his life Defoe never wavered in his belief that James II had not abdicated; see *Of Royall Educacion*, ed. Karl D. Bülbring, p. 23.

[22] *Observations upon the Late Revolution in England* (1689), in *Somers Tracts*, X, 345.

of government a totally new polity can be erected by the people, is not now discoverable in Defoe's thought[23] These admissions and absences ask that we consider what can proleptically be termed Defoe's "Lockean" political thought in 1689.

We ought, first, to be clear about Defoe's contract-compact-covenant language. It, too, is derivative, a consequence of his traditionalist reading of secularised covenant theology derived from 1 Samuel 10.25. "*Then Samuel told the People the manner of the Kingdom, and wrote it in a book, and laid it up before the Lord*" (p. 28). Defoe's language of contract is anchored, not in history or natural law, but specifically in Old Testament story; its meaning arises out of the corporate life of Israel. His terminology carefully differentiates between contract's testamentary denotation and its developing legalistic connotation. This scriptural foundation of Defoe's political thought is reasserted in his narrative of the first kings of England, who are also advanced to their thrones with an equivalent coronation ceremony, that of eating and drinking before the Lord. When Defoe styles the coronation day "the Marriage-day between the King and Kingdom" (p. 44), what is brought to the imagination is not the politico-secular moment of the seventeenth century but the feudal-sacramental world of medieval and Elizabethan history. In fact, Defoe's imagination here is at one, not with the political moderns of the seventeenth century, nor with those who were agents of revolution, but with the Old Testament prophets, who spoke "of the relationship between God and Israel as one of husband and wife, which in itself is also considered covenantal."[24] When Defoe quotes 2 Kings 11.17, "*And Jehoiada made a Covenant between the Lord, and the King, and the People, that they should be the Lords people; between the King also and the People*" (p. 32), it is not the language of contemporary political debate that we read; rather it is the language of Huguenot radicalism and the vision of England as an elect nation. Thus, while Defoe does admit that "the Kings of *Israel* and *Judah* were not Absolute, but were under Obligations and Conditions to their People, as well as subjected to the Laws of God" (p. 32), he can still ask "whether it is not possible to make a humane Contract so strong, that it shall be a Sin against God to break it" (p. 33).

Defoe's "humane Contract" is no social contract of individuals who come together to form a commonwealth; it does not posit a free community bound together by voluntary agreement to a covenant predating the existence of a ruling sovereign. The reader of the *Reflections* can never entertain the thought that the political community is a fixed and certain body with independent powers of its own antecedent to the creation, or the calling into office, of the king.[25] If kings are called to their thrones with God's approval and the

---

[23] See, e.g., Gilbert Burnet, *An Enquiry into the Measures of Submission to the Supreme Authority* (1688), in *State Tracts* (London, 1692), p. 483.

[24] *Encyclopaedia Judaica* (Jerusalem: Macmillan, 1971), V. 1021.

[25] See J. W. Gough, *The Social Contract: A Critical Study of Its Development* (Oxford: Clarendon Press, 1947).

people's consent, it remains for kings, and not the people, to establish government and to define its purposes. Defoe's language of contract and kingship is concrete and historical, rather than philosophic and theoretical. The *Reflections* is totally devoid of natural law and natural rights terminology. There is no mention of any self-evident rights, nor of any innate rule of creation that guarantees basic freedoms to the citizens of a commonwealth. The political societies in the *Reflections*, Israelite and English, are not founded on principles of natural obligation. No law of nature binds Defoe's subjects to their sovereign. Valid covenants, institutionalized and memorialized in coronation symbolism rather than in statute law, are sufficient protectors of the people's freedoms (p. 44). When the author of the *Reflections Upon the Late Great Revolution* seeks a secure basis for political legitimacy, he generally finds it not in nature but in God's text and human history.

In 1960 Peter Laslett published what has since become an indispensable edition of Locke's *Two Treatises of Government*. He there showed that the greater part of the text had been composed during the Exclusion Crisis of 1679–81. Since then, political scientists have learned to understand much of Locke's ideas by sorting out his silences; that is, they have considered the absences from his text, revised for publication in the aftermath of the Revolution, of those arguments and that political vocabulary that were the common concerns during the Revolution in general and the allegiance controversy in particular.[26] J. H. Elliott, examining the impact in the sixteenth and seventeenth centuries of the discovery of the New World on the Old, observed: "It is difficult not to be impressed by the strange lacunae and the resounding silences in many places where references to the New World could reasonably be expected."[27] And Frank Bastian's recent biography of Defoe's early years, which reconstructs Defoe's travels through a meticulous examination of his silences, must be seriously considered by all future biographers.[28] To seek the intentions of a masked author like Defoe and to define liguistic conventions in ordinary times are intensely chancy pursuits. But to search for absent languages of political debate in an author during a time of radical upheaval would appear fanciful.[29] Nevertheless it is essential that we be clear about what Defoe has *not* said in his *Reflections Upon the Late Great Revolution*.

[26] *Two Treatises*, ed. Laslett, pp. 77–78; M. P. Thompson, "The Reception of Locke's *Two Treatises of Government*, 1690–1705," *Political Studies*, 24 (1976), 184–91.

[27] *The Old World and the New, 1492–1650* (Cambridge: Cambridge University Press, 1970), p. 13.

[28] *Defoe's Early Life*. G. A. Starr, *Defoe and Spiritual Autobiography* (Princeton: Princeton University Press, 1965) considers Crusoe's silences (pp. 85–99). For a theory of silences in literature see Pierre Macherey, *A Theory of Literary Production*, trans. Geoffrey Wall (London: Routledge & Kegan Paul, 1978), pp. 82–101.

[29] See Lotte Mulligan, Judith Richards, and John Graham, "Intentions and Conventions: A Critique of Quentin Skinner's Method for the Study of the History of Ideas," *Political Studies*, 27 (1979), 84–98.

First, Defoe has said nothing about "the fundamental law." This is not the fundamental law of nature, or of reason, but the fundamental law of the ancient constitution, "that most important and elusive of seventeenth-century concepts," so deftly explicated for us by J. G. A. Pocock.[30] What this absence portends for Defoe's later accommodation to a strong and assertive monarch is revealed in Franklin L. Baumer's bold statement with which he introduced his study of early Tudor theories of kingship: "Where there is fundamental law, there cannot be absolute monarchy."[31] The proposition has not been stated with greater clarity or succinctness by later commentators on fundamental law in English history. J. W. Gough concluded that "fundamental laws . . . were valued for the protection they afforded against the arbitrary power of kings."[32] Professor Pocock observed that fundamental law, when tied to its almost cognate concepts of the common law and the ancient constitution, "became alternative to and incompatible with the sovereignty of the king."[33] A royalist like Filmer unequivocally rejected it, for it limited or adulterated the power of his "indivisible, all-encompassing, irresistible sovereignty."[34] The concept was momentarily jettisoned by parliament during the Exclusion crisis when it affirmed its right to limit or change the fundamental law of England's hereditary monarchy. (Parliament failed to do so.) But by 1688 it had become part of the bedrock of Whig political thought.[35]

Sir Robert Brady, a bulwark of royalist thought, sought to demolish the doctrine of a fundamental law of an English constitution. In doing so, Brady understood that he was challenging the mythic authority that was intoned to prove the antiquity, and thus the implicit sovereignty, of parliaments. Without the fundamental law, without the ancient constitution, "all the *Liberties* and *Priviledges* the People can pretend to, were the *Grants* and *Concessions* of the Kings of this Nation, and Derived from the Crown."[36]

The fundamental law came to be linked, albeit unhistorically and

---

[30] *The Ancient Constitution and the Feudal Law: A Study of English Historical Thought in the Seventeenth Century* ((Cambridge: Cambridge University Press, 1957), p. 48.

[31] *The Early Tudor Theory of Kingship* (New Haven: Yale University Press, 1940), p. 6.

[32] *Fundamental Law in English Constitutional History* (Oxford: Clarendon Press, 1955), p. 65.

[33] *The Ancient Constitution and the Feudal Law*, p. 234.

[34] Daly, *Sir Robert Filmer*, p. 23. See David Resnick, "Locke and the Rejection of the Ancient Constitution," *Political Theory*, 12 (1984), 97–114, Locke, it must be noted, rejected the concept to appeal to natural law and reason; Defoe, to appeal to Scripture and to English history that paralleled scriptural antecedents.

[35] Betty Behrens, "The Whig Theory of the Constitution in the Reign of Charles II," *Cambridge Historical Journal*, 7 (1941–43), 42–71. For fundamental law seen as a limitation on the King or "chief magistrate" during Exclusion see William Petyt, *The Ancient Right of the Commons of England Asserted* (London, 1680), pp. 57–58; and *A Dialogue at Oxford Between a Tutor and a Gentleman, Formerly His Pupil Concerning Government* (London, 1681), p. 7. *Touching the Fundamental Laws, or Politique Constitution of this Kingdom* (1643) was reprinted in *State Tracts* (1692).

[36] "To the Reader," *Complete History of England* (London, 1685), p. A4r. For Brady's importance see Pocock, *The Ancient Constitution and the Feudal Law*, pp. 182–228.

irrationally, with "custom, antiquity, native origin, the people's consent, reason, and truth," and it is by these equivalencies that we recognize the most recurrent ideological strands in the cable of Revolution whiggery.[37] This justification for revolution, that James II had broken the fundamental law, also legitimated submission to the present government of William, who had restored it. Significantly, the doctrine was not part of the political language of conservative royalists, Tories, and non-jurors writing in 1689 or thereafter. Those who did embrace the language of fundamental law and its contemporary equivalences implicitly appear to have accepted also the concept of immemorial parliamentary right and a regulated monarchy. In this camp we find defenders of the Revolution of nearly all persuasions: moderate Whigs, contractualists, constitutionalists, and moderate Tories, in addition to those radical Whigs with whom many readers have associated Defoe.[38]

Edward Cooke's post-Exclusion tract of 1682, *Argumentum Antinormanicum*, was republished in the spring of 1689. It carried a new title: *A Seasonable Treatise; wherein is proved, That King William (commonly call'd the Conqueror) Did not get the Imperial Crown of England by the Sword, but by the Election and Consent of the People.* A frontispiece that was etched for this new edition pictured William of Orange receiving the Scepter and the Crown – the Sword is absent – from Britannica and the Archbishop of York. The Explanation attached to the print informed the reader that the country's new king promised not to "violate, break, or alter, the Fundamental Rights of the Kingdom (as Tyrants do, who only design to enslave their People)" – obviously alluding to the joint declaration of the Lords and Commons a few months earlier, that "King James the Second [had] violated the fundamental laws."[39] In 1690, two radical Whigs, William Atwood and Daniel Whitby, in tracts affirming allegiance, both intoned "original contract" "for the Satisfaction of Those Who Scruple the Oath of Allegiance to King William and Queen Mary." Both implied that fundamental law confirmed the elective nature of the

---

[37] Reinhold Bendix, *Kings or People* (Berkeley: University of California Press, 1978), p. 314.

[38] Burnet, *An Enquiry Into the Measures of Submission* (London, 1688), p. 4; Stephens, *Important Questions of State, Law, Justice and Prudence*, p. 11; Samuel Masters, *The Case of Allegiance in our Present Circumstances* (London, 1689), p. 7; *A Friendly Debate Between Dr. Kingsman*, p. 49; James Wellwood, *A Vindication of the Present Great Revolution in England* (London, 1689), p. 2; Thomas Long, *A Resolution of Certain Queries Concerning Submission to the Present Government* (London, 1689), p. A4r; Peter Allix, *An Examination of the Scruples of Those Who Refuse to take the Oath of Allegiance* (London, 1689), p. 6; *A Political Conference between Aulicus, a Courtier; Demas, a Countryman; and Civicus, a Citizen* (London, 1690), p. 26; also p. 47. Charlwood Lawton shrewdly used the language of fundamental law to justify preserving the Stuart monarchy and hereditary succession, though, by 1694, his view appears to be an isolated one; see *The Jacobite Principles Vindicated*, in *Somers Tracts*, X, 523–41, esp. pp. 526–28.

[39] *A Seasonable Treatise*, p. A2v, and see p. 21 and n.1 for the joint declaration. For the significance of the metonymic crown, sword, and scepter in the language of political argument see chapter five below.

English monarchy.[40] In a word, to question or deny the concept of fundamental law, or its correspondent terms like ancient constitution, fundamental rights, or original constitution, was to encourage monarchical absolutism, to invalidate the thesis of the agelessness of parliaments, to undermine contemporary defenses of property rights, and to suggest that "the reasons of state" of the king carried greater weight and authority than the accumulated wisdom of countless generations of common lawyers. It was one of the standard Whig tenets of 1689, and in the paper wars of the next reign it was to remain an essential ingredient of Whig propaganda that affirmed the supremacy of the parliament over the king.[41]

This language of the fundamental law, or of the ancient constitution, is never intoned by Defoe, neither in the *Reflections* nor, in its traditional sense, in any of his later writings. When that language does appear – in 1689, 1692, 1694, 1701, 1706, and 1710 – the catchwords no longer retain their air of mystery and ambiguity which had enabled Whig writers to impose quasi-legal restraints on the wide ranging, if not absolute, powers of kings. For Defoe, fundamental law is always rooted in relatively recent history, or is anchored in statute law, the Magna Charta, or the Treaty between England and Scotland.[42] In the context of 1689, perhaps one could surmise that Defoe perceived the concept of fundamental law as an obstacle to constitutional renovation and even republican reform, but there is no hint of that in any of his later writings. Earlier, we distinguished Defoe's political vocabulary from the radical and revolutionary rhetoric of the social contract and individual rights. In this case his silence over one of the basic tenets of Whig political thought, his indifference, if not hostility, to the ancient constitution's immemorial magic that negated, in Professor Pocock's words, "the fear of some sort of sovereignty or absolutism," and his insistence on its modern, concrete embodiments, suggest an unconscious rejection of the time-honored concept with which his generation sought to bridle monarchical excess.[43]

[40] Daniel Whitby, *An Historical Account of Some Things Relating to the Nature of the English Constitution*, (London, 1690), and esp. p. 54; William Atwood, *The Fundamental Constitution of the English Government*, (London, 1690); Kenyon, *Revolution Principles*, pp. 35–36. Fundamental law was still a strong component of traditional Whig thought in 1695; see James Tyrrell, *A Brief Enquiry into the Ancient Constitution of England* (London, 1695), and esp. pp. 36, 43, 62. In 1697 King William founded his right to the English throne on fundamental law; see "A Memorial drawn by King William's special Direction, intended to be given in at the Treaty of Ryswick, justifying the Revolution, and the Course of his Government," in *Somers Tracts*, XI, 108.

[41] See, e.g., John Tutchin, *The First Volume of Observators* (London, 1703), nos. 2, 24, 98.

[42] *The Englishman's Choice, and True Interest* (London, 1694), p. 17; *The Danger of the Protestant Religion Consider'd* (London, 1701), in *A True Collection of the Writings of the Author of the True Born English-man* (London, 1703), p. 239; *The Case of the Protestant Dissenters in Carolina* (London, 1706), p. 31; *Seldom Comes a Better* (London, 1710), p. 11; *The Present State of the Parties in Great Britain*, pp. 237, 277, 279. But see *Review*, VI, 132 (9 Feb. 1710).

[43] *The Ancient Constitution and the Feudal Law*, p. 51.

. . . by the naturall lawe whereunto [God] hath . . . made all subject, the lawfull power of making lawes to commande whole politique societies of men belongeth so properly unto the same intire societies, that for any Prince or potentate of what kinde soever upon earth to exercise the same of him selfe and not *either* by express commission immediatly and personally receyved from God, *or* els by authoritie derived at the first from their consent upon whose persons they impose lawes, it is no better than meere tyrannye.[44]

This passage from Book I, chapter 10 of Richard Hooker's *Of the Laws of Ecclesiastical Polity* is one of the most quoted, and the concept is one of the most echoed, in the pamphlets of the allegiance controversy and those justifying the revolution.[45] As Robert Eccleshall has shown, Hooker's consensual account of political origins and his defense of English political and ecclesiastical institutions had been used earlier to justify manifold stances and to bolster a large variety of doctrinal postures.[46] The mutually exclusive categories of Book I, chapter 10 were echoed by Puritans, Laudians, Levellers, and Latitudinarians. In 1658 Edward Gee cited Hooker, not only to refute Filmer's divine right patriarchalism but to deny the legitimacy of the usurping Protectorate.[47] During the Exclusion controversy an Oxford graduate echoed the Hookerian dichotomy quoted above to counter his ex-tutor's arguments for divine right and conquest. From it he concluded to assert the supreme right of an English parliament to make and break laws, and to repeal the old and to make the new.[48]

But earlier, in 1648, Book VIII of the *Ecclesiastical Polity* had been published. Because of its anti-monarchical sentiments and its depiction of episcopacy as a human institution, Hooker became *persona non grata* to the conservative

---

[44] Richard Hooker, *Of the Laws of Ecclesiastical Polity*, ed. Georges Edelen, in *The Folger Library Edition of the Works of Richard Hooker*, ed. W. Speed Hill (Cambridge, MA: Harvard University Press, 1977), I, 102 (my italics).

[45] See, among others, Burnet, *An Enquiry into the Measures of Submission*, (1688), p. 2; Richard Claridge, *A Defence of the Present Government under King William and Queen Mary* (London, 1689), p. 2; *A Friendly Debate Between Dr. Kingsman*, p. 28; Long, *A Resolution of Certain Queries*, pp. 1, 2; Allix, *An Examination of the Scruples*, p. 21. A radical writer, William Denton, italicizes the "either/or" passage but does not give its source, expecting it to be recognized as Hooker's; see *Jus Regiminis: Being a Justification of Defensive Arms in General. And Consequently of our Late Revolutions and Transactions to be the Just Right of the Kingdom* (London, 1689), p. 20; also pp. 22, 23. For Locke and Hooker see *Two Treatises*, p. 57; II, 2 (p. 288). Locke cites the passage on II, 11 (p. 374). See also Algernon Sidney, *Discourses Concerning Government*, 3rd ed. (London, 1751) p. 85.

[46] *Order and Reason in Politics: Theories of Absolute and Limited Monarchy in Early Modern England* (Oxford: Oxford University Press, 1978), pp. 126–50; and "Richard Hooker and the Peculiarities of the English: The Reception of the *Ecclesiastical Polity* in the Seventeenth and Eighteenth Centuries," *History of Political Thought*, (1981), 63–117. I am indebted to Professor Eccleshall for his correspondence and his criticism of an earlier version of this chapter.

[47] *The Divine Right and Originall of the Civill Magistrate from God Illustrated and Vindicated* (London, 1658), pp. 22, 34–35, 138.

[48] *A Dialogue at Oxford Between a Tutor and a Gentleman Formerly His Pupil, Concerning Government* (London, 1681), pp. 5, 18. The royalist tutor supports "Jus Divinum" with the argument from conquest (p. 5); the whiggish gentleman uses fundamental law and compact in tandem (p. 7).

defenders of monarchy. Professor Eccleshall writes that "as far as I can ascertain, no royalist tract of the Restoration endorsed Hooker's view that communal consensus was the foundation of English polity."[49] He had been tainted by the uses which anti-royalist, even republican, writers had made of the tenth chapter of the first book of the *Polity*, which maintained that authority had been derived from the people.[50]

It was only natural, then, for the defenders of the Revolution to quote, cite, or paraphrase this most dramatic of Hooker's themes, not only to give respectability to the changed constitutional scene but to turn the flank of recalcitrant Anglican polemicists. One divine of the Church of England, defending the new government of William and Mary, abusively dismissed "a degenerous Race of Protestants" for whom God had determined but one true divine right model for civil government. Rather, he asserted, God has "left us, as *all other Nations*, to such a *Form* as shall be agreed upon by the People; and where this *Agreement* is not, 'tis not properly Government but Tyranny." Book I, chapter 10 is marginally glossed and the above quotation follows. "The Judgment of this great Man," he continues, "I could back with very many good Authorities; but there is no need, he alone being *Instar Omnium*, Equal to All, whose Five first Books of Ecclesiastical Polity have been received as Oracles, even by those very Persons who now differ from him."[51]

The quotation from Book I, chapter 10 of Hooker's *Polity*, to which nearly all writers of the Revolution except non-jurors and Jacobites were drawn, resembles the community-centered view of government that Corinne Weston and Janelle Greenberg have studied. (Hooker, of course, is not the father of it; it has an honorable lineage antedating him.[52]) It is a view that projects a society prior to and independent of representative authority; that human community moves mankind from its original natural state to a political order. To cite Hooker is to suppose the existence of a functioning community with certain rights and abilities existing in the multitude, or to accept the fact of a communal mind that was already in some advanced state of development before the establishment of a deliberate political order. In a sense, then, a social consensus, not a social contract, preceded a rectoral one; community preceded monarchy. "So that in a word all publike regiment of what kind soever seemeth evidently to have risen from deliberate advice, consultation, and composition betwene men, judging it convenient and behoofull."[53] Political society originates from a social-psychological need of the corporation, which then can transfer sovereignty to the one, the few, or the many. The state is

---

[49] "Richard Hooker and the Peculiarities of the English," p. 94.

[50] *Ibid.*, p. 95.

[51] Claridge, *A Defense of the Present Government*, pp. 2, 3.

[52] See J. W. Allen, *A History of Political Thought in the Sixteenth Century* (London: Methuen & Co., 1928), pp. 190–92; A. P. Entreaves, *The Medieval Contribution to Political Thought: Thomas Aquinas, Marsilius of Padua, Richard Hooker* (London: Oxford University Press. 1939).

[53] *Ecclesiastical Polity*, I, 100.

founded on the natural sociability of mankind, and government did not necessarily have to be monarchic.

The connection that can be seen between the Hookerian community-centered view of political origins and the belief in fundamental law is this: Hooker's historicism, his reliance on a mythic community and the evolutionary development of a political order from public consensus, and the concept of a mythic fundamental law-constitution, both dismiss the fact of an energizing and initiating warrior-king sanctioned by God to be the creator of the political order. For the believer in the fundamental law and for those taken in by the mythology enunciated by Hooker, a strange kind of corporate wisdom rooted in an unrecoverable past was the guarantee of the political grandeur of English polity. Both beliefs, we can conclude, "created a presumption that English laws were legitimate by suggesting that the collective wisdom of the nation as personified in its representatives in Parliament could not be thought defective in regard to the public welfare."[54] Kingly authority, then, could only be derived; it was never self- or God-initiated. No private act of will or valor could ever instigate monarchy. Conscious human design had always been the just foundation of monarchical authority. Logically, then, both beliefs appeared in tandem in 1689 in tracts that questioned the authority of, or sought limitations on, or justified resistance to, the king on the throne.

The variety of Defoe's arguments, I have noted, make it almost impossible to project a single target reader for his first political pamphlet. The doctrines he enunciates are both Whig and Tory shibboleths. He condones regicide yet extols the holiness of the episcopate. Whig propositions, such as contractual resistance – though founded on the Scriptures – rest side by side with desertion and non-resistance to the king in possession. But Defoe, as far as I can tell, never cited Hooker or the above-mentioned Hooker commonplace in any tract that we now ascribe to him.[55] His rejection of the community-centered ideology, added to his rejection of the fundamental law, reveal a disquietude with two contemporary propositions that devalorize the monarch or refuse to acknowledge the charismatic lawgiver-warrior-king of biblical, classical, and English tradition and myth. In the *Reflections* this disquietude is signaled in his analyses of the monarchies of Saul and David, whom "God Almighty does the most directly and immediately" raise to the throne (p. 14); or his insistence that "I would not be understood so, as if I meant to exclude God from having anything to do in the setting up or making of Kings" (p. 53). The significance of kingly activity comes up again in his reading of

[54] Robert Eccleshall, "English Conservatism as Ideology," *Political Studies*, 25 (1977), 71.

[55] Leslie in the *Rehearsal*, no. 337 (3 July 1708), remarks that Hooker is quoted by Locke, "by *Observators* and *Reviews*, and most of the republican writers." I have not found Hooker quoted in the *Reviews*. What is important, then, is that Leslie believed that Hooker would naturally be quoted by Defoe, since he was quoted by other Whig writers.

"our Ancient History," when "an Heptarchy among us," growing weary
of continual tribal wars, "*chose themselves One King, to maintain and defend their
Persons and Goods in Peace, by Rules of Law* (pp. 40–41).

Despite Professor Kenyon's aptly styled "blunderbuss technique," Defoe's
refusal to embrace a Hookerian model of society should be given its due. That
model, as we have seen, is of a corporate entity enfolding within a universal
framework of reason. Allowance is never given to the creative activity of the
monarch. For those who quoted the mutually exclusive terms of Hooker, and
for the community-centered ideologues, since the crown could not conceivably
descend from God, it had to come from the people. In Book I. chapter 10 of the
Ecclesiastical Polity, and with fundamental law, both God and king seemingly
disappear from any activity that brings a political society into existence.
Perhaps, then, when we consider Defoe's youthful flight to Monmouth's
romantic crusade, his admiration for the person of the king in the *Reflections*, his
deification of William III following his enlistment in his cause, and his later proposals to Harley that he assume a monarch's control in the councils of Queen
Anne, we can understand Defoe's intuitive rejection of an ideology that founded
communities on the gathered endeavors of its citizenry. We would then be able
to detect in Defoe's first significant pamphlet on the Revolution the beginning
presence of the warrior-king who will dominate Defoe's later imagination.
Some, like Robinson Crusoe, will initiate communities with little regard for
what has gone before them but God's plan. Others, like Charles XII of Sweden,
Peter Alexowitz, Czar of Muscovy, or Gustavus Adolphus, develop in his
biographies of them as shadowed modern equivalents of the heroes of classical
myth, who, visionary and unaided, lay a foundation of glory and greatness for
their obedient subjects. The controlling ideas in Defoe's *Reflections Upon the Late
Great Revolution* appear fairly consistent with his future political interests.

I would like now to consider one last aspect of the language of politics in 1689
and beyond, continuing into the following century, that can help to explain
Defoe's incipient eclecticism and point the way to his later political thought. Let
me begin by quoting a contemporary of Hooker, Robert Parsons, discussing the
varied modes of succession to the English throne. Henry IV, Parsons writes, was

called into the realm by general voice of all the people: his right gotten by arms upon the
evil government of the former king: the personal resignation and delivery of the kingdom
by solemn instrument made unto him by King Richard: his election also by parliament
and coronation by the realm: and finally the quiet possession of him and his posterity, for
almost three score years, with many confirmations of the whole realm, by diverse acts of
parliament, oaths and other assurances . . . And besides all this, that when King
Richard was dead, he was next in degree of propinquity unto him, of any man living.[56]

[56] *A Conference About the Next Succession to the Crown of England* (London, 1594), part II, p. 171. I
owe this quotation and the following paragraph to Professor Howard Nenner, who permitted
me to read and cite from a paper on monarchical succession in England.

Parson's retrospective assessment of the Lancastrian claim to the throne incorporated all the vocabulary of succession in his day: election, conquest, nomination, inheritance, and prescription, or quiet possession. Early seventeenth-century political debate added one more: James I and his defenders introduced a singular version of the divine right of kings.[57] In support of a theory of monarchical absolutism, they propounded the idea that the king was beholden to no one but God for his right to the throne as well as for the way he ruled. And, of course, the extraordinary events of 1688 engendered debates about, and searches in the law books for, the definitions of abdication, desertion, and a vacancy in the throne. While the succession issue was the immediate occasion for debate and polemics, allegiance controversialists went beyond narrow accounts of the nature of the English government to consider the origins of government itself and the first accession of a king to a throne. The earlier quotation from Hooker is about beginnings, not succession, but the distinction was blurred in many tracts. Defoe himself reveals this combined interest when he writes at the outset of the *Reflections* that "some [of his readers] may expect that I should by History trace Monarchy back to its Original source" (p. 7). He didn't, but many did; they settled on Hooker's lines to begin a discussion of the evolution of man to a full political society.

While admitting the validity of the blunderbuss technique in the publications of 1689, it can also be claimed that allegiance literature reveals a narrowing of options and a general hardening of positions. As William Pulteney intoned in the Convention debates, if the crown does not descend from heaven, it must then come from the people.[58] Conquest argument provides a clear example of the developing lines of the debate. In spite of the fact that William had issued an order in January, 1689, that any of his soldiers who suggested that he had conquered England be punished, the tenet proved too attractive and useful to neglect.[59] As we have seen, Defoe did not hesitate to legitimate a monarch's right to allegiance via possession gained by a conquest. Moderate Whigs and moderate Tories accepted the necessity to obey a conqueror in a just war. In May it was the main theme of Bishop Burnet's *Pastoral Letter* to the clergy in his diocese. Helping a friend write a history of the revolution in 1691, Defoe quotes from Burnet's *Letter*, and adds that "all [James's] Right and Title did accrue to the Prince in the Right of a Conquest over him. So that if he had then assumed the Crown, the Opinion of all Lawyers must

---

[57] See J. Neville Figgis, *The Theory of the Divine Right of Kings*, (Cambridge: Cambridge University Press, 1914).

[58] *Miscellaneous State Papers*, ed. Philip Yorke, Earl of Hardwicke, 2 vols. (London, 1778), II, 404.

[59] See Martyn P. Thompson, "The Idea of Conquest in Controversies over the 1688 Revolution," *Journal of the History of Ideas*, 38 (1977), 33–46; Mark Goldie, "Edmund Bohun and *Jus Gentium* in the Revolution Debate," *Historical Journal*, 20 (1977), 569–86; Lois Schwoerer, "Propaganda in the Revolution of 1688–89," *American Historical Review*, 82 (1972), 853.

have been on his [William's] side. And which way soever King *James's* Deserting the Government be turned, this Argument has much Weight. For, if he was forced to do it, then here was a conquest; and, if it was voluntary, it was a wilful Desertion."[60]

But in 1693, condemned by the House of Commons, Burnet's *Letter* and the argument from conquest no longer served the ideological needs of the defenders of the Revolution. It would appear, then, when the moderate voice of James Tyrrell concluded in 1694 that, since God no longer confers his divine authority on any persons whatsoever, "Election of the People, or Usurpation or Conquest" were the sole bases for accession and succession, he was stipulating only one morally legitimate avenue to the throne.[61] Tyrrell's terms appear to have been the mutually exclusive vocabulary of Whig argument into the next reign; they were also the Whig terms propounded at Sacheverell's trial in 1710. For example, in 1704, the Whig author of *The Occasional Letter*, attacking the patriarchal divine right theories of Charles Leslie, wrote that the English government, "so modelled, can never be said to be derived to us, by any *Divine* Right that I know of, or could ever hear of; and I fancy that those that contend most for the *Divine Right* of *Kings*, will allow that their Monarchs cannot be lawfully limited by the People, unless there can be a Pretence for Conquest."[62] And in Stanhope's defense of the Revolution at Sacheverell's trial, the mutually exclusive categories severing God from the origins of society conclusively revealed the distance that had been traveled from the accession and succession debates of the previous century: "I believe that there is not at this day subsisting any nation or government in the world, whose first original did not receive its foundation either from Resistance or compact."[63] For the Whigs, then, consent became the only model for government once conquest had lost its usefulness and when *jus divinum* became the text of an outmoded ideology.[64]

If, as Professor Kenyon asserts, Whig political thought could only attract a minority of Englishmen because of its illogical, extreme, and populist tenets, the Tory vocabulary emanating from 1689 defending Stuart claims and

---

[60] *A Compleat History of the Late Revolution* (London, 1691), p. 70. For Defoe's authorship see Frank Bastian, "Defoe and Guy Miege," *Notes and Queries*, n.s., 16 (1969), 103–05.

[61] *Bibliotheca Politica* (London, 1718), Dialogue III, p. 103, Unlike the 1694 edition, this one has continuous pagination. In his *A Brief Enquiry Into the Ancient Constitution*, Tyrrell presents consent or conquest as the two antithetical instigations of kingship and civil government following the Flood (p. 4).

[62] *The Occasional Letter, Number 1* (London, 1704), pp. 16–17. This was a Whig retort to the second part of Leslie's *The New Association* (London, 1703).

[63] *A Complete Collection of State Trials*, ed. T. B. Howell (London, 1809–1826), XV, 126–34. For this bedrock of Whig political philosophy see also *The Sentiments of our Fore-Fathers Relating to the Succession to the Crown, Hereditary Right, and Non-Resistance* (London, 1714), pp. 28–29.

[64] In *Cato's Letters*, consent or force, the latter defined by the law of the sword, are mutually exclusive terms; see no. 45 (16 Sept. 1721) and no. 60 (6 January 1721 [1722]).

questioning the rationale of the Revolution presented other problems. When it moved from attacking "revolution principles" it offered no practical alternative to a moderate electorate trying to move beyond the devoutly hierarchic principles that, once available, were tarnished and rendered obsolete by the searching inquiries and analyses of 1689.

That alternative vocabulary rested on a foundation of indefeasible hereditary monarchy intimately entwined in strands of divine right and brutal might equals right rationalizations. We have seen that conquest was only one of many possible lines of argument intoned by both Whigs and Tories in 1689 to reconcile their countrymen to the new regime. But it appears that allegiance controversialists perceived conquest as *the* argument used by Tories and Jacobites to deny William's legitimacy and the subject's right to resistance. Though Sir Robert Brady was rarely mentioned, the Tory argument rested on his historical research that there had been a conquest in 1066 and that William and successive monarchs, and thus James II, as a result of the revolution in feudal law and land tenure, could claim full and absolute legal authority over their subjects. Consequently, because of conquest and the Norman laws, "there is a clear Demonstration, that all the *Liberties* and *Priviledges* the People can pretend to, were the *Grants* and *Concessions* of the Kings of this Nation, and Derived from the Crown."[65]

A Political Conference, published early in 1689, is a dialogue among a republican, a moderate constitutionalist, and a courtier. The latter defends passive obedience and absolute submission to the authority of the monarch. Significantly it is also the courtier who rejects the language of the law of nature and consent by responding that, "in the most part of the Commonwealths, Kings set up themselves, forcing Provinces and Families to their obedience, and have never acknowledged any other Title, but Conquest and their Swords; so that it cannot hold as a General Rule, that in all Common-wealths there must be mutual Agreements, Engagements and Contracts betwixt Soveraigns and Subjects, and tho', in some cases, there were such, yet few of them do appear by authentick History or Record."[66] The Jacobite friend in White Kennet's *Dialogue Between Two Friends* – the other is a Williamite – dismisses the legalisms of Coke and Magna Charta by noting that "the Court of Wards is as signal as a Badge of Conquest, as undoubted a Character of Vassalage and Slavery, as any we can possibly instance in."[67] Turning consent on its head, he maintains that the unconditional and absolute authority of English kings derives from the "Agreement or Paction between the Conqueror and the English nobility." If mutual contracts of a protective sort follow the military despot, they are confirmed by the subjects among

---

[65] Cited in Pocock, *The Ancient Constitution and the Feudal Law*, p. 218.
[66] *A Political Conference*, pp. 14–15.
[67] London, 1689, p. 16.

themselves; the conquering king is no party to them. Thus, "the Prerogatives of the Crown, are a Divine Right, the Imperial Diadem settled upon the Royal Head by the Almighties own Appointment."[68] In 1689, as we have seen, conquest and divine right began the linkage that would continue into the next century. Contract and consent can be no basis for sovereignty, anti-Whig argument maintained, because they do "not comprehend the most Ancient beginning of Government, *viz.* Paternal Authority and Conquest." And, more specifically, "the Kings of *England* hold their Crown by right of Conquest and Succession; and consequently are no Trustees of the People." As a result of conquest, the Jacobite Jeremy Collier argued, "the Liberties of the Subjects are not founded upon the Reservations of an *Original Contract.* For a Conquered People must not pretend to make their own Terms. And therefore, their Priviledges are not of their own Creating, but Acts of Royal Favours, and Condescentions of Soveraignty."[69]

Conquest may have been proscribed by William's parliament in 1693 and may have become anathema to the Whigs, but it buttressed Tory-Jacobite arguments that denounced the Revolution. Scripture and the sword were the props of anti-Whig pamphlets refuting Locke and consent theories of government. In 1705, *An Essay upon Government*, the decade's most thoughtful refutation of Locke and Whig political thought, asserted that "Monarchy is the particular Form of Government, by God Established in Scripture, . . . [and] that the *English* Constitution is founded upon that Law of God, and therefore Hereditary Monarchy is the unalterable Power here Establish'd." And it was Romans 13 that proved conclusively that the sword of sovereignty had been placed in a single person, "*for he beareth not the Sword in vain; for he is the Minister of God*, etc. He bears it by the Ordinance of God, not by the Donation of the People; he bears it as the Minister of God, from whom he receiv'd it; and not as Minister of the People, who had no right to give it, because they never had it themselves."[70] When Leslie stopped mocking the Whigs' illogical and absurd vocabulary of the law of nature and consent, he too maintained that the power of the king is the power of the sword, and the king's sole possession of the sword is sanctioned by God.[71] In 1710, following the publication of the most Lockean tract of the decade, *Vox Populi*, someone reprinted Edward Fisher's

---

[68] *Ibid.*, pp. 17, 18.

[69] Jeremy Collier, *Vindiciae Juris Regii: Or, Remarques Upon a Paper Entituled, An Enquiry into the Measures of Submission to the Supream Authority* (London, 1689), pp. 4, 6, 14.

[70] *An Essay Upon Government. Wherein the Republican Schemes Reviv'd by Mr. Lock, Dr. Blackal, etc. are Fairly Consider'd and Refuted* (London, 1705), pp. 28–29. Here and elsewhere is repeated the royalist, orthodox, and "Tory" view of the University of Oxford; see *A Paraphrase and Annotations Upon the Epistles of St. Paul Written to the Romans, Corinthians, and Hebrews* (Oxford, 1675), p. 47.

[71] See *The Constitution, Laws and Government, of England, Vindicated* (London, 1709), p. 7. Cf. his *The New Association* (London, 1703), Supplement, p. 4; and his *Cassandra*, Num. 1 (London, 1704), p. 6.

intensely royalist tract of 1643, *An Appeal to Thy Conscience*, its new title page proclaiming it to be the answer to the secular political opinions championed by Hoadly, Defoe and a host of republican zealots.

From the Bible, the tract deduced that God made kings by both extraordinary and ordinary means. While God no longer chooses His kings by lot, or declares them by His special messenger, the ordinary ways and means still operate. Thus, "the King of *England* hath not his Crown from any but God alone; from whose gracious Hand he hath received it by the ordinary Means of Hereditary Succession; and was in the beginning obtained by the Sword."[72]

As the above citations reveal, in Queen Anne's reign the disputants in the debate over origins and monarchy had clearly and unambiguously staked out their terrain. God, scripture, and the military exploits of a conquering king were the tenets of those for whom sovereignty was unconditional and absolute. One extreme was countered by another. Since conquest, right gained through might, was abhorrent to the Whig mind, and since it was beyond belief that the first creation of God could immediately be monarch of the universe, whose inheritance was unalterably to be passed on to his posterity initiating hereditary and indefeasible monarchy forever, the only tenable position remaining was one that posited society, government, and succession determined by the consent of the people. This violent antithesis, this mutual exclusiveness of ideology, accounts in great part for the shrillness of political debate in Anne's reign.

It also accounts for the eclecticism and seeming contradictions in Defoe's later political writings. Once, policies, procedures, and political philosophies had been varied and complex, facilitating debate and helping to keep multiple options open. The hardening of views, the retreat to irreconcilable extremes, in the years following the Revolution closed these options and precluded a settling of disagreements on some middle ground. Defoe, it appears to me, refused to maintain a position on the origins of government and the accession of a sovereign that would lock him into either camp. The mutually exclusive categories of conquest or consent provided no singularly secure argument to an imagination taken with martial monarchs, and to one which at the same time yielded to the force of the community as a determinant of the supreme legislator. Neither was Defoe able to conceive of a vision of society and

---

[72] Edward Fisher's 1643 *Appeal* was republished under the following omnibus title: *An Appeal to Thy Conscience . . . An Unanswerable Answer to a Late Pamphlet Intituled, Vox Populi, Now Printed under the Title of The Judgment of Whole Kingdoms and Nations . . . Made Publick for the Defence of the Queen and Government, by a True Lover of Loyalty – – Challenges Dr. W – k – r, Dr. W – – st, Mr. H – d – y, Mr. B – s – t, de F – e, R – d – th, or any other Fanatical Round-head, and Republican Champion, to Confute this Appeal by the Word of God.* For the importance of *Vox Populi*, see Richard Ashcraft and M. M. Goldsmith, "Locke, Revolution Principles, and the Formation of Whig Ideology," *Historical Journal*, 26 (1983), 786–800, who inconclusively attributed it and other Lockean tracts to Defoe.

government that was silent on the intercession of God's voice in the nomination of the right ruler. Out of the events of William's reign Defoe reordered
and rearranged the arguments of the *Reflections*. In *Jure Divino* and *Robinson
Crusoe* he worked through the complex and contradictory issues of the
allegiance controversy to structure his coherent narrative of monarchy and
government.

3

Defender of the king, 1689–1701

The determination of Defoe's political stance during the years he was engaged as a government pamphleteer for William III is problematic because of his extensive resort to *personae*, aliases, and satiric voices, and the vexing problem of attribution. In addition, any secure judgment is rendered more difficult because it intrudes upon the larger and more contentious historical debate about the nature, extent, and consequences of the English Revolution of 1689. In what sense was it a revolution? Was there a significant shift in the balance of power between crown and parliament? If, as G. R. Elton maintains, "the royalist revolution came to grief in 1688," was 1689 the onset of a parliamentary revolution that decisively rearranged the political system that had governed England for almost two centuries?[1] Was the central characteristic of the Revolution the substitution of divine hereditary right by a temporarily elective monarchy? Or was the Revolution, as the citizens of London and the country wished to believe, a restoration of the balanced constitution that had protected the liberty and property of all Englishmen, a return to the original and ancient form of government?

The assured convictions of Macaulay and the Whig historiographic tradition, that saw events solely as progressive steps to parliamentary democracy, led to the inevitable generational reaction. Twentieth-century re-evaluations of England's bloodless and respectable revolution stressed the sovereign's independence and argued that no new limitations were imposed upon the monarchy at the accession of William and Mary. Not only were the conditions few and vague, but "what [the king] could do was not defined."[2] Even if the Convention Parliament had decided the rightful candidate to the vacant throne, this did not mean that it had become or was thought of as supreme.[3] In fact, as J. R. Western wrote in 1972, it was now a commonplace among historians that "nothing could have been more monarchical than William's government and that nobody could have been less like what he called 'a Doge

---

[1] G. R. Elton "The Stuart Century," *Studies in Tudor and Stuart Politics and Government*, 2 vols. (Cambridge: Cambridge University Press, 1974), II, 161.
[2] E. Neville Williams, *The Eighteenth-Century Constitution, 1688–1815* (Cambridge: Cambridge University Press, 1960), p. 7.
[3] See Williams, pp. 1–4.

of Venice.' He had an almost military idea of how a government should be
run and on a number of points his views coincided strikingly with those of his
uncle James.''[4]

As Alexander Hamilton observed of the American Revolution, "it is the
nature of war to increase the executive, at the expense of the legislative
authority.''[5] For the first eight years of his reign William was a warrior-
king. If, then, only in parliament and with parliament could William carry
out his wartime policies, in the shaping of those policies outside of parliament
he was mighty indeed. During the first half of his administration, up to the
Peace of Ryswick in 1697, William so dominated affairs that Louis XIV could
judge him a despot.[6] And even the distinguished Marquis of Halifax, no
lover of parliaments and radically supportive of William in the Convention
debates, could openly oppose his monarch as early as 1692 because "he saw
that the war with France, conducted on an unprecedented scale, could give
William the financial and military resources to make himself as absolute as
Louis XIV.''[7]

But Western's "commonplace among historians," of the sustaining
monarchical power of Willam III, had already been challenged in his time.
His contemporaries had seen a truly revolutionary character in the events of
1689; if not in the Revolution itself, then in the constitutional settlement that
followed. What Macaulay himself realized was one of the momentous and
least noticed consequences of the Revolution, the development of party
government through ministerial responsibility and the subsequent diminution
in the power of the executive, has been lucidly argued by Clayton Roberts.
"The Glorious Revolution of 1688 swept away the reluctance of many
members of the commons to interfere in the king's undoubted right to wield
the scepter.''[8] Through votes, impeachments, and addresses real or
threatened, and through the financial settlement of 1690, parliament "created
a new type of monarchy.''[9] Its intrusion in the heretofore sanctified domain
of executive sovereignty found justification in the "increasingly popular doctrine that supreme power, sovereignty, resides in the legislature, which then
entrusts executive power to the king.[10] A more extreme reassessment of
the Revolution of 1689, derived from a minutely detailed reading of the

[4] John R. Western, *Monarchy and Revolution* (Totowa, NJ: Rowman and Littlefield, 1972), p. 328.
[5] *The Federalist; Or, The New Constitution*, ed. Max Beloff (Oxford: Basil Blackwell, 1948),
   "Number VIII," p. 33.
[6] Mark A. Thompson, "Parliament and Foreign Policy," in *William III and Louis XIV*, ed.
   Ragnhild Hatton and J. R. Bromley (Toronto: University of Toronto Press, 1968), pp. 23–24.
[7] *Halifax: Complete Works*, ed. J. P. Kenyon (Baltimore: Penguin Books, 1969), p. 21.
[8] Clayton Roberts, "The Growth of Ministerial Responsibility to Parliament in Later Stuart
   England," *Journal of Modern History*, 28 (1956), 229.
[9] Clayton Roberts, "The Constitutional Significance of the Financial Settlement of 1690,"
   Historical Journal, 20 (1977), 75.
[10] Clayton Roberts, *The Growth of Responsible Government in Stuart England* (Cambridge: Cambridge
   University Press, 1966), p. 247.

Convention debates and the changing language of the Declaration of Rights, has been argued by Lois Schwoerer. Radical speeches and a radical document made radical changes in the nature of kings and in the relationship between monarch and parliament. "With the Declaration of Rights and the Bill of Rights the center of the constitutional and legal settlement, the Revolution is properly viewed as a real revolution that [not only] restored certain rights that had been assaulted by James II [but] also created a new kingship."[11] Parliamentary omnipotence was only an idea away.

The pendulum of historiographical examination has been noticed, not to stabilize it, but to admit that Defoe's varied, indirect, and camouflaged defenses of his king's policies, plotted against the divergencies of critics of the Revolution then and now, defy easy analysis. Compounding the problem is the political image of Defoe that has been derived from his writings during William's reign. Was he a political hack, a gutter journalist, the best but the most unscrupulous propagandist of his generation, writing only for ministries that would line his purse? Levelling complex political ideas for the less sophisticated trading interests? A Jacobin of radical leanings? A man whose political character is "Lockean," whose works "are articulate and lyrical renderings of Locke's ideas?"[12] Or do these modern tags of judgment not get us far from the quick analyses at the turn of the century in the *Cambridge Modern History*, which asserted that "of Whig principles, the most thoroughgoing exponent is Defoe. . . . It was Defoe who applied and popularised Locke, and drove home the philosopher's principles."[13] In 1966 J. Paul Hunter observed that "Defoe study has more often settled for the illusion of history than for a full, rigorous, and sensitive examination of the assumed contexts of a particular work."[14] Nowhere has this been more true – and does it continue to be true – than of his political writings and of his political career. The result has been a Defoe "strangely purged of all but Whig

---

11 "The Bill of Rights: Epitome of the Revolution of 1688–89," in *Three British Revolutions: 1641, 1688, 1776*, ed. J. G. A. Pocock (Princeton: Princeton University Press, 1980), p. 237; see also her *The Declaration Right of Rights, 1689* (Baltimore: Johns Hopkins University Press, 1981).

12 J. P. Kenyon, "The Revolution of 1688: Resistance and Contract," in *Historical Perspectives: Studies in English Thought and Society in Honour of J. H. Plumb*, ed. Neil McKendrick (London: Europa, 1975), p. 62. ("gutter journalist"); Kenyon, *Revolution Principles*, p. 123 ("Jacobin"); Goldie, "The Revolution of 1689," p. 502 ("radical"), also pp. 508, 509. See also E. W. Rosenheim, Jr., "The Text and Context of Swift's *Contests and Dissentions*," *Modern Philology*, 66 (1968), 65; Isaac Kramnick, *Bolingbroke and his Circle: The Politics of Nostalgia* (Cambridge, MA: Harvard University Press, 1969), p. 191; David Macaree, *Daniel Defoe and the Jacobite Movement*, Salzburg Studies in English Literature, no. 42 (1980), pp. 4–5.

13 Arthur L. Smith, "English Political Philosophy in the Seventeenth and Eighteenth Centuries," in *The Cambridge Modern History*, ed. A. W. Ward *et al.* (New York: Macmillan, 1909), VI, 816, 817. Cf. Charles Bastide, *John Locke: Ses théories politiques et leur influence en Angleterre* (Paris: Ernest Leroux, 1907), p. 347; Harold J. Laski, *Political Thought in England: Locke to Bentham* (London: Oxford University Press, 1920; rpt., 1955), p. 49.

14 *The Reluctant Pilgrim: Defoe's Emblematic Method and Quest for Form in "Robinson Crusoe"* (Baltimore: Johns Hopkins Press, 1966), p. 1.

philosophizing.''[15] In this chapter we will try to understand a more ambiguous and more complex Defoe as he discovers his political voice and
regulates his political postures in the tracts and poems he contributed to the
paper wars between William and his parliaments.

Jacobite plots, the first less than a year after William and Mary's ascension to
the throne, and assassination attempts during the reign, signified the enemy of
the monarch on the right, those who were ready to maim and murder to return
a Stuart to England. Proclamations calling for action against papists – read
divine right apologists – were issued annually from 1689 to 1692. And with the
death of William in 1702 and the accession of Anne, fed with romantic visions of
a dashing young prince capable of restoring the true hereditary line, Stuart
apologists reintroduced lively, if ineffectual, criticism of the fragile constitutional compromise that had been effected during the last decade of the century.
But during that decade the most sustained threat to the constitutional integrity
of England came from those who, seeking to end the abuse of royal power,
sought to diminish the exercise of that power. War was declared on the
monarch, even though William's adversaries perhaps believed that they did not
intend to change the constitution.[16]

Just as the early euphoria at the restoration of Charles II had all too quickly
degenerated into dissatisfaction, emnity, and contempt for the returned
monarch, so too did the nation's gratitude to William the Deliverer dissipate into
recrimination and rejection. Thomas Hanmer's observation, that ''the distrust
of the executive [is the] principle upon which the whole of our Constitution is
grounded,'' can serve as the epitaph for William's reign.[17] As if to counter the
nation's initial exuberance over its delivery from papist absolutism by a
wonder-working agent of divine providence, tracts were written and republished
asserting the total supremacy of English parliaments. Parliament was ''the
Soul'' of the Commonwealth; parliaments ''do make new, abrogate old Laws;
reform Grievances in the Commonwealth, settle the Succession, grant Subsidies; and in sum, may be called the great Physicians of the Kingdom.''[18]
''The Parliament of *England*,'' a document found among the Earl of
Shaftesbury's papers recited, ''is that *Supreme and absolute Power*, which gives Life
and Motion to the *English* Government. It directs and actuates all its various
procedures, is the Parent of our Peace, Defender of our Faith, and Foundation
of our Properties; and as the Constitution of this great *Spring*, and *Primum Mobile*
of Affairs, is in Strength and Beauty, so will also all *Acts* and Performances which
are derived from it, bear a suitable proportion and similitude.''[19]

---

[15] *TLS*, 10 April 1969 (no. 3502). An anonymous reviewer's comment of Kramnick's *Bolingbroke and His Circle*.

[16] Horwitz, *Parliament, Policy and Politics*, pp. 17–102, provides the best account of these years.

[17] Cited in Betty Kemp, *Kings and Commons, 1660–1832* (London: Macmillan, 1957), p. 5.

[18] *Vox Populi: or, The People's Claim to the Parliament's Sitting, to redress Grievances* (1681), in *State Tracts* (London, 1692), p. 220.

[19] *Some Observations Concerning the Regulating of Elections for Parliament* (London, 1689), pp. 5–6.

The earlier debates on the origins of the English constitution had hardened into a faith that parliaments had originated in the Anglo-Saxon *witenagemot*, so that, in tandem with common law, they became the foundation of English law and the safeguard of English liberties.[20] Even the king's appointees to power in the church were beginning to initiate subtle distinctions concerning the locale of power that was to be obeyed, distinctions that, as we shall see, overtook and subverted the more traditional language of authority and prerogative later in William's reign when the prospect of a Stuart queen and a truce in the European wars made the king *persona non grata* to his indignant and forgetful subjects. For example, John Sharp, recently appointed Archbishop of York, delivered a sermon before the Lords on 5 November 1691, the day commemorating the Gunpowder Plot and the arrival of William in England. Preaching on Romans 10.2, "For I bear them record that they have a Zeal of God, but not according to Knowledge," Sharp unleashed an attack on "the Bigots of the Church of *Rome*," following which he promised to "make such Application of it, as the Business of this Day calls for.[21] Beyond the elucidation of the text, Sharp addresses two subjects: he explains the role, not of the king, but of "*Law-givers* and *Magistrates* to see that *Nequid detrimenti respublica capiat*, to see that the Government be secured . . ." (p. 8); and he reminds his audience that the solemnity of the day was occasioned by "Popish *Zealots* [who] enter'd upon the most barbarous and inhuman Project that ever was undertaken by Men; even neither better nor worse, than the destroying the *King* and his *Parliament* at one blow" (p. 23). One isolated sentence recalls the deliverance of November 5, 1688, but no mention is made of William. Sharp simply alludes to the "horrible storm of late . . . impending over us" (p. 23). His subtle redirection of emphasis only hints at the devotion that will soon be paid not to William but to the loyal daughter of the house of Stuart, and to a parliament which, because it completely represents the freeholders of the kingdom and therefore cannot be suspected of illegal and unconsented power, has a divine right to its subjects' obedience.

The parliamentary history of these years, as Dennis Rubini details, is of a Country party, in its opposition to William, chipping away at the privileges of monarchy under the guise of a program for safeguarding the rights of the people.[22] By Christmas of 1691, stalwart Tories like Sir Thomas Clarges and Sir Christopher Musgrave were being called "commonwealthmen."[23] The debates in 1693 over the Triennial Bill, passed by both houses but vetoed by William – one of the five vetoes in his reign – reintroduced arguments for parliament's antiquity and thus its sovereignty.[24] The following year, it was the

[20] See William Petyt, *The Ancient Right of the Commons of England Asserted* (London, 1680).

[21] *A Sermon Preached Before the Lords Spiritual and Temporal in Parliament Assembled* (London, 1691), p. 2. Following citations will be noted in the text.

[22] *Court and Country 1688–1702* (London: Hart-Davis, 1967 [1968]), pp. 36–37.

[23] Downie, *Robert Harley*, pp. 19–20.

[24] Horwitz, *Parliament, Policy and Politics*, p. 114.

Junto Whigs who "recommended themselves to William by indicating that once the Triennial Act passed (December, 1694), they did not intend to put *further* restrictions on the prerogative."[25] Professor Kenyon remarks that "it is also unfortunate that no debates survive on the Demise of the Crown Act (1696), which by allowing parliament to meet and transact business after the king's death finally registered the legal and constitutional superiority of the one over the other."[26]

The direction of parliamentary opposition following the Queen's death in December 1694 can be clearly decoded in the Commons' debates over a new Board of Trade. Merchant frustration over the loss of naval convoys and the destruction of commercial shipping resulted in the proposal that the Admiralty, together with Commons' commissioners, assign naval cruisers to protect merchant ships along designated trade routes. It was a bold intrusion into the wartime decision-making prerogative of the monarch; its immediate result would have been to curtail the Admiralty's freedom of action. In 1696 parliament brought in a bill to create a council of trade. The action was seen by many as a clear usurpation of the monarch's functions. Bishop Burnet's partisan judgment has been borne out by subsequent commentators: "This was opposed by those who looked on it as a change of our constitution in a very essential point: the executive part of the government was wholly in the king: so that the appointing of any council by act of parliament, began a precedent of their breaking in upon the execution of the law . . . so that a king would soon grow to be a duke of Venice; and indeed those who set this on most zealously, did not deny that they designed to graft many things upon it."[27] Earlier in 1689 the Commons had declined the king's request that it name a commission to manage the sending of supplies to Ireland. Sir Edward Seymour, staunch Tory and defender of the prerogative, had supported the negative, noting "We have no part of the executive authority of the government, but we may advise the king . . . It is not in our power to remedy the miscarriages, but it is to represent them to the king to be remedied."[28] To consider the Commons' intrusion into the monarch's realm in 1696 is to realize how "republican" the parliament had become in its antagonism to the king.

Even new lands, *Terra Australis incognita*, were discovered that resembled England "both in Soil and Climate," in which her recent revolution was inscribed. In this free state of Noland, the royal line having failed, its peers united to install in power the great Aristaeus. He had reorganized the

---

[25] J. R. Jones, *Country and Court, England, 1658–1714* (London: Edward Arnold, 1978), p. 272. My italics.

[26] *Revolution Principles*, p. 42.

[27] *History of His Own Time*, IV, 294–95. See also R. M. Lees, "Parliament and the Proposal for a Board of Trade, 1695–6," *English Historical Review*, 54 (1939), 38–66; W. B. Gwyn, *The Meaning of the Separation of Powers*, Tulane Studies in Political Science, vol. IX (1965), pp. 134–37.

[28] *Commons Journal*, IX, 364.

kingdom and had created its new government, an imitation of Harrington's *Oceana*, but had significantly refused the crown offered to him. Noland's Great Council, the pinnacle of this administrative utopia and the kingdom's supreme legislative power, was composed of lords spiritual and temporal and the leading gentry in the kingdom. It was a "Government wherein all Sorts and Degrees of People shall find their Account, and feel their Condition better'd: Shall be enrich'd, advanc'd, and adorn'd with the Spoils of the Monarchy; and shall have those Advantages shared amongst them, which in a Monarchy are engross'd and swallowed up by one Man."[29]

From 1689 to 1697, the date of his *Essay Upon Projects*, amidst the confusion of business prospects and business failures, bankruptcy, imprisonment, and perhaps overseas travel, Defoe wrote little.[30] But what he did write enables us to continue to plot the political concerns that helped to make Defoe the most successful and dedicated propagandist of the last years of William's reign. By the end of that reign, Defoe had learned to confront parliaments concerned, not with legislation and remediation, but with opposition, conflict, and turmoil. Parliaments presented him with histories of encroachments, not co-ordinate and sympathetic activity, between England's elected representatives of the people and the crown. Defoe's parliaments are bodies dedicated not to the preservation but to the destruction of the perilous balance of the nation's constitutional compromise.

But it would take some years before Defoe recognized that the unbridled power of parliaments was the clearest threat to English stability. His early writings attacked the enemies of the moment. As the last decade of the seventeenth century began, these were Jacobites and half-hearted Tories. The former secretly plotted assassinations, rebellions, and invasions, the latter professed tepid allegiance to William's *de facto* authority. In July 1689, responding to the murmurs of discontent, Defoe wrote once again as a loyal member of the Church of England. His language in *The Advantages of the Present Settlement* is traditional and conservatively contemporary. His justification for the rebellion against James is founded on English tradition. If we hear of natural rights, it is the "natural Right" of noblemen, and "a deputed Right" of the commons, who come "from all parts of the Kingdom, to enact Laws for the good and profit of the Realm . . ."[31]

Echoing mainstream commentary, he admits that "Government in general, is of Divine and Natural Right; yet all the World will never be able to make either of these two things appear, *viz.* either that this or that Species of Government, is of such a right; for example, Monarchy in contradistinction to all other; or much less, that this family or person hath such a Divine or

---

[29] *The Free State of Noland* (London, 1701), p. 2. The first and shorter edition was published in 1696.

[30] Bastian, *Defoe's Early Life*, pp. 136–202; Moore, *Daniel Defoe*, pp. 68–103.

[31] *Advantages*, p. 12. Following citations will be noted in the text.

natural right to such or such a Kingdom or Dominion" (pp. 19–20). But he cursorily introduces two issues that would demand finer distinctions in subsequent publications. When he asserts that English history gives many instances of "the power of the Parliament to settle the Succession of the Crown," and also gave kings, like Henry VIII, "Power to settle the manner of Succession, and nominate the Successors as he thought fit" (p. 20), he muddies the distinction between nomination and election; the latter he was to distance himself from when later voices in and out of parliament argued for its omnipotence in the matter of disputed claimants to the throne. And in his zeal to dismiss the apologists for divine right, he simply states that "this Opinion that men would so fain impose upon us, is destructive of all Right and Conquest or Prescription; for against Divine and Natural Right, none of these are prevalent" (p. 20). After 1693, when tracts propounding the conquest argument were burnt and the theory proscribed by the administration, in the patriotism of the moment Defoe, like other pamphleteers, harshly attacked conquest's Tory and anti-Williamite proponents. Later, coming to understand the king's need to control his nation's army, Defoe never removed the sword of conquest and power from the hands of the monarch.[32]

The year 1691 saw the publication of *A Compleat History of the Late Revolution*, an anonymous tract of eighty pages, the first one-third of which traces the development of popery and the arbitrary power in the two preceding reigns, with the concluding two-thirds retelling England's deliverance by William in letters, proclamations, and other printed documents, the whole given order and coherence with tags of narrative and commentary. Though not yet persuasively attributed to Defoe, there is a Defovian voice in it, and that voice once again reveals a political imagination fervently discovering the immediate hand of the Old Testament God in the nomination of kings. It is also a voice that could just as comfortably allude to one of the radical tenets following James's flight and the vacuum in the executive office.[33]

Tis observed that, before the Theocracy of the Jews ceased, even in the time of extraordinary Revelations, the manner of the Divine Designation of their Judges was by God's giving the People some Deliverance by the Hand of the Person, to whose Government they were appointed to submit. Thus, *Othniel, Gideon, Jephthah, Samson*, and others, were invested by Heaven with the supream Authority, And, tho' *Joshua* had an immediate Command from God to succeeed *Moses* and an Anointing for that purpose by the laying on of *Moses* hands; yet the Foundation of the Peoples Submission to him was laid in *Jordan*. Now what History can give an Instance, since that

---

[32] See the useful bibliography in Goldie, "The Revolution of 1689," pp. 526–27. Earlier, in 1691, Defoe had called conquest "wicked" but accepted it as a legitimate basis for William's rule; see *A Compleat History of the Late Revolution*, (London, 1691), pp. 37, 70. As we have noted he embraced it in the *Reflections* (1689). He tried to resolve this ambivalence in *Jure Divino*, (1706).

[33] *A Compleat History of the Late Revolution* (London, 1691), p. 72. Following citations will be noted in the text.

Theocracy ceased, of a Designation of any Person to any Government more visibly Divine than this was? To see a Nation of so various Opinions, Interests, and Factions fall suddenly from a turbulent and fluctuating State into a serene Calm, and their Minds so strangely united on a sudden, it shews from whence the Nation was Influenced.''(p. 71)

Thus, though the finger of God clearly designated the choice the people were to make, the writer's paraphrase of the Convention's Resolution of 1689 and subsequent comment reveal a spokesman for the position that the administration being broken, government devolves back to the people and "the Throne thereby Vacant, They think fit to fill it again with the One who is not Immediate in the Line" (p. 72). But if Frank Bastian's surmise is correct, that Defoe had hurriedly assembled this history for a friend in need and had plagiarized nearly all of the above comment from a pre-allegiance tract, perhaps we can question somewhat his radical voice. In fact, in that tract Defoe found presented that position regarding monarchy and war that he would enunciate clearly in his own forthright voice as the martial and monarchical tensions of the reign came to the fore; for he noted ". . . the present State of *Europe* in general, so that of these Kingdoms in particular, required a vigorous and masculine Administration. To recover what was lost, to rescue what was in danger, and rectify what was amiss, could not be effected but by a Prince consumate in the Art both of Peace and War" (p. 73).[34]

Defoe's early pamphlets and his early political poetry reveal, not the ideology of court or country, Whig or Tory, but a voice that, as one early critic assessed, "would establish and defend, undeviatingly, from all sides, a King William."[35] His is also a voice that, despite assertions to the contrary, cannot move far from Old Testament patterns to support his defense of William's monarchy. For example, in *A New Discovery of an Old Intreague* (1691), an intensively contemporaneous poem on London politics, even though he writes, "No Parallels from Hebrew Times I take, / And leave the Jingling simily to speak," the following thirty lines attacking divine right and passive obedience veer to the Old Testament, to the statutes of Israel and the laws of a biblical God.[36] And even though most of the allusions are heavily veiled, it is odd to realize, as one commentator has written, that Defoe's William III is patterned after Dryden's Charles II.[37] Alan Downie concluded that "Defoe was not a hack in William's reign."[38] True; by 1694, Defoe has become his king's astute defender, attacking the parliamentary opposition

[34] "Defoe and Guy Miege," *Notes and Queries*, n.s. 16 (1969), pp. 103–05. In fact, Defoe took this critical position from *Reasons for Crowning the Prince and Princess of Orange, King and Queen Jointly, And for placing the Executive Power in the Prince alone* (London, 1689), in *Harleian Miscellany* (London, 1810), IX, 372–73.

[35] Mary Campbell, *Defoe's First Poem* (Bloomington: Principia Press, 1938), p. 187.

[36] London, 1691, p. 8.

[37] Gilbert P. Prince, Jr., "Poetry and Propaganda in Defoe's Three Major Verse Satires During the Reign of William III," *DA*, 33 (1972), 2340A.

[38] J. A. Downie, "Defoe in the Fleet Prison," *Notes and Queries*, n.s. 22 (1975), 344.

who were hostile to William and his land campaigns on the continent, who
defended a "blue water" policy, and who believed, anticipating the standing
army debates that were to erupt three years later, that the militia alone could
preserve England from invasion.[39]

In fact, Defoe's prescience and maturing political views can be better
understood when we examine *An Essay Upon Projects*, published early in 1697.
Twentieth-century editors, concentrating on Defoe's social, economic, and
feminist interests, have all but obscured the political bias of his first full-length
book.[40] From beginning to end, Defoe's projecting text is a song of praise and
triumph for William, William's wars, and his hated foreign officer corps; it is also
a program anticipating the future demobilization of William's trained but
unEnglish army; it offers reforms for militia training that were to be proposed
by republican pamphleteers of the anti-army ideology the following year;
and, in spite of a few token words respecting the activity of parliament, its
brief for the centralization and nationalization of power firmly endows the
executive with greater authority than it previously had.

Defoe's introduction to the *Essay* can be read, not only as a spirited defense
of his monarch's wars, but also as a defense of the Admiralty and the navy,
dissatisfaction with which had instigated the move to create the parliamentary
council of trade, making believable Defoe's confession that he had "kept the
greatest Part of it by me for near Five Years."[41] For Defoe, not necessity but
war in England's projecting age has been the mother of invention and the
cause for whatever improvement the nation has made in the seven years
following William's ascent to the throne. Not only is it easy to prove that "the
Nation it self, taking it as one General Stock, is not at all diminish'd or im-
poverish'd by this Long, this Chargeable War; but on the contrary, was never
Richer, since it was inhabited" (p. 2). Entering the decade's quarrel between
the ancients and the moderns, Defoe admits: "Nor am I absolutely of the
Opinion, that we are so happy as to be Wiser in this Age, than our
Forefathers; tho' at the same time I must own, some parts of Knowledge in
Science as well as Art, has received Improvements in this Age, altogether conceal'd from the former" (p. 2). And for Defoe, "the Art of War, which I take
to be the highest Perfection of Human Knowledge, is a sufficient Proof of
what I say, especially in conducting Armies and in offensive Engines" (p. 3).

Pointing his language to the landed gentry who were angered at the heavy
taxes necessary to support the land war, Defoe admits that "the Losses and
Depredations which this War brought with it at first, were exceeding
many . . ." (p. 4). Merchants, the trading part of the nation, suffered; many
fell into bankruptcy. As we would expect, Defoe has compassionate words for

[39] See *The Englishman's Choice and True Interest* (London, 1694), pp. 10–11.
[40] See, for example, Ernst Gerhard Jacob, *Daniel Defoe Essay on Projects (1697): Eine Wirtschafts-
und Sozialgeschichtliche Studie* (Leipzig, 1929).
[41] *An Essay Upon Projects* (London 1697), p. iii. Following citations will be noted in the text.

those who, "with difficulty bore up under the Loss of great part of their Estates" (p. 6). But, glancing backwards at the debates in parliament on a council of trade and the country's hostility towards the Admiralty, he is at pains to tell his reader that those losses and depredations were "suffer'd chiefly by the Ill Conduct of Merchants themselves, who did not apprehend the Danger to be really what it was: For before our Admiralty could possibly settle Convoys, Cruisers, and Stations for Men of War all over the World, the *French* cover'd the Sea with their Privateers, and took an incredible number of our Ships" (pp. 4–5).

Defoe's glorification of war, his theme that war invigorates man's inventive genius, his faith in war as the best academy in the world, his detailed proposal for a Royal Academy for Military Exercises – as carefully thought through as his computations for a national highway system or pension hall, or a seaman's hiring hall under the jurisdiction of the Admiralty – founded by William himself, "a Colledge for breeding up of Artists in the useful Practice of all Military Exercises; the Scholars to be taken in Young, and be maintain'd, and afterwards under the King's Care for Preferment, as their Merit and His Majesty's Favour shall recommend them; from whence His Majesty wou'd at all times be furnish'd with able Engineers, Gunners, Fire-masters, Bombardiers, Miners, and the like;" and all for the continuing glory of a king "of whom we have seen the whole World writing *Panegyricks* and *Encomiums*" (pp. 260–61; 231) – all this should remind us of Defoe's seventeenth-century milieu that has been generally overlooked when consideration is given to Defoe's political thought. His effusive defenses of war that seem so excessive and atypical of his age, his subsequent accolades to William III, his sympathetic identification with other soldier-kings like Gustavus Adolphus, Louis XIV, and, later, George I, all help us to recall that the principal function of a king in Defoe's day was fighting wars and judging subjects. The first line of England's still oft-quoted jurisprudential classic, Bracton's *On the Laws and Customs of England*, stated: "To rule well a king requires two things, arms and laws, that by them both times of war and of peace may rightly be ordered."[42] Defoe's seventeenth-century world is one still dominated by the triumvirate of Monarchy, Statecraft, and War.[43] As Michael Roberts and his students have made clear, war occupied the center of consciousness of seventeenth-century society. The governments of the period "were really giant warmaking machines, devoting their

---

[42] Samuel E. Thorne, *Bracton On the Laws and Customs of England*, II, 19. See also Sir John Fortescue, *De laudibus legum Angli*, ed. S. B. Chrimes (Cambridge: Cambridge University Press, 1949), p. 3. A note: Bracton and Smith cite the Vulgate Bible; thus their references to Saul and Samuel are to The First Book of Kings.

[43] See Donald Kelly's Introduction to Claude de Seyssel, *The Monarchy of France*, trans. J. H. Hexter (New Haven: Yale University Press, 1981). Also J. R. Major, "The Renaissance Monarchy as seen by Erasmus, More, Seyssel and Machiavelli," in *Action and Convention in Early Modern Europe*, ed. T. K. Rabb and J. Siegel (Princeton: Princeton University Press, 1969), pp. 17–31.

main efforts to the maintenance of large armed forces;'' and, with few excep-
tions, kings were soldiers.[44]

As seventeenth-century states became more and more organizations devoted
to fighting wars, the strategic and tactical innovations that were the consequence ''all matched the tendency of the age towards absolute government, and
may well have reinforced it; if discipline proved so successful in obtaining
results in the military sphere, it might be worth trying the experiment of apply-
ing it to civilian life.''[45] The new scale in the waging of war made it necessary
that the monarch ''take over the business of supplying material and supervising
war industries.'' As a result, ''the ruler was increasingly identified with the
commander-in-chief, and from the new discipline and drill would be born not
merely the autocrat but that particular type of autocrat which delighted in the
name *Kriegsherr*'' (p. 20). This military revolution reinforced the characteristic
of the age that did not find it easy to think of politics except in terms of persons
and power. Such is Defoe's distinctive seventeenth-century vocabulary. He
imbues his language with the monarch, not monarchy. His fascination is more
with the sovereign, the warrior-king, Glorious King William, Deliverer and
Saviour, than with sovereignty. And if we are reminded that ''it was perhaps
not the least of England's good luck that for the whole of the critical century,
from 1547 to 1649, she was ruled by monarchs with neither interest nor capacity
for military matters'' (p. 20), it should also be recalled that from the year of
Defoe's birth to 1713 England spent twenty-five years at war. His English experience before the Revolution is one of convulsions and successive national
crises. He wrote during a wartime economy; ''for twenty of the twenty-five
years from 1689 to 1714, England was locked with France in a struggle of
unprecedented dimensions and cost.''[46]

The Protestant revolution was as much a martial one as it was a political
and spiritual one. Magistrates, if not kings, fought for their people.[47] The
English cult of kingship that centered on Edward VI, when it imaged his
authority in prints, masques, and court and country spectacles, focussed on

---

[44] Michael Duffy, ''Introduction,'' in *The Military Revolution and the State, 1500–1800*, ed.
Michael Duffy, Exeter Studies in History, no. 1 (University of Exeter, 1980), p. 4.

[45] This paragraph derives from Michael Roberts, ''The Military Revolution, 1550–1660,''
Essays in Swedish History (London: Weidenfeld and Nicolson, 1967), pp. 56–81. The essay was
first printed by Queen's University (Belfast, 1956). I quote from p. 20 of the 1956 essay. See
also Geoffrey Parker, ''The 'Military Revolution', 1550–1660 – A Myth?,'' *Journal of Modern
History*, 48 (1976), 195–214.

[46] See Geoffrey Holmes, ''Introduction: Post-Revolution Britain and the Historian,'' in *Britain
after the Glorious Revolution, 1689–1714*, ed. Geoffrey Holmes (London: Macmillan, 1969), pp.
18–24.

[47] See Michael Walzer, *The Revolution of the Saints* (Cambridge, MA: Harvard University Press,
1965). William Perkins, the noted puritan theologian, immediately turns to the military
metaphor and analogy when he begins to discuss God's orders and man's calling (''A Treatise
of the Vocations or Callings of men . . .'' (1603), in *Puritan Political Ideas*, ed. Edmund S.
Morgan (Indianapolis: Bobbs-Merrill Co., 1965), pp. 37–38).

two symbols, the Book and the Sword.[48] The myth of the conqueror, Prince Henry Stuart, and the profound, almost incomprehensible, lament following his sudden death, substantiate a continuing faith in a warrior-prince, a Protestant champion, who would not only sustain the salvation of England but redeem the empire of the world.[49] A century later, William's enemies and Anne's Stuart visionaries likened her sole surviving child, William Henry, Duke of Gloucester, to the eldest son of James I. Anecdotes and Gazette accounts, less heroic than pathetic, told of this young Protestant prince soldiering at play in his artillery park. He too, many in England hoped and prayed, would wield a Protestant sword against England's Catholic enemies, and his early death precipitated deep anxiety and dynastic disruption to the same degree.[50] Educational and prescriptive treatises of English aristocrats from the beginning to the end of the seventeenth century linked the preservation of the kingdom to the education of its prince, especially his military accomplishments.[51] In the midst of the Exclusion crisis, a pamphlet detailing the offices and obligations of the supreme magistrate proclaimed the absolute necessity for the prince to be qualified to manage a war and conduct an army – perhaps directed at Monmouth's capability to lead England as its new Protestant prince.[52] The Marquis of Halifax, Defoe's "noble Author who was an eminent Tory, though a friend of the Constitution and of the Protestant interest (for such are consistent)," and whose views on party and parliaments Defoe echoed to the end of his life, wrote in 1695: "The truth is, the vigour of youth is softened and misapplied when it is not spent either in war or close studies; all other courses have an idle mixture that cometh to nothing, and maketh them like trees which for want of pruning run up to wood, and seldom or never bear any fruit.[53]

In his thoughtful study of the literature of mid-eighteenth-century England, John Sitter sought to discover the special sensitivity of the writers of that period. He defined it as a retreat from the hostile forces of history. But it is

---

[48] John M. King, *English Reformation Literature: The Tudor Origin of the Protestant Tradition* (Princeton: Princeton University Press, 1982), pp. 161–206.

[49] See J. W. Williamson, *The Myth of the Conqueror: Prince Henry Stuart, A Study of 17th Century Personation* (New York: AMS Press, 1978); Barbara N. Lindsay and J. W. Williamson, "Myth of the Conqueror: Prince Henry Stuart and Protestant Militancy," *Journal of Medieval and Renaissance Studies*, 5 (1975), 203–22.

[50] See M. R. Hopkinson, *Anne of England: The Biography of a Great Queen* (London: Constable, 1934), pp. 139–59; Edward Gregg, *Queen Anne* (London: Routledge & Kegan Paul, 1980), pp. 100, 107, 115–20.

[51] See four essays by Thomas Digges and his son, Sir Dudley Digges in the former's *Four Paradoxes, or Politique Discourses* (London, 1604); and *Maxims of State*, in *The Works of Sir Walter Ralegh, Kt. by Thomas Birch* (London, 1751), I, 20, Cf. J. A. Gunn, *Politics and the Public Interest in the Seventeenth Century* (London: Routledge & Kegan Paul, 1969), pp. 1–2.

[52] *The Sovereign: Or A Political Discourse upon the Offices and Obligations of the Supreme Magistrate* (London, 1680), pp. 19, 24–36.

[53] *Some Cautions Offered*, in *Halifax: Complete Works*, ed. J. P. Kenyon, p. 176; Defoe, *Rogues on Both Sides* (London, 1711), p. 1.

a history distinguished by warfare, occasioned by invading and destroying armies and power-crazy conquerors and kings.[54] It is a modern sensibility somewhat like our own. Defoe, who could write without a trace of irony that "the war is now like the Gospel, Men must be set apart for it," is no citizen of that world.[55] Nothing sets Defoe apart from it more and locates him in an earlier century than his incipient ideality of heavenly supported might, kingship, and right rule. Linked as crown, sword, and scepter, the triad would be inseparable in his later writings. Just as sovereignty was for him no metaphysical abstraction nor a political concept but embodied in the personality, presence, and power of a king, so too were the symbols of authority necessarily made concrete in his imagination and for his reading public. Like Bodin and other seventeenth-century writers, Defoe had no trouble in locating his sovereign and his sources of authority. They were there, real, physical, perceptible. Already at this juncture in his political development, from his wider reading in history and his immersion in the paper skirmishes in William's reign, Defoe understood the "absolute necessity that a Military Power must be made use of with a Regal Power."[56] He was never to modify that stance.

The history of the four last years of William III, and the record of speeches, resolutions, and bills passed by his fourth and fifth parliaments (August 1698–November 1701) provide some substance, as Keith Feiling observed years ago, "for that not wholly untrue reading of history, which would make the seventeenth-century a contest of King and people against oligarchy"[57] – oligarchy in the present instance redefined as an impassioned and xenophobic country gentry thwarting the sensible designs of a king and pursuing policies predicated upon jealousy, unrestrained abuse of the prerogative, and contempt for their monarch. And though he is most sympathetic to William, Stephen Baxter's judgment of the 1698 parliament, that it "was an unrepresentative and an increasingly detested body of men; but it held the reins of power, and for the moment neither the King nor the people could check it," has the support of innumerable other historians.[58]

Queen Mary's death in December 1694 had already severely lessened the

[54] *Literary Loneliness in Mid-Eighteenth Century England* (Ithaca: Cornell University Press, 1982), pp. 77–103.

[55] *A Brief Reply to the History of Standing Armies in England* (London, 1698), p. 14.

[56] *Some Reflections on a Pamphlet Lately Publish'd* (London, 1697), p. 5. See the observations of Heinz H. F. Eulau, "The Depersonalization of the Concept of Sovereignty," *Journal of Politics*, 4 (1942), 3–19. I have profited from an unpublished essay kindly sent me by Professor Stephen Baxter titled "The Professional Soldier in a Civilian Society."

[57] *A History of the Tory Party, 1640–1714* (Oxford: Clarendon, 1924), p. 21. Cf. D. T. Witcombe, *Charles II and the Cavalier House of Commons* (Manchester: Manchester University Press, 1966), p. 181.

[58] *William III and the Defence of European Liberty, 1650–1702* (New York: Harcourt, Brace & World, 1966), p. 370. Cf. J. P. Kenyon, *The Stuarts: A Study in English Kingship* (London: B. T. Batsford, 1958), pp. 192–93.

attachment of the Crown's supporters who had been able to rationalize their allegiance to William by maintaining that they were only being loyal to a daughter of a Stuart king. William's authority, unassailable as long as foreign affairs and continental wars dominated parliamentary sessions, waned as a result of the peace negotiations that had been secretly begun in the spring of 1695, and which the English plenipotentiaries were actively engaged in by the end of 1696. Once the political nation learned of the signing of the Peace Treaty at Ryswick in September 1697, a grateful parliament began dismantling the king's army, resumed the grants he had made to loyal but foreign favorites, and threatened impeachment of his ministers. So disheartened – or disgusted – was England's Deliverer that he had written out an abdication speech in January 1699 and had prepared to return to Holland.[59] By November 1700 the Bishop of Derry observed that the king was becoming "only a sort of sheriff to execute their [parliament's] orders."[60]

A volatile London reading public once again found readily available the most immoderate tracts written during earlier immoderate times. *Killing No Murder*, an anti-Cromwell tirade that condoned the assassination of an usurping prince and that reappeared with frightening regularity at tumultuous political moments, was reprinted in 1698. Defenses of the civil war parliaments also were reprinted, perhaps to counter the developing cult of Charles, the Martyr. The cult itself helped to erode the sympathy that was still generated toward the Williamite crown.[61] The 1698 elections brought a "flood of country pamphlets on the importance of free parliamentary proceedings in 'a house of commons chosen truly by the people, incapable of pension and place'."[62] By many, this new Country party was seen to be Jacobite, its purpose to bring back popery and King James. But many other moderate royalists and erstwhile supporters of monarchy were echoing commonwealth principles, seemingly ready to make any sacrifce in order to emancipate the nation from the domination of the soldiers and their warrior-king. Between 1697 and 1700, Harrington's *Oceana*, Milton's commonwealth tracts, and Sidney's *Discourses Concerning Government* found their way into print. Vindicators of an omnipotent parliament confuted William Molyneaux's assertions of the legislative independence of Ireland.[63] Memoirs of prominent civil war politicians and soldiers were discovered, printed, and commented upon.[64] Their intent was clear, one contemporary defender of the court realized; they were

59 See Baxter, *William III and the Defence of European Liberty*, pp. 322–64.
60 Cited in Rubini, *Court and Country*, p. 202.
61 See Kenyon, *Revolution Principles*, pp. 61–82.
62 Downie, *Robert Harley*, p. 35.
63 See John Carey, *A Vindication of the Parliament of England* . . . (London, 1698); Michael de L. Landon, *Erin and Britannia* (Chicago: Nelson-Hall, 1981).
64 See *The Memoirs of Edmund Ludlow*, ed. C. H. Firth, 2 vols. (Oxford: Clarendon Press, 1894); Edmund Ludlow, *A Voyce From The Watch Tower, Part Five: 1660–1662*, ed. A. B. Worden, Camden Fourth Series, vol. 21 (London, 1978).

"all on the same subject, and tending to promote the design of lessening and reproaching monarchy . . . for subverting monarchy itself . . ."[65]

The pamphlet war over William's professional standing army and its demobilization when hostilities ended was initiated in October 1697 with the publication of Trenchard and Moyle's *An Argument, Shewing a Standing Army is Inconsistent with a Free Government.* The seventeenth-century background and the controversy itself have been ably documented by Lois Schwoerer.[66] As she has observed, the question of maintaining a standing army in peacetime inevitably led to questions of greater import. If, as *An Argument* realized, 'Sword and Sovereignty always march hand in hand," then the demand that the arms machinery be taken out of the hand of the king was an implicit attack on one of the most vital prerogatives of the crown.[67] In 1653 "the question never was whether we would be governed by arbitrary power but in whose hands it should be."[68] In 1697, as one anti-army pamphleteer wrote, "Now the sole Debate between us is, In whose hands these Weapons should be put."[69]

Defoe's prepossession for the military, his infatuation with soldier-kings, his passionate commitment to William III, and his intelligent comprehension of the changing conditions of diplomacy and war, all would have conduced to make arguments of the anti-standing-army pamphleteers misguided and simplistic. In addition, the antiquarianism of the faction, its dedication to "the old English Constitution" and the "glorious Commonwealth of Rome," would have provoked Defoe's ire. Still, in his responses Defoe is "the moderate Whig" that Professor Schwoerer presents him to be.[70] But once again, as in 1689 and as we shall continue to see, the Janus-face of Defoe is evident. What can be called his deeply felt ideology of monarchy and war and the practical politics of the moment come into conflict. Defoe never modified his belief that sovereignty and the sword in the hands of the king march hand in hand. The whiggish philosophy of government that advocated a restricted monarchy and a powerful parliament, and resulted in many of William's ministers arguing his case half-heartedly, committed Defoe, once again, to language revealing the idiosyncratic nature of his political thought. Thus, to support the prevailing argument that "*tis not the King of England alone, but the*

[65] *Cursory Remarks Upon Some Late Disloyal Proceedings* (1699), in *Somers Tracts,* XI, 149–91. Cf. George Stepney, *An Essay Upon the Present Interest of England* (1701), in *Somers Tracts,* XI, 195–227.

[66] *"No Standing Armies!" The Antiarmy Ideology in Seventeenth-Century England* (Baltimore: Johns Hopkins University Press, 1974).

[67] London, 1697, p. 7.

[68] Quoted in George Mosse, *The Struggle for Sovereignty in England* (East Lansing: Michigan State College Press, 1950), p. 175.

[69] John Trenchard, *A Letter From the Author of the Argument Against a Standing Army, To the Author of the Balancing Letter* (London, 1697), p. 7.

[70] "The Literature of the Standing Army Controversy, 1697–1699," *Huntington Library Quarterly,* 28 (1965), 195.

Sword of England *in the Hand of the King, that gives Laws of Peace and War now to* Europe,'' he returns to The First Book of Samuel: "God himself, when the *Israelites* would have a King, told them this would be the Consequence; as if it might be inferr'd as of absolute necessity, that a Military Power must be made use of with a Regal Power; and as it may follow *No King, No Army,* so it may as well follow, *no Army, no King.*"[71] And, countering the sympathy shown by the anti-standing-army pamphleteers to the Gothic model of government, with its citizen army and its elective monarchy, Defoe rehearses once again the history of the Revolution, deliberately avoiding the language of contract and parliamentary monarchy:

> Now if King *James* Deserted the Nation, so did his Son with him, and thereby the Throne became Vacant, and the power of Government devolv'd upon such as were next Heirs; and who they were was to be decided by the Parliament, who have been allow'd to be the Judges of the Right of Succession in all Ages. Now the Parliament did not upon this Vacancy of the Throne proceed to Elect a King, *as some People are mighty fond of saying,* and so alter our Constitution to an Elective Monarchy. But they proceeded to Examine whose the Right of Government was, and to make a Declaration of that Right by Authority of Parliament . . .[72]

If, as I have suggested, a war mentality and the struggle for parliamentary omnicompetence are the distinctive conditions of the period, conditions which Defoe recognized and wrote about in three reigns and for innumerable ministries, his tendency to delimit the power of parliaments, and to reject their continuing and increasing antagonism to the institution of monarchy – or at least William's monarchy – should be given its due value. One of the commonplace justifications for a large standing army was that parliament's power of the purse and its consent to a peacetime army would preclude any danger to the constitutional balance and reduce any threats to the liberties of the subject. Defoe echoed this when he wrote: "In this Establishment of a Parliament, the Sword is indeed trusted in the Hands of the King, and *the Purse in the Hands of the People*, the People cannot make Peace or War without the King, nor the King cannot raise or maintain an Army without the People, and this is the True Ballance."[73] Defoe's "Ballance" of king and people, sovereign and subject, sounds old-fashioned and also distinguishes English parliaments from the whole people of England. His language is obviously different from the language of the king's enemies, but it is also different from the language of the king's lukewarm ministerial supporters writing in defense of the standing army. John, Lord Somers, for example, in his *Letter, Ballancing the Necessity of Keeping a Land-Force In Times of Peace*, asked his English readers to put their full trust

---

71 *An Argument Shewing, That a Standing Army, With the Consent of Parliament, Is Not Inconsistent with a Free Government* (London, 1698), pp. A2r–A2v.

72 *Some Reflections on a Pamphlet Lately Publish'd, Entitled, An Argument Shewing that a Standing Army is Inconsistent with a Free Government* . . . (London, 1697), p. 5.

73 *An Argument Shewing*, pp. 12–13. But cf. Kenyon, "The Revolution of 1688," who argues that Defoe was using "Original Contract" language (p. 56).

in parliament: "Our Representatives do well to secure our Constitution, by the most effectual Means they can think on: But after all, we must trust *England* to a *House of Commons*, that is to it self."[74] This tendency to discover omnicompetence in English parliaments because they were equated with the electorate, or the people of England, was not now and never was to be Defoe's position. For him, "Parliaments are Magnipotent, tho' they are not Omnipotent."[75] Perhaps we can pause to consider Defoe's word about the magnipotence of parliaments because it *is* Defoe's word.

Defoe, it could be said, first discovered the magnipotence of parliaments in the standing army debates of 1697. In 1700, in an essay minimizing the strength of Louis XIV's armies, since England might once again have to engage in a continental war to protect its commercial interests and dynastic stability, Defoe, perhaps unconsciously, connected his heady parliaments with the arbitrary despot by calling the latter "magnipotent."[76] In 1701, challenging the Commons' intimidation of the Kent petitioners, he scathingly and consciously attacked "the arbitrary methods" made use of by this "*Arbitrary Parliament . . . to Ruine those who have felt their Magnipotent Indignation . . .*"[77]

In what have been defined as his most radical years, in 1707 and 1709, writing on behalf of the unrestrained Whig ministry of Anne's reign, whether the subject was the Treaty of Union or a bill for the creation of a new East India trading company, Defoe maintained: "I allow the Parliament is a Magnipotent Power, but I must not call them Omnipotent; no, not in every thing relating to civil Government."[78] And during the Sacheverell trial in January 1710 and at the end of a year that was to bring in a parliament, under the ministry of Harley and Bolingbroke, that was to be zealously and defiantly Tory, Defoe kept reminding his *Review* readers – he was now one of Harley's pensioners – that "the Parliament is indeed a Magnipotent Creature."[79] Magnipotent, as far as I have been able to tell, is a term totally absent from the age's voluminous debates on monarchy, sovereignty, and the power of the people. It is no part of Locke's vocabulary, nor of any Lockean one that proclaims the supremacy of the legislature. John Tutchin, Country Whig and the author of the aggressively whiggish *Observator*, while he can censure the ideas of both Defoe and Somers, whom he calls "modern" Whigs, nevertheless, defending the sovereignty of parliament, approximated the language of the

[74] London, 1697, p. 15.
[75] *Some Reflections on a Pamphlet*, Preface. p. A2v.
[76] *The Two Great Questions Consider'd* (London, 1700), p. 4.
[77] *The History of the Kentish Petition* (London, 1701), p. 8. The British Library copy of the first edition prints "*Magnificent.*" All subsequent issues and editions print "*Magnipotent.*" That Defoe cared enough to correct this egregious misprint reveals his conscious preoccupation with a word he had made his trademark.
[78] *Review*, IV, 69 (22 July 1707). See also V, 156 (26 March 1709).
[79] *Review*, VI, 122 (17 Jan. 1710) See also VII, 115 (19 Dec. 1710).

latter but not the former. "It was a noted Apothegm of Sir *William Cecil*, Lord *Burleigh* and High Treasurer of *England*," Tutchin frequently wrote, "*That he knew not what an Act of Parliament might not do*; For their Power is Prescrib'd by no law, because it is Antecedent to all Law. *ab mundi Origine* . . ."[80] Legislative sovereignty and Whig veneration for parliament, "the highest Power in England," is one of the supreme touchstones of the ideology and language of Whiggism. Defoe's terminology divides him from the vaunted and necessary party shibboleths of the period to reveal the problematic radicalism of his early pamphlets and the ambiguous whiggism with which he has been labeled.

Defoe was virtually silent for the next two years, from September 1698 till November 1700. Except for *The Pacificator* (November 1700), his poetic response to a literary squabble among the poetasters of 1700, which contains strange but characteristically sympathetic couplets on absolutism, albeit in art, Defoe remained aloof from political pamphleteering.[81] The anti-Williamite momentum of 1697–98 did not abate. Defoe had remarked in 1698, upon the publication of Lieutenant General Ludlow's *Memoirs*, that not only were they blasphemous but they also were directed against the rule of William, for "the Conduct of the Parliament against the King is exceedingly magnified; the Government of a single Person opposed covertly, under the Person of *O. C.* but in general, of any single Person whatever; and all the Common-Wealth-Principles advanced and defended."[82] But the voices undermining the integrity of his monarch were not only coming from the republican left; conservative ex-defenders of hereditary monarchy and the Stuart line were also advancing and defending principles that could terminate in the loss of a balanced constitution and thus in tyranny and slavery. Perhaps this explains the scathing tones of an *Encomium Upon a Parliament* (May [?] 1699), which has been attributed to Defoe. The poem, Frank Ellis rightly comments, "is neither Whig or Tory or, more exactly, . . . is anti-Whig and anti-Tory."[83] As the hostility to a widowed William increased, perhaps heightened by the hope of an anticipated Stuart restoration under a chastened if not Protestant Prince of Wales, Tories and Whigs, Anglicans and Dissenters, advanced arguments that prompted Defoe's most forthright defenses of the king and resulted in his most controverted political pamphlets.

On 30 January 1699, the anniversary of the martyrdom of Charles I, "the King's Day," three sermons were preached and later published. Offspring Blackall, chaplain-in-ordinary to the king, preached before the House of Commons; William Fleetwood, also chaplain-in-ordinary to the king, preached at St. Paul's before the mayor, aldermen, and citizens of London; and Samuel

80 *Observator*, no. 24 (11–15 July 1702). Cf. no. 23 (8–11 July 1702). Tutchin's vocabulary is of the "Antient Constitution" (no. 99), and of election and consent (no. 100).

81 See *The Pacificator*, POAS, VI, 178–79.

82 *A Brief Reply to the History of Standing Armies in England* (London, 1698), p. 24.

83 POAS, VI, 47.

Bradford preached before the king in St. James's Chapel. These sermons begin to reveal tendencies and anticipate developments that would soon be exploited over the nature and locale of sovereignty. Blackall's is the most traditional and needs little comment. Its fulsome exaltation of the martyred Charles could scarcely have surprised his audience. Preaching on John 9.3: "*Jesus answered, Neither hath this Man sinned nor his Parents; but that the Works of God should be made manifest in him,*" Blackall opened the text by remarking Charles's "great Example," calling him "the Lord's Anointed" and the "Father of their Countrey," put to death by impious and hypocritical judges and subjects. From beginning to end his theme is of a suffering Job and the wickedness of a past day.[84]

Fleetwood's and Bradford's sermons are other matters. The first had as its text 1 Samuel 26.10, 11: "David *said furthermore, as the Lord liveth, the Lord shall smite him, or his day shall come to die, or he shall descend into Battel and perish. The Lord forbid that I should stretch forth mine hand against the Lord's anointed.*" Fleetwood's narrative is about Saul and David, a heavenly appointed king of Israel and his servant, of a father, son-in-law, and a barren wife. But Fleetwood's sermon lays the stress on the "young aspiring Hero," a David whose virtue and merit "had not acquir'd him a considerable Party, and a well-grounded Interest at Court."[85] The son-in-law of the king is also "a mighty Man of Valour, he fought *the Lord's Battels*; he was the Sword and Shield, the Horsemen and the Chariots of *Israel.* He was the Scourge of the *Philistines*, and indeed of all the Idolatrous Nations round; the great Defender of the *Jewish* Faith, and the Supporter of God's Worship. And 'tis hard to think a Man thus qualified, should fail of bearing sway amongst the Soldiery, and being gracious in the Camp; and all Men know, how far that tends to the promoting and securing any great Designs" (p. 12). The heart of Fleetwood's theme, though, is restraint, the restraint exhibited by a man of valor, a conqueror, a king-designate, who repeatedly refuses to "*stretch forth my hand against the Lord's anointed*," against his father-in-law, the King of Israel, "the Man that was by God's designation and appointment, anointed King or Captain over all the People" (p. 17). In spite of the fact that Saul was a king who had "abandon'd common Honesty, broken the sacred Cords that knit Societies, and keep up Governments and mutual Correspondences, together with Relations Natural and Civil, and by his Perjuries, provok'd the Vengeance of God, and is delivered into the Hands of those whose Innocence and good Credulity he had impos'd on, and abus'd almost to their Destruction," the young prince could still say, "*The Lord forbid that I should stretch forth my hand*

[84] *A Sermon Preached before the Honourable House of Commons . . . January 30th. 1698/9* (London, 1699), pp. 9, 12, 25.

[85] *A Sermon Preach'd at St. Paul's Cathedral, January 30. 1698/9. Before the Right Honourable The Lord Mayor and Court of Aldermen* (London, 1698/99), pp. 7, 12. Following citations will be noted in the text.

against the Lord's anointed" (p. 9). Scripture-Examples, as Fleetwood observed, govern the world; thus it is almost impossible not to believe that his audience interpreted his tale as another example of parallel history that so adversely reflected upon William's conduct to James II. A. B. Worden has reminded us that "it was difficult for politicians, however suspicious they might be of William III, to criticize openly the deliverer of 1689. They could, however, disguise their criticisms in historical parallels. That is one reason why so much political controversy in the 1690s was conducted as a debate about the 1640s."[86] Scripture-Instances and Scripture-Examples enabled the critical voices of the Anglican church to implicate the present king and his establishment innocently and with impunity. Perhaps the sermon explains why Fleetwood, a so-called zealous Whig, received no mark of royal favor until just before William's death.

For David's devotion to the principle of obedience is founded less on "the Laws of God" and more on "the fundamental Constitutions of the Nation" (p. 18). Thus, as Fleetwood warms to his interest, his language moves away from those traditional approximations of authority, God and king, and shifts the agency of obedience from the crown to "the *Civil Constitution*," magistrates, and *"Rulers"* (p. 18). Obedience, Fleetwood begins to insist, is paid to governments; governors exercise power and justice over subjects who are bound to obey and reverence them and submit with patience and contentedness. Echoing then the justification for the Revolution we have observed in the allegiance pamphlets, Fleetwood concluded by exhorting his countrymen, *"Look to the Constitution, look to the Laws and Customs of a Country,* if you would know the Prince's Power or People's Privilege" (pp. 23–24). Divine right may have died on the scaffold with Charles I, but Christianity came "to urge the Subjects to obey the Laws *made* by the Legislative Power, where-ever that resides" (p. 23).

Bradford's sermon before the King was on Proverbs 24.21: *"My Son, fear thou the Lord and the King: And meddle not with them that are given to change."* Defoe, if he had heard or read it, might have gotten some satisfaction that a sermon on a text that was one of the old warhorses of royalist Church of England ministers lambasting dissenters and exhorting passive obedience and non-resistance to Stuart monarchs was now being reworked by a staunch Whig.[87] But Bradford's Whig message could hardly have received Defoe's enthusiastic approval, because the Solomonic text was, like Fleetwood's the same day, put to serve an argument for passivity, obedience to the status quo, and a shifting authority in government. That authority is, in fact, no longer the monarchy or the monarch, but, ominously, "the Civil Government under which we

---

86 Edmund Ludlow, *A Voyce From the Watch Tower*, p. 49.
87 See, for example, Thomas Cartwright, *A Sermon preached to the Gentlemen of Yorkshire, At Bow Church in London, the 24th of June, 1684* (London, 1684); John Fitzwilliam, *A Sermon Preach'd at Cutenham near Cambridge, On the 9th. of September, 1683* (London, 1683).

are plac'd, [which] is to be regarded next to Almighty God, the Supreme Lord and Governor of all.''[88] Except for the reiteration, *"Fear thou the Lord and the King,"* the present sitting king is never mentioned in Bradford's text. William III is lost among "Law-makers" and "Governors." Expounding his text, Bradford writes: "So that *to fear the King,* is to have a great regard to the Government we live under, to yield a ready obedience to all its wholsome Laws and Customs, never willingly to deviate from either, unless the Commandments of God, and the Laws or Customs of Men, should interfere: and if at any time we should fall into such unhappy circumstances, in that case either peaceably to withdraw from the Society, and remove to some other, where we may enjoy both a good Conscience and our Liberty together; or if that may not be, then quietly and patiently to submit to such Penalties as by the Laws of our Country may be inflicted upon us" (p. 7). Always, then, in Bradford's terms, to fear the king is to fear the governors. And his presentation of the commonplace adherence to the powers that be is firmly and finally grounded in the language of Peter and Paul that was the stock-in-trade of seventeenth-century royalist rhetoric (p. 9). Some months later, a fervent defender of William III, in what James Ralph termed "a reviling declamatory pamphlet," attacking the cabals in and out of the Commons, amazedly asked: "Who that ever knew, how in the late reign our laws were suspended, our properties seized, our rights and liberties invaded, and protestants insulted by furious papists, could ever think to see the day, that any English protestant could requite good with evil, and industriously slander the footsteps of the Lord's anointed, that healed our breaches, and restored us to liberty?"[89] He could more easily have been directing his questions to the pulpit oratory of 30 January 1699.

These sermons of 1699 are of more than minor significance, for they reveal the manner in which the right and the left, so to speak, the enemies and friends of William's monarchy, Tory constitutionalists and Whig contractualists, were shunting the location of sovereignty to diminish the power of the monarch. And this old wine of passive obedience and non-resistance to the powers that be, poured into the new bottle of the legislature, was not suddenly a Tory scheme, as one recent historian suggests: "The first clear sign that the Tories were prepared to preach obedience to the legislature appears in the famous sermon which John Sharp, Archbishop of York, preached to the House of Commons on 30 January 1700."[90] Sharp's text, Titus 3.1: *"Put them in*

---

88 *A Sermon Preach'd before the King, In St. James's Chappel, January 30th. 1698/9* (London, 1699), p. 6. Following citations will be noted in the text.

89 *Cursory Remarks upon some late Disloyal Proceedings,* in *Somers Tracts,* XI, 149, 154. The *Dictionary of National Biography* attributes *Cursory Remarks,* on his admission, to Richard Kingston. But see Ellis's account of Defoe's *Encomium upon a Parliament (POAS,* VI, 720–21), where, discussing the manuscripts, Ellis suggests that Defoe might have had a hand in the writing of the *Remarks.*

90 H. T. Dickinson, *Liberty and Property: Political Ideology in Eighteenth-Century Britain* (London: Weidenfeld and Nicolson, 1977), p. 47. Dickinson's study is most astute in explaining the political climate of the age. Note his observations about the "divine right of the sovereign legislature" (pp. 44, 47). Cf. Kenyon, "The Revolution of 1688," pp. 54–55.

mind to be subject to Principalities and Powers, to obey Magistrates,'' and his insistent concern for "the *Supreme Civil Governours,''* and *"Magistrates,''* and "the standing *Laws* of every Country,'' as we have seen, were already the content of Whig sermons; in fact, Sharp repeats the stern injunctions of Romans 13.1, 2 and Proverbs 24.21 that his London audience had heard and read a year before.[91] The powers that be were once hereditary monarchs ordained of God. In 1689 the detractors and even the supporters of William III had dismantled that religious scaffolding upholding the great Deliverer who Defoe believed had been sent by Providence to secure his English nation. Now in 1699 and 1700 the new powers that be were English legislators, divinely sanctioned and above the criticism of the populace without doors.

Over in the House of Commons that same King's Day of 1700, a sermon more destructive to England's balanced government of kings, lords, and commons was being preached by one "tainted with Republican principles.''[92] Coincidentally, Rev. William Stephens's text, like the Archbishop of York's was also Titus 3.1. Before a Tory-dominated Commons, Stephens too anchored a doctrine of civil obedience to the supreme magistrates on Romans 13 and Peter. While it has been suggested that the denunciation that followed Stephens's sermon was caused by his presentation of the Whig doctrine that the foundation of government lies in the consent of the people, it is just as likely that the furor that followed resulted from Stephens's omission of the prayer for the king and the royal family and his questioning the continuation of the anniversary observance of the execution of Charles I.[93] Surely the Commons found no radical notion in his assertion that obedience is due, not to the king, but to the civil magistrates, the "Governours" or rather the "Inferior Authorities.'' "For tho' the superior and inferior Powers differ greatly, if compared among themselves; yet, with respect to the Subjects Obedience, they are to be regarded alike; so that we cannot wilfully disobey the Inferior, without affronting the Sovereign Authority.''[94] The monarch thus is nothing more than the first dignitary of the state; his distinguishing characteristics removed, he becomes unexceptional and reducible to his subordinate and derivative powers. The redefining of the magistrates of the state has concluded in the diminishment of the image and the constitutional importance of the king. A decade after the Revolution, for Defoe's contemporaries, the legislative power, that mythical and traditional safeguard of the old English constitution, had become the resurrected absolute and almost arbitrary authority to whom the English were to yield abject obedience. This significant redistribution of the balance of power could be of comfort to many who had

[91] *A Sermon Preached before the Lords, Spiritual and Temporal in Parliament Assembled . . . On the Thirtieth of January. 1699/1700*, 2nd. ed. (London, 1700), pp. 10, 14, 18, 23.

[92] William Cobbett, *The Parliamentary History of England* (London, 1809), V, 1224.

[93] See Kenyon, *Revolution Principles*, p. 73.

[94] *A Sermon Preach'd Before the Honourable House of Commons, January 30. 1699/1700* (London, 1700), p. 10.

their thoughts directed to the future; on the one hand, Tory moderates who might have been willing to accept the claims of a chastened prince of the House of Stuart to his English throne, and, on the other, Whig contractualists who already could anticipate the accession of a Hanoverian warrior-prince disturbingly similar to William III. As one historian has pointedly concluded, "by changing the location of sovereignty they found an absolute and irresistible power, the Legislature, which was more able than an absolute monarch to protect the interests of propertied men."[95] This is the context in which Defoe's "Lockean" tracts in the last year of William's reign have to be viewed.

The dissolution of William's fourth parliament in December 1700, the return of an emboldened House of Commons, and the growing recognition by Country interests of the king's vulnerability unleashed a rage of party that revealed a nation more threatened internally than at any time since the Revolution.[96] "The Act of Resumption [April 1700] constituted a humiliating setback for the king and an assertion of parliamentary authority in a field in which the royal prerogative had appeared to be firmly established."[97] The issue had further ramifications in what appeared to be a concerted design of Stuart apologists and old-stamp republicans to subvert the monarch, for, as Professor Ogg noted, by printing and publishing the report of the Irish Commissioners on the forfeited estates in Ireland, the Commons had taken "an unusual step which implied an appeal to the nation against the crown."[98] The death of the Duke of Gloucester in the summer had provoked a major crisis for Tory consciences, for those who returned to William's fifth parliament, which convened in February 1701, were pulled toward Hanover on the one hand and St. Germains on the other. The Convocation controversy, which began that same month, led to an irreparable breach between the High Church and Low parties. A turbulent Convocation and a turbulent Commons greeted a king who was once again preparing his adopted country for a major war with France, but without a standing and prepared army and without his superior officers, who had also been rejected by xenophobic legislatures. During 1701 an attempt was made to limit the king's control over the Church with a bill to forbid the translation of bishops.[99] Even the sympathetic House of Lords, while defending its privileges during the impeachment proceedings in the spring, asked for the creation of a special council to advise the king about matters of importance, domestic and foreign, which was to be made up of

---

[95] Dickinson, *Liberty and Property*, p. 44.

[96] See Horwitz, *Parliament, Policy, and Politics*, pp. 275–310.

[97] J. D. Simms, *The Williamite Confiscation in Ireland 1690–1703* (London: Faber, 1956), p. 82.

[98] David Ogg, *England in the Reigns of James II and William III* (Oxford: Clarendon, 1955), p. 451.

[99] See G. V. Bennett, *White Kennett, 1660–1728, Bishop of Peterborough* (London: S. P. C. K., 1957), pp. 26–55. Also G. V. Bennett, *The Tory Crisis in Church and State, 1688–1730: The Career of Francis Atterbury, Bishop of Rochester* (Oxford: Clarendon Press, 1975).

"natural born subjects."[100] Pamphlets deluged the London reader, ostensibly supporting William and attacking only those who were making him an autocrat, but in reality asserting the moral superiority of parliaments and undermining the king's control in matters of foreign policy and war.

If, as Frank Bastian has ventured, Defoe was "already deep in William's confidence by the beginning of November [1700]," his profusion of Williamite propaganda over the following year is explained.[101] In addition to *The True-Born Englishman* (January 1701), more than a dozen moderately lengthy and well-reasoned tracts were published; and the year concluded with *The Original Power of the Collective Body of the People of England, Examined and Asserted* (December 1701), seemingly Defoe's most radical and "Lockean" essay. It now remains to be seen if Defoe moderated or revised his stance on power, parliaments, and the monarchy, and whether, as Professor Kenyon believed, "it is difficult to imagine the king countenancing any of Defoe's writings over [these] . . . twelve months, or condoning his *Legion Memorial*" (May 1701).[102]

Defoe's opening salvo in defense of William's foreign policy, *The Two Great Questions Consider'd. I. What the French King will Do, with Respect to the Spanish Monarchy. II. What Measures the English ought to Take* (November 1700), is a cogent analysis of the dynastic crisis in Spain that was to bring on the War of the Spanish Succession, a subject that Defoe had discussed three years earlier. Both tracts argue for his intelligence in issues of diplomacy, continental history and dynastic complexity, and the economics and politics of European trade.[103] He had already understood that "Titles to Crowns are generally disputed by the Sword, not by Deeds and Instruments."[104] Thus, understanding that England would have to be, once again, involved in a land war on the continent, his supportive words for William were matched by his insinuations that England's dangerously present weakness, a land divided in temper and impotent in forces, resulted from that cabal of republican pamphleteers who had disbanded the king's armies and had thus made it impossible for him to thwart French ambition and maintain the balance of power. His moderate suggestion that England re-arm for a land war on the continent immediately was answered and rebutted by a Country pamphlet that continued the contemporary attacks on the king. It denied the legitimacy of the Treaty of Partition, castigated the king's ministers – who were to be impeached the

---

[100] John, Lord Somers, *Jura Populi Anglicani* (London, 1701), Preface, in *Parliamentary History*, V, 1,242.

[101] *Defoe's Early Life*, p. 225.

[102] *Revolution Principles*, p. 57.

[103] For Defoe and diplomacy see William Roosen, *Daniel Defoe and Diplomacy* (Selinsgrove: Susquehanna University Press, 1986). But see Frank Ellis's review in *American Historical Review*, 93 (1988), 146–47.

[104] *The Interests of the Several Princes and States of Europe Consider'd, With Respect to the Succession of the Crown of Spain* (London, 1698), p. 7.

following April – proclaimed that England's security lay with her fleet alone, and came to a resonant defence of England's parliament, "by whom Kings reign, and from whom proceed all the legal Rights of crowned Heads."[105]

To this Country-republican attacker, who could quote Algernon Sidney, proclaim a Tory "blue-water" policy, and detect his "squint-ey'd Reflections" on the parliament, Defoe immediately responded.[106] In *The Two Great Questions Further Considered. With some Reply to the Remarks* (December 1700), Defoe stressed the traditional power of the monarch over foreign policy. It is he who makes leagues and treaties, engages in war and sues for peace. Parliaments can withhold funds if they wish to but the ordering of diplomacy, foreign negotiations, and commerce is solely in the king's jurisdiction. Behind the scenes Defoe detected a "Pamphleteering Club" that was undermining the very being of the English monarchy by declaiming "the People's Right to make Kings, which is what these Gentlemen are so fond of."[107] And once again Defoe rejected without qualification the whiggish assertion that an English monarch, or at least his English monarch, was a "King by Modern Contract," that is, a king created and to be disposed of by parliaments.[108] Despite the ministerial changes of the next reign, which forced Defoe to change his tune to accommodate successive court patrons, he never passed up an opportunity to continue to look "squint-ey'd" at the Commons. In the following year he defined them as "those Wonderful and Unintelligible Assemblies . . ."[109] When the Commons held up funds for the war, Defoe responded sarcastically about their plans to break down modern walls of Jericho with rams' horns.[110] Defoe is an anomaly among his contemporaries, who could not suspect parliaments – or at least the Commons – of a grab for illegal or unconsentual power. "[I]t is not to be imagin'd," Mackworth wrote, "that a Majority of so numerous a Body of Gentlemen,

---

[105] *Remarks Upon a Late Pamphlet Intitul'd, The Two Great Questions Consider'd* (London, 1700), p. 11. That a good case can be made for Defoe's authorship of these *Remarks* (Bastian, *Defoe's Early Life*, p. 311) brings us to the heart of any study of Defoe's politics. If we see him writing on both sides of an issue, publishing answers to himself, controverting his "own" positions in immediate contexts, impersonating completely his antagonists and enemies, it then becomes vital that we attempt to distinguish in those works of propaganda, on both sides of the question, the few tenets of politics that can be said he securely held.

[106] *Remarks*, pp. 4, 11, 12, 20–21, 23.

[107] P. 12. Defoe appears to be attacking views expressed in *Gloria Cambriae* (London, 1702); see *Somers Tracts*, XI, 393. The author was Richard Price; the tract is his speech delivered to the Commons in 1696 attacking William's land grants. It was twice reprinted; in *A Choice Collection of Papers Relating to State Affairs* (London, 1703) and in *A Collection of Scarce and Valuable Papers Relating to State Affairs* (London, 1712).

[108] *Gloria Cambriae*, p. 9.

[109] *The Free-Holders Plea Against Stock-Jobbing Elections of Parliament Men* (London, 1701), p. 3.

[110] *The Danger of the Protestant Religion Consider'd, from the Present Prospect of a Religious War in Europe* (1701), in *A True Collection*, p. 240. See also J. A. Downie, "An Unknown Defoe Broadsheet on the Regulation of the Press?" *The Library*, 5th ser., 33 (1978), 51–58.

can be Influenc'd against Reason and Justice."[111] More than any writer of his time, Defoe realized a new tyranny, the tyranny of parliaments, which was to become a major preoccupation of English political commentators only after his death in 1731.[112] A judgment he made in defense of the Protestant dissenters in Carolina in 1706 makes clear his life-long attitude. He, like those able progenitors of the colony, "did not forget, that even those Representative Assemblies, especially in the Infancy of the Government, might be corrupt, or might by Bribery or other ill Practices, be Modell'd and Influenc'd in Matters of Parties, to Oppress and Injure the People they acted for."[113] It could also be noted that Defoe, unlike nearly all of his contemporaries, rarely sought to dismiss the English parliament's responsibility for the outrages of the rebellion of the 1640s. While the blame was generally laid on sectarians, fanatics, or republicans, men mad with destructive principles, Defoe kept reminding his readers that the civil war had been a "Parliament War," and that "Parliament-Men" had rebelled and destroyed their king.[114]

Defoe's two tracts of late 1700 might help us to put in better perspective the "Lockean" terminology of *The True-Born Englishman*, published early in 1701. In those tracts he had posited explicitly the threat to England's past and present military insecurity, and had singled out the two factional interests whose xenophobia and reinterpretation of English history were behind the humiliation of the king, the libeling of his countrymen and counsellors, and the continued questioning of the Revolutionary settlement of 1689. One was "our *Jacobite-Protestant*-Brethren," now "deplor[ing] the Ruins they ha' made, / And Murmur[ing] for the Master they Betray'd."[115] The other was the anti-standing-army contingent of 1697–98, comprised of Socinians, freethinkers, and Calves Head republicans who were behind the end-of-the-century publications of Sidney, Milton, and Harrington. If Defoe really believed that William was being squeezed between the pincers of a Tory-Jacobite and republican confederacy, he would have found such evidence in the poems of the past summer that provoked his rage and resulted in *The True-Born Englishman*. For Tutchin's *The Foreigners* and Dennis's *The Reverse* epitomize the ideological extreme of an axis to which Defoe was providing a middle and moderating position.

Supporting the right of the Spanish people to dispose of their throne as they saw fit – and thus undermining the Second Partition Treaty and denying

---

[111] *A Vindication of the Rights of the Commons of England* (London, 1701) pp. 23–24. Cf. *Of the Fundamental Laws, or Politick Constitution of this Kingdom*, in *State Tracts* (1692), p. 25.

[112] See Gunn, *Beyond Liberty and Property*, pp. 7–42.

[113] *Party-Tyranny: Or, An Occasional Bill in Miniature; As Now Practiced in Carolina* (London, 1705), p. 3.

[114] See *Jure Divino*, pp. viii–ix; XI, 24. The irony oozes in *King William's Affection to the Church of England Examin'd* (London, 1703), p. 8. For Defoe's other mockeries directed at the Commons see Downie, *Robert Harley*, p. 69. For Defoe's low opinion of Parliaments in 1715 see *A Hymn to the Mob* (London, 1715), p. 7.

[115] *The Two Great Questions Consider'd*, p. 20; *The True-Born Englishman*, POAS, VI, 290.

that England had any interest in, or was threatened by, Europe's dynastic chaos – Tutchin had advanced a dangerously democratic argument in his interpretation of William's ascent to the English throne:

> Have not Mankind on equal Terms still stood,
> Without Distinction, since the mighty Flood?
> And have not [Carlos II's] Subjects a free Choice
> To chuse a King by their united Voice?
> If [England's] People cou'd a Monarch chuse,
> A living King at the same time refuse;
> That [Carlos II's] People, shall it e'er be said,
> Have not the Right of Choice when he is dead?
> When no Successor to the Crown's in sight,
> The Crown is certainly the People's Right.
> If Kings are made the People to enthral,
> We had much better have no King at all:[116]

Dennis, appalled at the *"Common-wealth"* message of *The Foreigners*, rose to defend the Stuart past – James I, "a Monarch Wise and Good," Charles I, a "Father *Martyr'd*," and James II, "the Son *Mislead*" – but his reversal of Tutchin's excess led to a counter excess:

> If King's are made the Product of our Choice,
> And owe their Grandeur to the Peoples Voice,
> Whence is their *Right Divine*, and whence is giv'n
> A *Sacred* Pow'r, unless their *Voice* is *Heav'n*.
> God first appointed Kings, and God ordain'd
> That should be fix'd which He alone sustain'd,
> Well knowing from his Providential Mind,
> That [England] could not *chuse*, since she was *Blind.*[117]

The True-Born Englishman is vintage Defoe. Defending William and boisterously contemptuous of the ingratitude and insane pride of the lineage exhibited in *The Foreigners*, Defoe reiterated themes that already were, and would continue to be, staples of his political journalism. He mocked antiquity and stale custom; he dismissed the conquest argument that would legitimate a *de facto* monarch; he scorned the Anglican clergy who disowned their preachments of passive obedience and non-resistance when James's tyranny was seen as a threat to their wealth, power, and perquisites of office; and he revealed his disgust at the courtier corruption and whoredom "throughout [Charles II's] Lazy, Long, Lascivious Reign."[118] But also, in the middle of his 1,216-line poem, he reaffirmed his earlier reflections on 1689. Unjust kings are tyrants and can be resisted; subjects and kings are bound together by "the *Mutual Contract*;" "*That Kings, when they descend to Tyranny, / Dissolve*

---

116 *The Foreigners, POAS*, VI, 242,
117 *The Reverse, POAS*, VI, 231, 243, 245.
118 *The True-Born Englishman, POAS*, VI, 274.

the Bond, and leave the Subject free. / . . . Till Laws revive, and mutual Contract ties:"[119] – these tenets, as we have seen, are less verifications of Locke's *Two Treatises* than they are the commonplaces of allegiance pamphlets. What Defoe wrote could bring little anxiety to his king, for scarcely any idea challenged the constitutional order of the day. That "Laws superior are to Kings," that "Justice is the End of Government," or that private self-defense is a public right and can explain a national response to tyranny, are tenets that move beyond the difficult moment and serve as the basis for all legitimate government.[120] There is absolutely no mention of the English legislature as the supreme authority in the nation; and in fact, if parliament is mentioned by Defoe, it is "Nature's Universal Parliament," which sanctions the mutual oaths that subjects and sovereigns pledge to one another and supports the dissolution of governments when authority is abused by usurping kings.[121]

As we have observed, the death of the Protestant Stuart heir-presumptive to the throne, William, Duke of Gloucester, in July 1700 turned Tory eyes towards France. Although the evidence is still somewhat obscure, it has been suggested that Rochester and Godolphin were actually dallying with the idea of restoring the exiled Prince of Wales.[122] Fear, uncertainty, and the possibility of civil strife were increased with the news that Sophia, the Dowager Electress of Hanover, had reported that her martial and princely son, who was part of the Hanoverian link to the blood of James I and who, in the event of his elderly mother's death, would be most likely to succeed upon the death of Anne Stuart, was indifferent to the crown of England. Given this disturbing admission and her favorable disposition to the Prince of Wales, it is "no wonder that William began to think of alternative candidates to George . . ."[123] Retrospectively, then, perhaps one can find something sinister in Francis Atterbury's sermon preached before a Tory-dominated Commons on 29 May 1701, the anniversary of the restoration of King Charles the Second. Discoursing on the wisdom of God manifested in the revolutions of government, Atterbury noted that "the chief way, in which God hath been pleas'd to give Extraordinary Indications of his Power and Providence, hath been by such Signs of the times, such Wonders of Government" as the age's great political upheavals. Such freak changes were God's way of achieving "Political Justice."[124]

If Tory-Jacobite royalists were buoyed by the present conflicts that could

[119] *The True-Born Englishman, POAS*, VI, 292. For the "Lockean" influence see *POAS*, VI, xxxi; 291–93.
[120] *POAS*, VI, 293.
[121] *POAS*, VI, 293.
[122] Baxter, *William III and the Defence of European Liberty*, p. 385.
[123] Ragnhild Hatton, *George I, Elector and King* (London: Thames and Hudson, 1978), p. 73: cf. p. 74. See Horwitz, *Parliament, Policy and Politics*, pp. 276–77; Leopold von Ranke, *A History of England Principally in the Seventeenth Century*, 6 vols. (Oxford, 1875), V, 228–31.
[124] Cited in Gerald Straka, "The Final Phase of Divine Right Theory in England, 1688–1702," *English Historical Review*, 77 (1962), 646.

prefigure a dynastic resolution or revolution, republicans also, as we have seen, were responding radically to the same domestic confusions. Tracts reappeared with alarming frequency that identified William's intractable Commons with the body of the people, the political nation, in language similar to that which had preceded the outbreak of England's civil wars in the previous century. An extended and more detailed exposition of the commonwealth utopia, *The Free State of Noland*, was reissued. One writer, attempting to control the corruption of parliaments by place-men, argued that parliament itself should elect ministers of state and exercise a veto over the crown's appointments to office.[125] Another, citing Samuel Johnson, Sidney, and Tyrrell, and recurring to England's Saxon past, envisioned a new order, a parliamentary order, emanating from the restrictive limitations that could be now placed on a foreign successor to the House of Orange.[126] John Toland gave his readers a course in English history, explaining that Henry VII "believ'd an Act of Parliament cou'd limit, transfer, supersede, or annul all other Titles whatsoever." As such, "Henry the Eighth was only a Trustee appointed by the Parliament; and it makes their Power to be the greater that they can at pleasure delegate it to another."[127] Reading this mood of his fellow countrymen, who now hopefully imagined "that when our present settlement is run out, a commonwealth may be set up," the career diplomat and consummate statesman George Stepney proclaimed the need for providing greater security for the Hanoverian succession.[128]

In the midst of the country's debates and the innumerable books and tracts deconstructing again the monarchy of William III and redefining the Revolutionary settlement, Defoe contributed a most daring essay: *The Succession to the Crown of England, Considered* (January [?] 1701). Ostensibly an objective examination of the many claimants to the English throne, the tract is really an impassioned brief for the suitability of James Scott, the son of the Duke of Monmouth, as king of England. Seemingly offering foreign claimants an invitation to reside in England to acquaint themselves with the particular and peculiar attributes of the nation, Defoe in reality stresses the awkwardness, difficulties, and perhaps the impossibility of these continental competitors to ever adapt to the special genius of the nation. All elements – the intricate articles of England's government, the knowledge of different men and things – militate against a successful reign. As a foreigner, Defoe concludes, with a jab once again at William's xenophobic adversaries, all his mistakes would be magnified "to his Disadvantage."[129]

[125] G. Sharpe, *The Claims of the People of England; Essayed* (London, 1701). For the importance of this tract see Gwyn, *The Meaning of the Separation of Powers*, p. 89.

[126] *Limitations For the Next Foreign Successor, Or New Saxon Race* (London, 1701), esp. pp. 19–20.

[127] *Anglia Libera: Or, The Limitations and Succession of the Crown of England Explain'd and Asserted* (London, 1701), pp. 121, 123. For election language see pp. 118–19.

[128] *An Essay upon the Present Interest of England* (1701), in *Somers Tracts*, XI, 209.

[129] London, 1701, p. 23. Following citations will be noted in the text. For a different interpretation of this pamphlet see Moore, *Daniel Defoe*, pp. 56–57, 73.

As Defoe warms to his real intent, he recalls for his readers – as we would expect him to – the English courage and gallantry of Scott's parent. But the son also, as Defoe makes clear, has fought honorably under William in Flanders in 1692. Thus, "there is no fear but he may come to be *a Glory to the English Throne*, and be fitly qualified to *Succeed his present Majesty*, both at the Head of *English Armies*, as well as at the Helm of *English Councils*" (p. 28). Is it not likely, at this dangerous juncture in English history, that Defoe has discovered his ideal warrior-prince, "consummate in the arts both of peace and war"?

Defoe's reiterated request to the parliament, "*That the Legitimacy of the Duke of* Monmouth *may be Examined into, and the Title of his Son consider'd*" (p. 33), presented him once again with the opportunity to challenge those adherents of an emasculated monarchy who would, in Burnet's phrase, legislate "such extravagant limitations, as should quite change the form of our government, and render the crown titular and precarious."[130] Defoe, once again, countered the radical contract and election language of the time, as we have seen him counter it undeviatingly since the Revolution. In a career of incessant turnabouts to satisfy the needs and demands of fickle and pragmatic men and ministries, Defoe's consistency concerning the limitations of an English parliament cannot be ignored: "And tho' we have some who are very fond of calling our Government an *Elective Monarchy*, yet they cannot give us one Instance in all the last *Settlement*, wherein the Parliament, whatever Right they have to *alter* it, have not kept close to the *Right of Descent*, and followed the Right Line, unless they will suppose that the *Administration* remaining in King *William* during his Life, be an Infraction into the *Line of Succession*, which if the Doctrine of the *Abdication* be true, would be hard to make out" (p. 20). But once again, as he did in the *Reflections*, backing off from too assertive and dogmatic a position he appears to be deeply committed to, he concluded with concessive clauses that do little to diminish the integrity and rhetorical authority of the previous argument: "But I shall not *Concern* my self, Whether our Succession shall be guided by *Descent* or *Choice* of the *People*: Only I shall suppose, if the Hereditary Descent of the *Crown* be observ'd, who the Persons are to whom it so Descends, and if not, out of what Families we may Direct the Choice of an Heir, so as that the *Right* of *Descent*, and the *Right of Election* may go hand in hand, and kiss each other" (pp. 20–21). Unlike so many of the more extreme Whig journalists, Defoe never denied the hereditary principle altogether. In fact, his language here anticipates his later affirmation that it is parliamentary hereditary right that validates any claimant's right to the English throne. Defoe's moderation here, or his attempt to bridge two seemingly mutually exclusive extremes, is characteristically his *modus operandi*. His political tendency, like his fictional, is to be inclusive, compendious,

---

[130] *History of His Own Time*, IV, 499. Cf. an astute foreign diplomat's similar assessment in *POAS*, VI, 327n.

equivocal, and seemingly contradictory. One is thus compelled to discover and to insist upon the few sustained allegiances that are recognizable in his variegated presentations. The benign participation of a providential deity in the creation and the succession of kings appears to be one. A monarch's merit established by gallantry and courage on the field of battle is now developing as another. And a concurrent right of a parliament to participate in the determination of the crown is a third. If kings do not yet drop down from heaven in Defoe's *Succession to the Crown of England, Considered*, they still retain a quasi-mystical aura from the hereditary principle: "I might Examine here, *Whether a Right by Birth has so much in it, that it cannot be in the Peoples power to reject it, or whether it be in the People to stipulate with their Princes on what Conditions they shall ascend the Throne?*" (p. 20). Twelve years before, moderate voices had enunciated the somewhat illogical view that the parliament's elevation of William and Mary to the throne had *not* made any new law and that it had *not* extended the power of the legislature. Parliament had *not* created a new dynasty. It had *not* arbitrarily and innovatively selected a person or persons to settle the crisis of 1689. Rather, it had responded to an unique occasion, and had restored the ancient rights of the subjects by restoring the constitutional balance. It had functioned then, as Defoe was asking it to function now, as a court of examination, determining among many appropriate candidates, and not as a revolutionary legislature freely and randomly selecting a new leader. Then as now, it was less innovative and initiatory, more restrictively responsive to an uniquely sensitive external event; now as then, it was to evoke a conservative judicial opinion. Finally, in *The Succession to the Crown of England, Considered*, Defoe seems to have pulled out all the stops, suggesting a serious commitment to his audacious proposal. "Here would be an *English King*, born among us . . ." (p. 27). Not only that, but the young Monmouth's Scottish birth would obviate England's need for a standing army to protect her borders from her vengeful neighbor; his elevation would counter Scotland's turn to French subsidies and independence. It would placate their trading interests, who, with the failure of the Darien scheme still fresh in their minds, felt ill-used by the English. It would negate the claims of foreign princes and thus diminish, if not dismiss, the chances of war. Defoe is also rhetorically effusive. His praise for the martyred prince equates him with his heroic King William, for the former fell attempting what the latter succeeded in, rescuing the nation from popery and slavery. Daringly, Defoe appears to admit for the first time in print his active participation in the rebellion of 1685: "I do no where enter into the *Merit of the Cause*, however I may be *Convinc'd my self* of the *Legitimacy of the Father*, and the *Right of the Son*, which indeed I never doubted of, and *freely ventured for*" (p. 32). Stylistically, Defoe resorts to those series of introductory subordinate clauses that characteristically carry him to plateaus of deeply felt emotions. Gratitude – that second quintessential quality in Defoe's honorific vocabulary – to such a renowned and noble father would give to England "A *Phoenix*, rais'd out of the *Ashes of his Father*, who Sacrificed *his*

Life, to save the *People* his Son wou'd *govern*" (p. 28). Here, then, characteristically we once again see Defoe attempting a conciliation between contrastive arguments of the moment. He holds no brief for an elective monarchy determined by parliament. He maintains monarchical succession in right of blood, though that right was neither automatic or indefeasible. Parliament's right is to examine and determine among legitimate and limited blood heirs for the public good and as the immediate occasion demands.[131] Later, in the word wars with the defenders of Henry Sacheverell, when a Tory victory was presaged at the polls and the conservative cause dominated the pamphlets, Defoe clarified his theory of succession. Blood and the votes of the representatives of the people gave Queen Anne a hereditary and parliamentary claim to the throne of England.

Under the pressure of events as they unfolded during this most turbulent year of 1701 – the Legion controversy, the jailing of the Kent petitioners, and the immoderate and extravagant turn in the language of political debate that followed the publication of Sir Henry Mackworth's *Vindication of the Commons of England* (August 1701) – Defoe published some of his most strident tracts. To discern only their "populist" or "democratic" tendencies is to see them in a limited context. Defoe's line – which may or may not have been a party line – during these tumultuous months never deviated: The threat to England's liberties now came from an absolute and arbitrary House of Commons, not from a tyrannical king. The Commons' high-handed imprisonment of the petitioners from Kent and the subsequent defense of their actions by Mackworth moved beyond the immediate discussion of the privilege of the Commons to the undoing of the balance of the constitution. While Mackworth and his Tory supporters could intone the commonplace language of the three estates, and accept that the legislative authority, as per tradition, was lodged in the bodies of kings, lords, and commons united, in the final analysis their contention asserted the infallibility of the Commons: "Power in this Government is chiefly Lodged in the Commons."[132] Not only did Mackworth's legalistic analysis displace the Lords from their traditional position as the fulcrum of the balance, it effectively cut into the power of the prince. Redistributing the balance, Defoe and others could hardly fail to see, would not only set five hundred self-centered egos in the place of one tyrant, but would efface the constitutional royalism and the leadership of a unitary sovereign that was to be Defoe's ideal governance.[133] Mackworth, by going back to the language of Smith, Coke, and the jurists, and with some

[131] See his *An Argument Shewing, That the Prince of Wales, Tho' a Protestant, Has No Just Pretentions to the Crown of England* (London, 1701), pp. 11–12.

[132] *A Vindication of the Rights of the Commons of England*, p. 20.

[133] For Defoe's later comments on the balance of government see my "Defoe, Political Parties, and the Monarch," in *Studies in Eighteenth-Century Culture*, ed. O. M. Brack, Jr. (Madison: The University of Wisconsin Press, 1985), pp. 187–97. For Mackworth on the concept of the three estates and the balance see his *Vindication of the Rights of the Commons of England*, pp. A3v, A4r, 2, 3, 6, 38.

distortion of their intent, had made Defoe's monarch, still an agent of the Lord, a cypher, at the mercy of a half-thousand fragmented, self-seeking individuals. In *A New Satyr on the Parliament* (June [?] 1701), Defoe ridiculed the Commons' reach for parliamentary omnicompetence; and, for the first time in his writings, jingled the three attributes of monarchy – crown, sword, and scepter – that would resonate later in nearly all his considered narratives whose subject was the origin of monarchy and political society, and the right rule of the king:

> You shou'd find out some other word
> To give the Crowns *Accepter*,
> To call him King would be absurd,
> For tho' he'l seem to wear the sword,
> 'Tis you have got the Scepter.[134]

Frank Bastian, in the most lengthy and, I believe, balanced appraisal of Defoe's publications of this year, concluded that "Defoe's radicalism, such as it was, was only a passing phase, hastily adopted to meet the situation of 1701, and equally quickly laid down."[135] Perhaps a detailed analysis of Defoe's last grand statement for the year 1701, *The Original Power of the Collective Body of the People of England, Examined and Asserted*, can better reveal where that radicalism, such as it was, rests.

We can best begin by observing, once again, exactly what Defoe is not saying. Unlike the extreme republicans, Defoe is not opposed to monarchy; he has no desire to remodel the English constitution. Like them, he shares a belief in the balance of the constitution, but he never hints at any program to redistribute the powers of the Crown in order to increase the powers of the Lords and Commons. Nothing in Defoe's canon gives any indication that he would strip the king of his separate but equal powers in the state.[136] Nor do we find anywhere a phrase that the vital executive powers of the monarch should be diluted to strengthen the natural aristocracy of the Lords or the representative nature of the Commons. Seemingly radical statements of the *Original Power*, reiterating its title, are scattered throughout the text, yet nothing is written or implied to undermine Defoe's preference for a single person ordering the kingdom in its most essential affairs: war and peace, the militia and the army and navy, the nomination of officers and the control over the revenue, though with the advice and support of the other two estates of the realm. Defoe's monarch, in spite of the language that gives *original* [my italics] power to the people, rightly rules for the sake of the ruled, managing his signal authority for the welfare of the community. For Defoe the monarch is and always will be the principal component of government. I think that he

---

[134] See *POAS*, VI, 327. Professor Frank Ellis's attribution is made more firm by this vocabulary of monarchy uniquely Defoe's.

[135] Bastian, *Defoe's Early Life*, p. 263.

[136] See *Review*, V, 25 (25 May 1708).

would have hugely appreciated Michael Walzer's aside, that "it is hard to imagine a politically active and interested God who works his will through Parliaments.[137] Defoe seems to have believed, as did Bolingbroke and Hamilton later in the century, but for diverse reasons, that a hereditary monarch would be less likely to sacrifice his nation to private inordinate demands, that, given the present circumstances of history, he could provide the most resolute barrier against domestic faction, insurrection, and the tyranny of the majority.[138] As I have observed, Defoe's contract language is somewhat archaic; he speaks generally of a "mutual compact between king and people," language less of Locke and the allegiance controversy than of his forebears earlier in the century. And though Defoe seems to be writing "a tract for the times," though his role is to be a "Whig propagandist," much like his earlier influences and less like his contemporaries "he does not go deep into constitutional history," as Paul Kelly shrewdly observed. "His arguments, indeed, are more theological in tone than legal or historical."[139] For whatever reason – and I have suggested that the necessity for martial leadership was one – Defoe never developed that inordinate prejudice against the executive arm of government that characterizes Locke's *Two Treatises*. Locke is, of course, aware that it is naive to think that tyranny and arbitrary government are faults peculiar only to monarchies, but, reading him, one cannot avoid the sense that, more often than not, those conditions of illegitimacy arise from the encroachments of the executive. Locke appears to have no plans to legislate kingship out of existence – though the examens of Richard Ashcraft maintain that [140] – and his ferocious and savage attacks on monarchy, as Laslett has pointed out, are later interpolations directed at the despotism of James II.[141] Even so, Locke's monarch is usually divested of the traditional powers of the crown and is a hereditary successor as long as he acknowledges his dependence upon popular consent. It has been remarked that "the archetypal whig sought to curtail the prerogative of the Crown."[142] If so, Defoe rests uncomfortably in his camp.

In 1649 a Commons resolution had proclaimed that "the People are, under God, the Original of all just Power." Even though that tenet can be attributed

---

[137] *Regicide and Revolution* (Cambridge: Cambridge University Press, 1974), p. 15.

[138] See Max Farrand, *The Records of the Federal Convention of 1787*, 4 vols., rev. ed. (New Haven: Yale University Press, 1937), I, 289; *Federalist*, Numb. 22; Gerald Stourzh, *Alexander Hamilton and the Idea of Republican Government* (Stanford: Stanford University Press, 1970), pp. 38–48.

[139] "Constituents' instructions to Members of Parliament in the eighteenth century," in *Party and Management in Parliament, 1660–1784*, ed. Clyve Jones (Leicester: Leicester University Press, 1984), p. 177.

[140] See his "The Two Treatises and the Exclusion Crisis: The Problem of Lockean Political Ideology as Bourgeois Ideology," in *John Locke* (William Andrews Clark Memorial Library, University of California, Los Angeles, 1980); and "Locke, Revolution Principles, and the Formation of Whig Ideology," *Historical Journal*, 26 (1983), 773–800.

[141] *Two Treatises*, p. 154n; and II, 172 (pp. 400–01).

[142] Downie, *Robert Harley*, p. 7.

to almost all English political writers of the day except the ultra-radical proponents of the divine original of the English throne, perhaps one can claim a Commonwealth residue in Defoe's thought. But all the evidence indicates that Defoe had rejected outright the concluding clause of the resolution, "that the Commons, being chosen by, and representing the People, have the Supreme Power in this Nation."[143] Henry Parker, too, had written of the original collective power of the people, but that power, translated to their elected representatives, then negated whatever original power had initially resided in the people. His purpose was to elevate a parliament. Defoe's is to relegate parliaments to a continuous trust, with the original power of the people lingering as a threat to prevent their grab at sovereignty. And, of greater import, Defoe never gives any hint that the people, the creators of parliaments, are also the creators of kings. Thus, whether he is discussing the power of parliaments or the power of the people, neither essentially weakens or intrudes upon the power of the holy office of kingship. In the 1701 debates over the locale of sovereignty, it is Mackworth's analysis which is ultra-radical; for he, like Henry Parker earlier, averred that parliaments are seemingly infallible and that their acts are indisputable to all but other parliaments.[144] For this moment, Defoe saw clearly that parliamentary tyranny had replaced the royal tyranny he had invested his life and fortune to forestall. He confessed in 1708 that he had "liv'd under luxuriant Tyranny and Popish Tyranny, . . . and Regal Tyranny, Instrumental Tyranny, Parliamentary Tyranny, and Party Tyranny." His ideal legal "method of Government" was "a just Supream Power, a regulated subordinate Power," and the history of his political development reveals that he has in mind a just supreme king and a regulated subordinate parliament.[145] But in 1701, the representatives of the people had gradually assumed and had finally usurped the powers of government.

In 1701 and continuing throughout his career as a political journalist, Defoe raised this insistent warning to his nation, that the representatives of the people could very easily become arbitrary and absolute. "That England can never be thoroughly ruined but by parliament" was Lord Burleigh's maxim, frequently quoted by Defoe's contemporaries.[146] But it was only Defoe who was able to sense the sinister and ironic undercurrent to the phrase. Defoe cited and referred often to Sidney and the standard Whig martyrs of the Stuart repression, but he never subscribed to the theme of the *Discourse Concerning Government* as it was fixed in the minds of his contemporaries, that the sole power of government lay in the English parliament and

---

[143] *Meoirs of Edmund Ludlow, Esq.*, 2 vols. (Switzerland, 1698), I, 274.

[144] See Margaret Atwood Judson, "Henry Parker and the Theory of Parliamentary Sovereignty," in *Essays in History and Political Theory in Honor of Charles Howard McIlwain*, ed. Carl Wittke (Cambridge, MA: Harvard University Press, 1936), pp. 138–67.

[145] *Review*, V, 25 (25 May 1708).

[146] *Considerations upon the Choice of the Speaker of the House of Commons* (1698), cited in *Cursory Remarks, Somers Tracts*, XI, 170.

the people. Bertrand de Jouvenal attributes to Rousseau at the century's end the insight "that, once the possibility of the sovereign being represented was admitted, it would be impossible to stop the representative laying claim to sovereignty . . . More especially, he foresaw . . . that the authority of Parliament, though for the time being it would grab at the expense of the executive and so act as a brake on Power, would come in the end first to dominate the executive and then to fuse it with itself, thus reconstituting a Power which could lay claim to sovereignty."[147] At the beginning of the century, Defoe already understood the absolutist tendencies infiltrating the English parliament. Isaac Kramnick illuminated a Bolingbroke for whom a fantasy of a patriot king was necessary to maintain and even restore the past. For Defoe a king was vital to steady the political present and even safeguard the political future.

In 1704, declaiming against the bill outlawing occasional conformity, Defoe wrote: "Acts of Parliament depend upon the Opinions of different Men, whose Breath, like themselves, is Frail and Uncertain; they are frequently chang'd, and frequently change their Opinions; one House often Repeals what a former House Enacts, they very often alter and disanull what they have Enacted themselves . . ."[148] Later, in his own personal voice in the *Review*, he supported the Commons on the issue of controverted elections, but then continued with the following; that though he was aware that those selected are the "best, ripest, ablest, wisest, and wealthiest of our Gentry" – the irony fairly oozes – nevertheless, "in their assembled State, as well as in their separate State, [they] are subject to Mistakes, capable of acting contrary to the true Nature of their Constitution, capable of abusing their Trust, betraying their Country, tyrannizing over the Liberties of the People, ruining those they are sent thither to defend, and in short, of all the most fatal Errors that can be Suggested – *Pray mark it*, – for I shall not be misconstrued here, I will not leave Room for a Possibility of it, I say as Men, they are capable of Error, Capable of Mistakes, capable of abusing their Trust, and capable of all Manner of Corruption."[149] The gratuitous commentary in context, the rush of emotion, and the anaphoric intensity of the prose reveal that we are once again as close to Defoe's deeply felt and realized beliefs as we can get.

What Defoe did write in *The Original Power* reveals little direct indebtedness to the *Two Treatises of Government*, to which it has been generously compared and which has been long considered its "source." Defoe enumerated the themes of *The Original Power*: 1) "*Salus Populi suprema Lex*;" 2) government dissolves when it forsakes the public good and power retreats to its original;

---

[147] *On Power* (Boston: Beacon Press, 1962), p. 41.

[148] *A Serious Inquiry Into this Question; Whether a Law To prevent the Occasional Conformity of Dissenters, Would not be Inconsistent with the Act of Toleration, And a Breach of the Queen's Promise* (London, 1704), p. 14.

[149] *Review*, V, 106 (30 Nov. 1708).

3) the fallibility of all collective or representative bodies of men; and
4) "Reason is the Test and Touch-stone of Laws."[150] Nearly all of these
tenets in *The Original Power* either antedate Lockean principles or are in some
opposition to Lockean thought. For example, Defoe articulates what J. R.
Western has observed to be traditional whiggish doctrine; it "distinguished
between the state and society: the state was the product of deeper social forces
and its dissolution did not mean that society was dissolved."[151] Controversialists as diverse as Samuel Rutherford, Philip Hunton, and George Lawson,
even radical Whigs and Jacobite Tories, had made it a commonplace idea
throughout the seventeenth century.[152] Defoe's language is threatening, his
tone admonishing, yet he never reaches the crescendo of that radicalism that
asserts that "all power is *Originally*, or *Fundamentally* in the People, Formally
in the *Parliament*," and thus, "if the Government be dissolved, the Power
devolves on the People; no one can claim the Crown; the Royal Family is as
it were extinct; the People may set up what Government they please; either
the old, or a new; A Monarchy absolute or limited; or an Aristocracy or
Democracy."[153]

It might also be presumed that Defoe's insistence that the political state "was
originally design'd, and is maintain'd, for the Support of the Peoples Property"
(p. 2), is a page right out of *Two Treatises*. But Defoe's supreme interest is Power.
Thus, when he starkly asserts that "*Property is the Foundation of Power*" (p. 20), or
"that Property is the best Title to Government in the World; and if the King was
universal Landlord, he ought to be Universal Governor of Right, and the People so living on his Lands ought to obey him, or go off of his Premises" (p. 18),
he is more an echo of Harrington and Brady. Of Defoe's seventeenth-century contemporaries, it is James Tyrrell and Henry Neville for whom property is the essential ingredient of any political presence. Neville, in fact, could even be cited as
Defoe's "source," for to him "Dominion is founded in property," and a monarch
who has no sharers in the dominion or possession of the land likewise has no sharers
in the sovereignty.[154] For Defoe also, land ownership, *ipso facto*, confers authority, power, sovereignty. "Locke's distinctiveness lay in his consistent position that
all men had a positive political interest through their non-material possessions,
their self-propriety, and their natural rights."[155] Defoe's language runs counter

[150] *The Original Power of the Collective Body of the People of England, Examined and Asserted* (London, 1702
[1701]), pp. 2–3, 6, 16. All further citations will be noted in the text.

[151] *Monarchy and Revolution*, p. 31.

[152] See Julian H. Franklin, *John Locke and the Theory of Sovereignty* (Cambridge: Cambridge University
Press, 1978), pp. 53–86; Gough, *Fundamental Law*, pp. 106–07, 122.

[153] *A Letter to a Friend* (London, 1689), pp. 14, 15.

[154] *Plato Redivivus*, in *Two English Republican Tracts*, ed. Caroline Robbins (Cambridge: Cambridge
University Press, 1969), pp. 87, 89; cf. Defoe, *The Original Power*, p. 18. For Harrington see *The
Oceana of James Harrington, Esq.; And His Other Works . . . by J. Toland* (London, 1700), p. xviii,
where it is presented as a dangerous Tory tenet.

[155] Judith Richards, Lotte Mulligan, and John K. Graham, " 'Property' and 'People': Political
Usages of Locke and Some Contemporaries," *Journal of the History of Ideas*, 42 (1981), 39.

to that Lockean argument. In fact, it turns on its head and contradicts a major premise of what is the most significant contemporary pamphlet paraphrasing, even plagiarizing from, the *Two Treatises of Government*. The anonymous Lockean author of *Political Aphorisms* wrote: "If the Possession of the whole Earth was in one Person, yet he would have no Power over the Life or Liberty of another, or over that which another gets by his own Industry, for Propriety in Land gives no Man Authority over another."[156]

Perhaps one way to suggest the limited novelty and the traditional and unexceptional political doctrines of Defoe's 1701 treatise is to examine it in the larger context of "*the Paper-War* in England" to which it was a signed contribution. One important tract in that war was *The Source of Our Present Fears Discover'd* (1703). Its author was a Tory stalwart defending from a traditional Tory position the activities of the Tory-dominated Commons that had sought to extend its rights and jurisdictions, and to thwart the policies of William and the Whig-dominated House of Lords. It is, as Frank Ellis has commented, "a kind of group analysis of some fifteen Whig pamphlets."[157] In those it saw evidence of a Whig conspiracy, but also it perceived doctrines that redefined the constitutional traditions of England; their intent was to elevate the monarch to a commanding position in the ordering of political affairs.

Among the "Dangerous Pamphlets" noted are Defoe's *Legion's Memorial* and *The History of the Kentish Petition*, both published earlier in 1701 to defend the right of petition by freeholders and to protest the arrest and imprisonment of those Kent petitioners by a scandalized Commons. Defoe's *Original Power* is completely overlooked, which irked Defoe exceedingly.[158] Seemingly, the Tory establishment found its political philosophy conventional enough not to warrant a rebuttal. It is Jonathan Swift's *Discourse of the Contests and Dissentions Between the Nobles and Commons in Athens and Rome*, published two months before Defoe's *Original Power*, that drew extended fire from this vigorous Tory pamphleteer. He devoted nearly a third of the volume, thirty pages, to his denunciations of Swift's allegorical reflections upon the Tory Commons. Perhaps it could be suggested that the author's motivation was less ideological and political, more personal and spiteful, for he assumes that he is answering Bishop Burnet; thus the putative author of the *Discourse*, rather than its political principles, evoked his animadversions and sharp corrections. Perhaps Daniel Foe – *The Original Power* not only quoted obtrusively seventeen lines from *The True-Born Englishman* but was also signed "D. F." – was not yet a name to contend with, was not deemed worthy of serious and extended rebuttal. After all, *The Original Power* was initialled by a doggerel poet

---

[156] 3rd ed. (London, 1691), p. 29. For the importance of this pamphlet see Ashcraft and Goldsmith, "Locke, Revolution Principles, and the Formation of Whig Ideology," 773–86.

[157] *A Discourse of the Contests and Dissentions Between the Nobles and Commons in Athens and Rome*, ed. Frank H. Ellis (Oxford: Clarendon Press, 1967), p. 228. All following citations from Swift's *Discourse* and *The Source* will be taken from this useful edition and noted in the text.

[158] See *Some Remarks On the First Chapter in Dr. Davenant's Essays* (London, 1704), pp. 6, 17, 23.

and occasional scribbler for the now-dead king. Yet many others of Defoe's pamphlets during these frenzied years had been immediately answered by Defoe's Tory adversaries. But perhaps also the commonplace tenets politely adumbrated by Defoe were perceived by an astute Tory mind as no immediate challenge to contemporary political thought; less an affirmation of "Lockean" principles and more a defense of the old English constitution. Perhaps, then, a consideration of the Tory response to Swift's *Discourse*, and a comparison of the latter's themes as they were reshaped in Defoe's *Original Power*, could provide us with, if not a formula for Whig and Tory rhetoric, at least another insight into Defoe's developing political thought.

The supreme issue of the moment was the authority and the relative significance of the House of Commons. Both Swift and Defoe had addressed themselves, in one form or another, to this immediate constitutional debate. Much of the *Source* is taken up with corrections and reinterpretations of the Greek and Roman instances with which Swift, in his allegorical history, decried the despotic tendencies of the Commons. Two issues, one general and one parochial, get us close to the political Defoe. The first is the concept of the people, the other is the concept of the balance of power that distinguished England's mixed constitution.

For Swift, the people can do no right. Always differentiated from the Tribunes, or the Nobles, or the Patricians, and always equated with the Commons of 1701 synonymously or allegorically, the people of Athens and Rome are resentful, volatile, jealous, rash, inconstant and gullible, tricked continually by every popular agitator or insurrectionist. The devolution of political order follows a well-traveled path: popular tumults lead to a "Tyranny of the People, . . . which as perpetual Experience teaches, never fails to be followed by the Arbitrary Government of a single Person" (p. 106). The Tory author of *The Source of Our Present Fears Discover'd* perceived "the Design and Tendency of this pernitious Libel . . . By Representing the Collective Body of the People, as a Giddy, Violent, unjust Rabble, unfit for the Exercise of any Power, he does consequently, endeavour to deprive 'em of that Share in the Government, which by our Constitution they ought to have" (p. 240). And he concludes correctly, as F. P. Lock realized, "that the 'drift' of the *Discourse* 'is to shew the Preferrableness of a Government by one or a few Persons.' "[159]

Swift's "People Collective" (p. 84) is indistinguishable in his *Discourse* from the Commons. Defoe's "Collective Body of the People of England," every one of whom has a portion of the free-hold of England, choose a few from their midst to become the original of the Commons. His "populism" of the moment allots a political voice only to those who have a comfortable stake in the land wealth of England. If Swift is contemptuous of the people, Defoe appears

---

[159] *Swift's Tory Politics* (Newark: University of Delaware Press, 1983), p. 160, citing *Source*, p. 233.

indifferent to the multitude, the vulgar, the popular, or the plebian. He not only differentiated the "Collective Body of the People" from the Commons; his Collective Body is also differentiated from the common people, for "the *Freeholders*" he writes, "are the proper Owners of the Country: It is their own, and the other Inhabitants are but Sojourners" (p. 18), "Servants" (p. 19). Though Defoe does seem to suggest that the king and his heirs have a property in their office, that office appears to be dependent upon the real property the crown holds. And while Defoe can remark about "the Liberties and Religions of the People" (p. 11), throughout his text property is always the equivalence of power and right. In fact, the running title of *The Original Power* is *The Original Right of the People of England*, and both are synonymous with freehold. For Defoe "*there can be no Legal Power in* England *but what has its Original in the Possessors; for Property is the Foundation of Power*" (p. 20). Even the radical tenet, *Salus Populi suprema Lex* is explicated thusly: "[A]ll Government, and consequently our whole Constitution, was orginally design'd, and is maintain'd, for the Support of the Peoples Property" (p. 2). This attribution of political value only to men of estates is indicative of the conservative cast of Defoe's political thought, which is a far cry from any Lockean radicalism that, as we have noted, gave membership in the political community to all men "through their non-material possessions, their self-property, and their natural rights." And though many astute commentators have observed how party rules, party doctrines, and political ideologies were confused and randomly eclectic at the time, it should be noted that Defoe shares here the major tenet of Charles Davenant, called by Frank Ellis "the Field marshall of the Tory forces," for whom "the Ballance of Property . . . is the Ballance of Power."[160]

Four years later, Defoe wrote to reassure the Scottish electorate about the limited power of the Union parliament to invade the natural rights of the freeholders of both nations. His reasoning is pointed, his language clear. His reaffirmation of the doctrine in *The Original Power* is almost a programmatic note for *Robinson Crusoe*:

The Reason is plain, the Right of a Freeholder is an Original, 'tis claim'd by his Possession, which is to be trac'd back to God Almighty's first Donation, when he gave Man Possession of the Earth to him and his Heirs, and bid him possess and subdue it, *Gen.* 11. [sic: 1.28] that is, Govern it; from whence 'tis easie to deduce the Right of all Government in the World, to depend upon the Legal Possession of the Solid, *Anglice*, the Freehold. If any single Man was able to purchase, and had purchased all the Land in *England*, he would be King by Divine Right, he would be himself the whole Parliament by natural Consequence, and the whole Power of Legislature would be in himself.[161]

Defoe's "Collective Body of the People of England" excludes from political participation all who do not have a material stake in the culture. Nevertheless,

---

[160] *A Discourse*, pp. 10, 133.
[161] *Review*, III, 151 (19 Dec. 1706).

given Defoe's "Fundamental Maxim" that he poetically and prosaically rendered in *The Original Power*, that tyranny dissolves the bonds of government, frees the subjects, and "Power retreats to its Original" (p. 16), enabling the people to arrange for themselves a government more to their liking, one could read his political philosophy as a threat, an undermining of the represented authority of parliaments. In point of fact, though, Defoe does not give his "Collective Body" much to do besides holding a residue of original power, which would only be exercised in the last resort, in the most extreme of emergencies. It interferes little with the ongoing activities of government, debated and executed by the traditional three estates of the realm. Defoe's "Collective Body" does not make laws or even silently assent to laws. Its participation is limited to a pacific acquiescence to the decisions of its betters; and sometimes to petitioning. Little significant activity is committed by it. As a collectivity, Defoe's "People of England" (p. 8) intrude upon their government and its representatives at rare and unusual moments of emergency and distraction; and even those very occasional intrusions carry the voices and petitions, not of the multitude, but of the gentry and freeholders of esteem and wealth.

The Tory author of *The Source of Our Present Fears Discover'd* not only chastised Swift for his odious and misread parallels from "Ancient *Roman* and *Greek* Histories" (p. 233) and present English politics; he reserved his most scathing criticism for this whiggish defender of the ministry's extensive commentaries on "the true Meaning of a Balance of Power" (p. 84), that most traditional and also cherished of English political tenets. Swift had begun his *Discourse* with the commonplace analogy between the body natural and the body politic, the former and the latter both moving with the "Consent of all its Parts." Though his immediate concern is with the "Executive Part" of each, which accords with "an absolute unlimited Power," as he develops the metaphor of the body politic he introduces the three-fold Polybian division of the one, the few and the many – king, lords, and commons – and concludes quite inoffensively that "Power in the last Resort was always meant by Legislators to be held in Balance among all three" (p. 84).

But trouble arises when Swift attempts to reaffirm the "true Meaning of a Balance of Power." As he redefined the balance with the image of a scale and its fulcrum, he explained:

In order to preserve Peace between these [three] States, it is necessary they should be form'd into a Balance, whereof one or more are to be Directors, who are to divide the rest into equal Scales, and upon Occasions remove from one into the other, or else fall with their own Weight into the Lightest. So in a State within itself, the Balance must be held by a third Hand; who is to deal the remaining Power with utmost Exactness into the several Scales. Now, it is not necessary that the Power should be equally divided between these three; For the Balance may be held by the Weakest, who, by his Address and Conduct, removing from either Scale, and adding of his own, may keep the Scales duly pois'd.   (pp. 84–85)

That the "Weakest third Hand" is the monarch's is everywhere implied by the text and was understood by the Tory critic.

As F. P. Lock realized, a commonplace constitutional tenet has been rendered topsy-turvy by Swift, who "gives the monarch the really decisive role, for he is not (as might have been expected in a 'mixed' government) a king with fixed and limited powers but a free agent able to alter the balance of power at will.[162] And Swift had also turned around the traditional concept of the three estates and England's balanced constitution as it had been understood since Charles I issued his *Answer to the Nineteen Propositions of the Parliament* in 1642; "The equipoise in the balanced constitution was maintained by the House of Lords, an excellent Screen and Bank between the Prince and People." Nothing is more Roman in the writings of seventeenth- and eighteenth-century English political theorists than the argument that the wise, the landed, the leisured aristocracy of the Lords, was the pivotal element in the triad King, Lords, and Commons, the balancing force for English freedom. From James Harrington to Blackstone, it remained an enduring faith.[163]

The Tory author of the *Source* immediately perceived the ideological and the metaphorical unbalancing that Swift had perpetrated on the constitution:

By this Notion of a Ballance, it is plain that the whole Power is in the *hand* that holds the Ballance; and that the Powers weigh'd in the *Scales*, are no more than dead weights to be dispersed or tumbled backwards and forwards at the Pleasure and Discretion of the *Weigher*.
If this be the Scheme of Government which he has contriv'd for us (if it should prevail) we might have the most *Arbitrary Despotick* Government in the World; nay, and must have, if it should please the person, or persons into whose hands he would put the Ballance. For what is it that gives any single Man the power of *Tyrannizing* over any Countrey? Surely not the Strength and Force of the single person of the Prince, but the Means of using one part of the people, to serve as Instruments to obtain his ends and purposes upon all the Rest. And what is this more than holding and turning the Ballance (according to our Authors Phrase) as he pleases?   (p. 231)

Swift's sudden overturning of the metaphorical balance, of hands holding and thus arbitrarily manipulating a pair of scales, has then to be metaphorically and ideologically corrected:

[This notion of balance, the notion of a free state] supposes a Harmony and Symmetry of Parts, Constantly and Regularly Co-operating to the same Ends and Purposes, any one of which parts being Check't, are disorder'd, the Action of the whole Machine is disturb'd, if not destroy'd.   (p. 232)

This digression to Swift and his Tory critic has been taken to serve two purposes. The first is to reveal the traditional basis of Defoe's thinking about English politics. It is Swift, rather than Defoe, who radicalizes received notions

---

[162] *Swift's Tory Politics*, p. 153.
[163] See my "Defoe, Political Parties, and the Monarch," pp. 190–91.

and contemporary political thought. In fact, Defoe's language of the balance
in *The Original Power* can almost suggest it as a "source" for the argument of
Swift's Tory antagonist. For Defoe also, the three heads of the Constitution
work in a mystic tandem. While he too introduces the analogy between the body
natural and the body politic (p. 20), and though he momentarily animadverts to
the scale image (p. 21), his words are the common currency of his time. Law and
order depend on the "mutual Consent of the Parties," so "That if either of the
Three Powers do Dispense with, Suspend, or otherwise Break any of the known
Laws so made, they Injure the Constitution; and the Power so acting ought to
be restrained by the other Powers not concurring according to what is lately
allowed, *That every Branch of Power is designed as a Check upon each other*" (p. 3). It is
England's unique mixed government that reveals "the Beauty of our Constitution, and the exact Symetry [sic] of its Parts" (p. 8). Later he repeats: "The
Excellency of our Constitution consists of the *Symitry* [sic] *of Parts; and the
Ballance of Power*; and if this Ballance be broken, one Part grows too great for the
other, and the whole is put into Confusion" (p. 20).

Defoe, then, we can say, did not share completely in what has been rightly
called the "tory, authoritarian nature of Swift's political thought."[164] Swift,
though rebuked for his ignorance of English constitutional language in 1703,
never deviated from this position. For he still believed, when he wrote *The
History of the Four Last Years of the Queen*, that "in such a Government as this,
where the Prince holds the Balance between two great Powers, the Nobility and
the People; It is of the very nature of his Office to remove from one Scale into
Another; or sometimes put his own Weight into the lightest, so to bring both to
an Equilibrium."[165]

If Swift never deviated from his "tory authoritarian" position, what is quite
remarkable is to see Defoe tending that way.[166] In *The Pacificator* (1700), Defoe
tried to settle, mock-heroically, the literary war of the moment that had been
raging between "the Men of Sense against the Men of Wit;" thus the political
content of his thought is offset, and diluted of subversive possibilities by the
comic and aesthetic context:

> Let them to some known Head that strife submit,
> Some Judge Infallible, some *Pope in Wit*,
> His Triple Seat place on *Parnassus* Hill,
> And from his Sentence suffer no Appeal:
> Let the Great Balance in his Censure be,
> And of the Treaty make him *Guarantee*,
> Let him be the Director of the State,
> And what he says, let both sides take for Fate:
> *Apollo's Pastoral Charge* to him commit.
> And make him *Grand Inquisitor* of Wit,

[164] Lock, *Swift's Tory Politics*, p. 157.
[165] *Prose Works*, ed. Herbert Davis (Oxford: Basil Blackwell, 1951), VII, 20–21.
[166] For the following paragraphs see my "Defoe, Political Parties, and the Monarch," pp. 192–94.

Let him to each his proper Talent show,
And tell them what they can, or cannot do,
That each may chuse the Part he can do well,
And let the Strife be only to Excel.

Sixteen years later, in 1717, after a lifetime in the trenches of political journalism and commitment first to a "prime minister" and now to a new king, in both of whom he saw the possibilities of a singularly firm and vigorous masculine leadership, Defoe once again wrote to resolve a factional dispute between two warring parties – and coincidentally in a fictional construct two years before *Robinson Crusoe. The Quarrel of the School Boys at Athens* is Defoe's mocking commentary about, and resolution of the bi-polar split in the Whig party that came about as a result of the defection of the Walpole-Townshend faction from the reigning Sunderland-Stanhope ministry. With Walpole and his followers caballing with the Jacobites, the Whig split demanded a thoughtful and bi-partisan approach. Defoe's solution was a bold narrative fiction of an authoritarian schoolmaster on a vacation from his school, which is divided into upper and lower classes, and the "meer Bedlam" that ensued. Civil war disrupts the classroom, when the schoolmaster suddenly returns, appearing at the door with his rod in his hand. The factions "no sooner saw the Master and his Rod, but they all sat down as quiet and as still, as if nothing had happened at all; not a Word was spoken, not the least noise heard, all was perfectly calm and quiet in a Moment; the Master went peaceably up to his Chair of Instruction, and laid down his Rod; the Scholars fell very lovingly to their Books, and have been very good Boys ever since." And in *Applebee's Journal*, four years after the publication of *Robinson Crusoe*, Defoe organized a series of political essays that fully and coherently stressed the essential Tory notion of the monarch as supreme mediator, manipulating the polar tensions of the political community, for " 'tis his *Interest*, by employing them indifferently according to their *Parts* and *Loyalty*, to keep the *Ballance* in an equal *Liberation*; that while they are at enmity amongst themselves, they shall have no *Aversion* to him, who impartially rewards them in proportion to their *Deserts*."

Christopher Hill remarked of the political Defoe that he "found himself a radical in a society in which there was no alternative to the corrupt rule of a gentry parliament."[167] Defoe's languages, explicit and implicit, and his silences, would ask that we question that extreme claim. His political imagination intuited, his political experience dictated, the domination and control of the state by a benevolent autocrat, a gallant and courageous soldier-king. The creation and the sustaining "well-being of a realm . . . depended on the virtue, the patriotism, and the energetic leadership of the sovereign."[168] What there is of a

---

[167] Christopher Hill, "Robinson Crusoe," p. 16.
[168] Ralph Ketcham, "The Transatlantic Background of Thomas Jefferson's Ideas of Executive Power," *Studies in Eighteenth-Century Culture*, vol. II, ed. Harry C. Payne (Madison: University of Wisconsin Press, 1982), p.165. I have reversed the intent of Professor Ketcham's phrase, the purpose of which was to deny Defoe any monarchical or royalist vocabulary.

"populist" tendency in his "Lockean" pamphlet of 1701 only serves to undermine the integrity, the authority, and the sovereignty of parliaments when those parliaments misrepresent the people to whom they must remain decently subservient. Defoe's "radical" language, we discover, is generally heard only when the political context involves parliaments and people. His king has no standing, so to speak, in the populist debate. Throughout *The Original Power*, Defoe's king remains strangely and totally absent, inviolate, distanced from the Lords and Commons, scarcely the subject of critical evaluation, political diminution, or ideological disrespect. In 1701 the king remains a potent and equi-partnered member of a mystic English triad of king, lords, and people, his glory intact, his sovereignty untouched by the omnipresent squabbles of importunate and error-ridden men. Defoe closed his discussion of *The Original Power of the Collective Body of the People of England* with the stirring words of King William's last speech to his parliament. With those words, Defoe added, the "Restorer of *English* Liberty" gave "a Sanction to the natural right of his People" and to "those just Rights which . . . we doubt not he will hand down unbroken to our Posterity" (p. 24).

4

From the death of William III to
Jure Divino, 1702–1706

On the last day of December 1701, following a moderate Tory election victory in a nation geared for renewed hostilities on the continent, King William addressed his sixth and final parliament. Conciliatory, eloquent, and candid, aware of the "new war" he was to prepare his subjects for and the funds that would be necessary to finance it, he prayed for the cessation of "disputes and differences" and concluded: "I have shewn, and will always shew, how desirous I am to be the common father of all my people."[1] Ten weeks later, on 8 March 1702, the *pater patriae* of his adopted nation was dead.

As Defoe intimated in 1700, "real kings" (the phrase is Carlyle's) like William find it easier to rule in times of war than peace.[2] England had not only lost her greatest king in an age of kings – one who was ready and able to temper those unhappy and almost fatal animosities that were dividing the nation at home – it had also been deprived of its mythic military leader at the onset of what was clearly seen to be a major European conflagration. "It was expected that . . . before the end of April the King was to appear in Holland in order to open the campaign in person."[3] And the accession of Queen Anne compounded this already disquieting situation, for, as one sympathetic biographer conceded, no other English queen had been "less tutored in queenship."[4] Her early letters reveal a somewhat bewildered and simple woman, practically uneducated in anything beyond the narrow familial and feminine interests, whose political consciousness might have been aroused after her family's breakup in 1689, but whose interests devolved into personal relations and domestic matters.[5] It could have occurred to some contemporaries, as Henry Snyder has noted, that "a new constitutional situation was created in 1702 by the accession of Queen Anne. Anne was disqualified by

[1] *Parliamentary History*, V, 1331.
[2] Cited in Gerald M. Straka, *Anglican Reaction to the Revolution of 1688* (Madison, WI: 1962), p. 92. Cf. Defoe, *The True-Born Englishman*, *POAS*, VI, 287.
[3] Leopold von Ranke, *A History of England Principally in the Seventeenth Century*, 6 vols. (Oxford, 1875), V, 296.
[4] David Green, *Queen Anne* (London: Collins, 1970), p. 11; also pp. 15, 69.
[5] See *The Letters and Diplomatic Instructions of Queen Anne*, ed. Beatrice C. Brown (1935; rpt., London: Cassell, 1968).

sex, health, education, and intelligence from acting as the head of the executive."[6]

Perhaps Anne herself had given some thoughts to her succession upon the demise of England's soldier-king. Such thoughts could account for the parallel Anne had begun to make as early as 1692 between herself and her Tudor predecessor, Elizabeth I.[7] The greatest of England's female monarchs, Elizabeth could become more than a sexual role model for England's new queen. For in the political tracts of the Restoration and continuing beyond Anne's death in 1714, the one refrain that remains constant is the assertion of England's military greatness under the Tudor prince and her martial efforts in defense of a militant and crusading Protestantism.[8] She may not have been able to lead her troops into battle, but she did everything else that a war leader could do; she supported her armies, exhorted her soldiers, and was invested with the aura of a king. "In her famous Armada speech before the troops massed at Tilbury in 1588, for example, she offered herself as a model of kingly courage: 'I have the body of a weak and feeble woman, but I have the heart and stomach of a king, and of a king of England too.' On this martial occasion her costume gave visual embodiment to her verbal appeal. She carried a truncheon as she rode between the ranks and wore upon her breast a 'silver cuirass' – appropriate covering for the heart and stomach of a king. Poets commemorating the occasion praised her 'tough manliness', her '*masculine vis*', and likened her to her father Henry VIII, 'Whose valour wanne this *Island* great renown'."[9]

Her stirring "Golden Speech" of 1601 was printed and disseminated throughout England. It was also republished in the 1690s. In it we hear the variation of the rhetorical formula that had served her well for forty years; and we too can see the image, the icon, that remained undiminished and untarnished to Defoe's generation:

I know the title of a King is a glorious title: but assure yourself that the shining glory of princely authority hath not so dazzled the eyes of our understanding, but that we well know and remember that we also are to yield an account of our actions before the great Judge. To be a King and wear a crown is a thing more glorious to them that see it, than it is pleasant to them that bear it. For myself, I was never so much enticed with the glorious name of King or royal authority of a Queen, as delighted that God hath made me His instrument to maintain His truth and glory.[10]

[6] *The Marlborough-Godolphin Correspondence*, ed. Henry L. Snyder, 3 vols. (Oxford: Clarendon, 1975), I, xvi.

[7] Edward Gregg, *Queen Anne* (London: Routledge & Kegan Paul, 1980), p. 96.

[8] See, for example, Richard Daniel, *The Dream: A Poem on the Death of His Late Majesty, William III* (London, 1702), p. 23.

[9] Leah S. Marcus, "Shakespeare's Comic Heroines, Queen Elizabeth I, and the Political Uses of Androgyny." I would like to thank Professor Marcus for permitting me to read and quote from her paper before its publication in *New Perspectives on Medieval and Renaissance Women*, ed. Mary Beth Rose (Syracuse: University of Syracuse Press, 1986).

[10] *The Golden Speech of Queen Elizabeth to Her Last Parliament, November 30. Anno Domini, 1601. With*

To Queen Anne's countrymen her Tudor ancestor, in spite of her sex, embodied unassailable princely authority and stood for their nation's military prowess. Thus, in his elegy for William, Duke of Gloucester, comparing him to the great pantheon of war leaders in England's past, William Browne wrote of Elizabeth that "tho' she wore a Female Dress . . . Her vast Heroick Soul was Masculine."[11] Upon William's death a recurring theme was the recollection of the Protestant "Arms of Eliza."[12] Defoe too spoke of the great Tudor queen's "more Masculine Spirit . . . tho' in the Person of a Woman."[13] Following the death of Henry VIII, she gloriously assumed the role of common protector of all her people, a civil head in lieu of the Pope, a fixed center of England, "notwithstanding," Defoe also wrote, "the disadvantage of her Sex."[14] He extolled King George I, who came "to restore the *British* Throne to the same Grandeur, which it once possess'd in the Days of Glorious Queen ELIZABETH" because he, like her, gave every indication that he could retain in his princely hands the dignity and power of monarchy, made concrete in the crown, sword, and scepter of right rule.[15]

Defoe's assessment of Queen Anne told a much different tale. Following her death his retrospective evaluations of her reign generally concentrate on her feminine incapacity, her inability to reject the zealous demands of her most frenzied supporters in parliament. What they were able to make most use of was her "Female Weakness, and the timorous Nature of a Woman, to enforce their importunate Measures."[16] In *Proper Language For the Tories*, Defoe served up a concise history of England: William "the Warrior" was followed by Anne, during whose reign chaos immediately ensued for she replaced the faithful ministers of the late king with "Persons who deceiv'd her; they imposed upon her; for she was but a Woman."[17] And being but a woman, she only wore the crown, losing control of her government to destructive factions because the sword and the scepter were put in other hands.[18]

Upon her accession, then, with the onset of war, public policy was served by identifying the Stuart queen with the remembered masculine and martial

---

Observations Adapted to These Times (London, 169?), pp. 7–8. The observations appear directed at extremists hostile to King William, those who wish to set up an "Arbitrary Government" and a "Democracy" (p. 11).

[11] *An Ode on the Death of William Duke of Gloucester* (London, 1700), p. 10.

[12] Daniel, *The Dream*, p. 23. For the sermons see, for example, Francis Hext, *A Funeral Oration Sacred to the Immortal Memory of our Late Most Serene, Most Puissant Prince William III* (London, 1702), p. 12.

[13] *The Danger of Court Differences* (London, 1717), p. 9.

[14] *Considerations on the Present State of Affairs in Great-Britain* (London, 1718), p. 17; cf. *Review*, I, 13 (18 April 1704); VI, 83 (15 Oct. 1709).

[15] *Secret History of State Intreagues in the Management of the Scepter* (London, 1715), p. 64.

[16] *The Secret History of the White Staff. Part III* (London, 1715), pp. 28–29. For Defoe's crude proverb see Morris Tilley, *A Dictionary of the Proverbs in England in the Sixteenth and Seventeenth Centuries* (Ann Arbor: University of Michigan Press, 1950), p. 306.

[17] London, 1716, p. 21.

[18] *Secret History of State Intreagues in the Management of the Scepter*, p. 23.

grandeur of Elizabeth's reign. In December 1702 it was requested "that whenever there were occasion to Embroider, Depict, Grave, Carve, or Paint her Majesty's Arms, these Words, SEMPER EADEM should be us'd for a *Motto*: it being the same that had been us'd by her Predecessor Queen *Elizabeth*, of glorious Memory."[19] Months earlier, in March 1702, when she made her first formal speech to Parliament, not only did she model her costume on a portrait of Elizabeth, but in pledging that "I know my own heart to be entirely English," she deliberately echoed Elizabeth's resoundingly patriotic and jingoistic tag, of being "mere [i.e. pure] English."[20] The queen's phrase, "Entirely English," in fact, when printed as the legend on her accession medal, "was held by some to be in doubtful taste, for it was thought to reflect upon the late king."[21]

But other Englishmen had made other reflections on their late king, and their anxieties can be understood when we examine the elegies that appeared immediately upon William's death. As in the panegyrics of the earlier decade, the monarch was compared to the great warrior kings of history: Alexander, Caesar, and Augustus; or he had come to surpass the great commanders and leaders of the Hebrew host: Joshua, Moses, and David.[22] A few elegists before, but, understandably, many more after the coronation of Anne in April invoked themes of renewal and recalled memories of Elizabeth's illustrious victories. But all realized that the loss of a national saviour had been intimately connected with William's role as military commander, and the loss to England of his sword is the dominant theme of nearly all the elegies. As Defoe himself intoned, "Crowns know no Sexes," and Anne could easily wield William's "Glorious Scepter," but "who shall for us weild the Military" sword?[23] Though another sincere lover of his queen and country wishfully wrote that Anne "will Outvie the Fam'd ELIZA in her Love," he nevertheless had to inquire, "*Who / Shall lead our Troops against the Common Foe? / Since* WILLIAM's *gone, that did our Battles fight, / Who shall our* Counsels, *who our* Arms *unite?*"[24] Even after the Queen's declaration of war against France and Spain and Marlborough's return to the continent to take command of the army in the field, Joseph Stennett could still anxiously inquire:

[19] Abel Boyer, *The History of the Reign of Queen Anne, Digested Into Annals* (London, 1703), I, 162.

[20] Gregg, *Queen Anne*, p. 152.

[21] John Oldmixon, *History of England during the Reigns of King William and Queen Mary* (1735), cited in Helen Farquhar, "Portraiture of our Stuart Monarchs on Their Coins and Medals, Part V. Anne," *British Numismatic Quarterly*, 1st ser., 10 (1915), 224.

[22] Hext, *A Funeral Oration*, p. 3. Cf. *A Pindaric Ode Dedicated to the Lasting Memory of the Most Illustrious and Pious King William III* (London, 1702), pp. 7, 16. For earlier panegyrics see *Poems on the Reign of William III*, ed. Earl Miner, Augustan Reprint Society, no. 166 (University of California, Los Angeles, 1974).

[23] *Mock-Mourners* (1702), *POAS*, VI, 391, 393. Further citations will be incorporated in the text.

[24] *The Mournful Congress, A Poem on the Death of the Illustrious King William III . of Glorious Memory* (London, 1702), p. 7.

> Who now shall Head your Armies in the Field?
> Who wave his Sword, and who shall bear his Shield?
> Who shall your Troops with generous Courage fire,
> And all around him Martial Rage inspire? . . .
> His Army was the Body, He the Soul
> T'inform, direct, and animate the Whole.[25]

The elegiac refrains of desultory poets and sermonizers, merging with Defoe's imaginative vision of kingship, enable us to begin to see the formulation of his myth of politics. Two months after William's death, breaking four months of publishing silence, Defoe published *The Mock-Mourners. A Satyr By Way of Elegy on King William*, the title page defiantly proclaiming his authorship. To a great extent Defoe's lines echo those of previous mediocre poetasters, but his signal variations of those themes underscore his more consistent views. For example, all earlier English history pales before William's descent upon England. "*William* laid the first Foundation Stone: / On which the stately Fabrick soon appear'd" (p. 377). In Defoe's myth of his king, time begins with William's coming; he is always the "first," "the Mighty Founder," the "first proposer" of grand legislative enactments like the Union.[26] William's birthday is "the initial Day of *Euroupe's* [sic] Liberty, the great Dawning of this Age's Glory."[27] On his birthday, Defoe proclaims, life began for man and for nation. Defoe's king is something more than the clichéd Deliverer of twenty years of panegyrics and elegies; he is, as Defoe stated and restated in *Review* essays and innumerable tracts, the "Saviour" of England, God's unique and "eminent instrument to us for Good."[28]

Searching in the Old Testament and classical literature for a type of William, Defoe can find no single figure to compare him to. Neither Joshua, nor David, nor Solon, nor even Moses – "God needed not to part the Waves for him" – comes up to "William's Modern Character":

> The *Pompeys, Caesars, Scipios, Alexanders*,
> Who croud the World with Fame, were great Commanders:
> These too brought Blood and Ruin with their Arms,
> But *William* always fought on other Terms.   (p. 391)

Defoe's William is no paradigmatic monarch, for his attributes are God's: "'Terror indeed might in his Front appear, / But Peace and Plenty follow'd

---

25 *A Poem To The Memory of His Late Majesty King William III* (London, 1702), p. 8. Tutchin spoke for the mass of Defoe's contemporaries who believed that "there seems more Encouragement to Bravery under a Queen, than under the most Valiant King" (*Observator*, III, 10 [22–26 April 1704]). Cf. the Russian nobility and tsarinas in Leonard Krieger, *Kings and Philosophers, 1689–1789* (New York: W. W. Norton, 1970), p. 9.

26 *Review*, III, 39 (30 March 1706); III, 154 (26 Dec. 1706).

27 *A Commendatory Sermon Preach'd November the 4th, 1709 Being the Birth-Day of King William of Glorious Memory* (London, 1709), p. 2.

28 *A Commendatory Sermon*, p. 5.

in his Rear'' (p. 391). Thus, in spite of the convention that would place this
modern king in modern times, as warrior, restorer, and architect who "laid
the first Foundation Stone" of a government founded on law and the constitution, there is seemingly no irony nor contradiction in Defoe's mind when the
Goddess Britannica admits her inability to find any parallel ancient or
modern to her "Son," her "Darling," and her "King":

> If back to *Israel*'s Tents I shou'd retire,
> And of the *Hebrew* Heroes there enquire,
> I find no Hand did *Judah*'s Scepter wear,
> Comes up to *William*'s Modern Character.
>   (p. 389)

Perhaps one can make too much of Defoe's hyperbole on the occasion of
the death of England's Deliverer, but his special relationship to and unique
judgment of William had a bearing on his notion of sovereignty and monarchy.
His inability to move beyond the language of divinely ordained kingship, his
metaphors that reveal his refusal to divorce the idea of divinity from the figure
of his monarch, have their roots in his Williamite model of authority and rule.
Defoe was unable to depersonalize sovereignty; that is, he does not seem to
be able to visualize authority transferred to an unsubstantive legislative body.
His is no abstract vision of sovereignty. The king and the people are his now
almost anachronistic dyads whenever he lists the ingredients of a political
community. And his model for his king remains the superlatively immediate
yet biblical one, William of Orange grafted to an Old Testament trunk.

In 1704 Defoe published a scathing response to those critics who had belittled
the recent publication of *A Form of Prayers used by His Late Majesty King William
III, when he received the Holy Sacrament.* Just as the authorship and the spirituality
of *Eikon Basilike* had been caustically questioned by the republicans, so now
High Churchmen such as Leslie were mocking the piety of Defoe's monarch,
who, in Defoe's unique terminology, had so religiously laid "down the
Scepter" and resigned "the Crown."[29] In the king's death Defoe saw the
source of the political and moral degeneration of England. His king, once
again, is *sui generis*, distinct from the earth-bound monarchs of history. He is
"a *Star* in the *East*," his "Temper," his "Charity," and "the Healing Principle, which on all occasions appear'd in him" (pp. 4, 27), make William not
only the pattern that the whole English nation could profitably imitate, but
also an *imitatio Christi.* Before recounting examples of impious and
vainglorious monarchs, classical and modern, past and present, English and
continental, Defoe considers William's life. "We Challenge," he writes,
"History of Times past, or Experience of Time within Memory, to match the
Instance before us" (p. 12). King William's life and actions, his performance
as king and his prayers as a man, give us "a Prince of the greatest

---

[29] *Royal Religion* (London, 1704), p. 16. Further citations will be incorporated in the text.

Piety, Sincerity, and unfeigned Religion, as either History relates, or Memory informs of in the World" (p. 21). When he concludes, Defoe characteristically joins those two components that valorize this king's, or any king's fitness for that holy office. "And whenever this Nation is blest again with a Praying and Fighting Monarch; may they treat him better, betray him less, and love him more; least Heaven serve them then, as he has done now, and take him from them when they have most need of him" (p. 27).

As William receded from the memories and prayers of his ungrateful English subjects, he increased in glory in Defoe's eyes. On the sacred day of 5 November 1709, "a Day set apart by me to celebrate the Immortal Memory of King *William*," Defoe printed an eulogy in the *Review* which was separately reprinted as *A Commendatory Sermon Preach'd November the 4th, 1709. Being the Birth-Day of King William, of Glorious Memory*. The biblical text appended was Samuel 1.24: "*Ye Daughters of Israel, weep over Saul, who cloathed you in Scarlet, with other Delights; who put on ornaments of Gold upon your Apparrel.*" It is a revealing text for two reasons: first, the death of Saul was part of a biblical sequence previously reserved for the solemnization of the anniversary of the martyred Charles I, lamenting as it does the destruction in war of "the Lord's annointed;" secondly, the biblical analogue asserting William's correspondence with Saul allied Defoe with his hated enemies, as he well knew, for Saul had also become, in the political debates of the decade, the type of the divine-right king as interpreted by Tory Highchurchmen.[30] As we shall see when we look at *Jure Divino*, the Sauline model of kingship was to become the salient characteristic of Defoe's Miltonic epic on the origins of monarchial government and the pervasive model for the evolution of civil and political society in *Robinson Crusoe*. Here we can only note that Whig commentary of the time was clear and unambiguous: Saul was an apostate from God and from the people who had accepted him as their king. Denigrated in the Revolution debates, Saul had, in Whig ideology, become the archetype of a monarch who governed by his single will without the restraint of any co-ordinate legislative power. Desacralized, then, in Whig political propaganda, it was Defoe's ideological enemies who asserted that Saul had come to exercise his authority by express commission immediately and personally received from God.

Masculinity, affirmed by military leadership, glory in battle, and divine right, appear to have become the defining characteristics of Defovian monarchy. In his contributions to Miege's *Compleat History of the Late Revolution*, we have observed how Defoe justified lodging complete executive power in William "because a Man, by Nature, Education, and Experience, is generally rendred

---

30 See Richard Newman, *A sermon preached in the parish-church of St. Sepulchres, on Monday the 30th of January, 1693/4. Being the anniversary solemnity of the martyrdom of King Charles I* (London, 1694); and Edward Lake, *A Sermon preached at the church of S. Mary le Bow . . . on the Thirtieth of January MDCLXXXIII. Being the Anniversary Day of Humiliation for the Martyrdom of K. Charles the First* (London, 1684). Newman's biblical text was 2 Samuel 1.14; Lake's, 2 Samuel 1.18.

more capable to Govern than a Woman. And, as the present State of *Europe* in general, so that of these Kingdoms in particular, required a vigorous and masculine Administration. To recover what was lost, to rescue what was in danger, and rectify what was amiss, could not be effected but by a Prince consummate in the Art both of Peace and War."[31] Again and again Defoe concentrated on the soldierly attributes of his monarchical ideal. The minister of his youth, Dr. Samuel Annesley, we recall, was "a willing Soldier in the Sacred War;" in his Christian vocation "the vigorous Combat he began."[32] Later, in 1716, in his parodic biblical narrative of English history, Defoe's first observation about King William reminds his readers that "he had been a Warrior from his Youth upwards."[33] The essentiality of this divine characteristic is just as clearly revealed two years later in his *Memoirs of Publick Transactions in the Life and Ministry of his Grace the D. [uke] of Shrewsbury.* In his glowing narrative of this model statesman Defoe was forced to confront immediately the most glaring deficiency in this hero's, or any hero's, life: "The Person whose Actions we are to write of, . . . has not added to the Fame of his Illustrious Ancestors by Martial Deeds, and has not been much of a Man of the Sword . . ." Defoe qualified Shrewsbury's limitation in his distinctive linguistic pattern: "But as his Ancestors have been Men of War, he has been a Man of Council."[34] Unlike Monmouth's son, who, we recall, was "fitly qualified to *Succeed his present Majesty,* both at the Head of the *English Armies,* as well as at the Helm of *English Councils.*" As he wrote of Charles XII of Sweden, political leaders must have "extraordinary Genuis" both "in the Camp [and] in the Cabinet."[35] Thus by a telling recognition of its absence, Defoe betrays the extraordinary worth and necessity of the sword of martial valor in his determination of political greatness.

To understand Defoe fully, then, we must understand some less considered aspects of his age that we have touched upon earlier, aspects that have as much bearing on his political thought as his Calvinism or his proto-bourgeoise leanings. Leonard Krieger has written that "it was an age of kings" but kings

---

[31] P. 73.

[32] *The Character of the Late Dr. Samuel Annesley,* p. 5.

[33] *Proper Lessons for the Tories,* p. 18; cf. Defoe, *An Impartial History of . . . Peter Alexowitz, Czar of Muscovy* (London, 1723), p. 118.

[34] London, 1718, p. 3. George I, by contrast, arrived in England "for Counsel form'd as well as Fight" (*A Poem on the Arrival of the King* [London, 1714], p. 9). Cf. also William Lee, *Daniel Defoe, His Life and Recently Discovered Writings,* I, 231–32.

[35] *The History of . . . Charles XII . . . The Second Edition* (London, 1720), p. 7. For another instance of Defoe's favorite "Field/Cabinet" dyad see *Royal Religion,* p. 9. In his Preface to *The General History of the Pyrates* Defoe wrote: "I presume we need make no Apology for giving the Name of a History to the following Sheets, tho' they contain nothing but the actions of a Parcel of Robbers. It is Bravery and Strategem in War which makes Actions worthy of Regard" (ed. Manuel Schonhorn (London: Dent, 1972), p. 6). Till the end of his life Defoe believed that only men of martial genius are "destined to great action" (*Of Royall Educacion,* ed. Karl Bülbring, p. 3; cf. p. 9).

of a special kind.[36] In European history, it was the last hurrah of personal monarchs like William III, Louis XIV, Charles XII, and Gustavus Adolphus, common fathers of their people, who sustained – or attempted to sustain – military dictatorships, covert or explicit. Or kings like Charles XII, who adjured court for the campaign, society for the saddle and sword, "a chivalric preference that made [them] the last of the kings to retain personal leadership of [their] men in battle as the most continuous, the most characteristic, and the most exalted duty of a King." And it was still an age of the divinity of kings, not only in the sense of "the sacred origination of the royal office," but also in its conception of the monarch as embodying the ethos of God.[37] At times it is this dual notion of kingship – one whose crown is immediately derived from God and who affirms that crown by wielding his sword in defence of his people – that invigorates, if only metaphorically, Defoe's political propaganda, and is the political assumption underpinning *Robinson Crusoe*.

Defoe's special relationship to William imaginatively shaped his deep-seated conception of kingship in general. We have seen how his portrait of the right monarch had been developing over the years, challenged, modified, and refined by the changing history of England internally and externally. But now consider Defoe's first allusion to William, selected in the summer of 1689 as the euphoria of the Revolution inevitably gave rise to a fuller and more down-to-earth realization of the fictions and frustrations of the constitutional settlement. In *The Advantages of the Present Settlement, and the Great Danger of a Relapse*, Defoe took on the "Murmurings and Whisperings" of those in church and state – they are never fully identified – those forgetful backsliders who have begun to have second thoughts about the "Divine Contrivance" of the Revolution.[38] Their intent is clear; they would have, Defoe submits, "King WILLIAM and Queen MARY dethroned again, and have them either voluntarily to return back from whence they came, or else to be sent back again by force; [they] would have King JAMES the Second restored to his Crown and Dignity, and reinstated in his Throne and Government" (pp. 4–5). He follows with the commonplace review of England "before the happy arrival of their present Majesties" (p. 5): the corruption of judges, the quartering of troops, the suborning of witnesses, the closeting of judges, the trial of bishops, the invasion of corporations – in short, James's co-ordinated program for absolute and despotic power that was to undermine "the Religion and Civil Rights" of all Englishmen through a deliberate policy of Catholicizing English culture. To counter this corrupt ideology of *jure divino* government,

---

36 Krieger, *Kings and Philosophers*, p. 1. See also Stephen B. Baxter, "The Age of Personal Monarchy in England," in *Eighteenth-Century Studies Presented to Arthur M. Wilson*, ed. Peter Gay (Hanover, NH: University Press of New England, 1972), pp. 1–11.

37 Krieger, *Kings and Philosophers*, pp. 43 and 7.

38 London, 1689, pp. 3, 4. Further citations will be incorporated in the text.

"God raised up this mighty Deliverer, our present King, to put a stop to those unhappy Proceedings" (p. 23). To England, "this famous Island," "this *British* Island," came "the greatest Hope" of the Protestant religion, William of Orange, "like another *Titus*, the Delight of mankind" (pp. 24, 26).

The Titus allusion was no doubt selected with careful understanding of some of its associations. Defoe's *persona*, once again, is a Church of England man who has already revealed his old-fashioned zeal for England's reformed religion in particular and its haven as "the Bulwark of the Protestant Religion in general"(p. 33). And he knows his Bible; in fact, his last words are the Psalmist's voice of God responding to the prayer of his anointed king, "*that your Enemies may be clothed with shame, but upon your Head the Crown may long Flourish*" (p. 38).[39] Such a speaker would likely know that Titus was seen as a magistrate, a presbyter, even a bishop of the Church, placed in his holy seat by God. Calvin's sermon on Paul's Epistle to Titus set the direction for the ensuing Protestant commentary and comprehension: "For it is his prerogative to give the sword, & also to unbuckle the sword girdle, when hee listeth to put downe those that had the sworde of Justice before."[40] Titus taught that Christians must obey those in high places; together with Romans 13.1 and 1 Peter 2.13, it was the fashionable text of royalists and *jure divino* apologists: "Put them in mind to be subject to principalities and powers, to obey magistrates."[41] Quite traditionally, Titus's orders from the apostle of God to reform the denizens of Crete – all of whom were liars – and to evangelize a heathen island, legitimated him in the eyes of the Anglican establishment as the first bishop of Crete and served as the text for the nature, origin, and divine right of the episcopacy. Titus, at great peril to his life, came to an island community to perfect what had been left unfinished, to restore the spiritual foundations of that community.[42] He was, as George Stanhope, preaching before the Sons of the Clergy in 1697 defined him, "a Power, by St. *Paul*'s own Appointment lodged in one Single Person, at whose Hands the rest should receive their Authority, and to whom, as their Superintendent, they were accountable for the Use of it.[43]

Early in his writing career, Defoe's unique analogue for his king coincided

---

[39] Psalms 132.18.

[40] L. T., *Sermons of M. John Calvin, on the Epistles of S. Paul to Timothie and Titus* (London, 1579), p. 1205. STC no. 4441.

[41] See, for example, Jonathan Clapham, *Obedience to Magistrates Recommended, In a Discourse Upon Titus 3.1* (Norwich, 1683); Thomas Grey, *Loyalty Essential to Christianity: Being a Sermon Preached the Thirtieth of June, 1685. Upon the Occasion of the News of the Damnable Rebellion in the West* (London, 1685).

[42] See, for example, Robert South, *A Sermon Preached at Lambeth-Chappel on the 25th of November* (London, 1666). Cf. *Annotations Upon the Holy Bible, Wherein the Sacred Text is Inserted, and Various Readings Annex'd . . . Vol. II. Being a Continuation of Mr. Poole's Work by Certain Judicious and Learned Divines. The Third Edition* (London, 1696).

[43] *A Sermon Preach'd in St. Paul's Cathedral, at the Annual Meeting of the Sons of the Clergy* (London, 1698), p. 1.

with the authoritative sacerdotalism of a peculiarly idiosyncratic New Testament prophet, steward of God. But he is also one who, significantly, is devoid of heirs.[44] Defoe's hero-king, like Calvin's Titus, mirrors the shepherd of his flock, or the *pater patriae*, or the mentor to his pupils. But William and Titus are also prime examples of Defoe's true and enduring leaders,

> . . . always born *to stand alone*;
> *Caesar* and *Alexander* left no Son,
> And *David's* but eclips'd by *Solomon*:
> Fate seems to make it look *like Nature's Law*,
> From Great *Gustavus* down to Great *Nassau*.
> That where consummate Vertue shall remain,
> The *Last of every Line* shall be the Man.[45]

In imagining his king as the New Testament evangelist, Defoe underscored William's heaven-sent mission and his validation by spiritual authority. Defoe, then, has once again – and very early in his career – refused to distinguish between the secular and spiritual roles of his soldier-king. His ideal monarch from the beginning remained somewhat independent of human creation, carrying inseparably within himself the earthly and heavenly orders that enabled him to succeed in his role as unitary and military monarch. But also as early as 1689 Defoe envisioned this charismatic leader of the body politic as one who would be unable to perpetuate dynastically his unrivalled authority. William, and Titus, and perhaps Robinson Crusoe, are all aliens in a strange land, childless heaven-sent initiators but transitory governors of their respective communities. Though sanctioned by the divine, they sadly disclose the inevitable discontinuity in the transmission of the power and authority of the king.

The year that began with the death of William III was one of the most dramatic and traumatic in Defoe's life. In May 1702, two months after the unexpected demise of his Protestant hero, the Deliverer of England, Defoe was in debtors' jail. In the first week of 1703 Defoe was a hunted felon, the publication of the controversially ironic *Shortest Way with the Dissenters* having led to the issuance of a warrant for his arrest for writing "a scandalous and seditious pamphlet." His flight from justice, his incarceration, time in the pillory, and eventual release; the creation of the *Review*; even his recognition of his cowardice and anxieties – all have been admirably discussed elsewhere.[46] It was a time of excess and extreme – the success of his tile works, his pride in becoming the voice of England as signified by the

---

[44] I say unique despite the fact that I have discovered one other allusion to Titus in panegyrics to William: John Guy, *On the Happy Accession of Their Majesties King William and Queen Mary, To the Throne of England* (London, 1699), p. 3. In his Preface Guy, seemingly in need to defend his loyalty to William, explains that he wrote the ode in 1689, four months before the publication of Defoe's pamphlet.

[45] *Jure Divino* (London, 1706), XII, 12.

[46] See Moore, *Daniel Defoe*; Bastian, *Defoe's Early Life*; and Downie, *Robert Harley*.

publication of a half-dozen tracts over the sobriquet of "The True-born Englishman," the pirating of his first collection of poetry and prose; then business failures, abject fear, the scandal of the pillory, finally succeeded by freedom and "employment in the government's service, but at the price of almost absolute dependence on the good will of Robert Harley."[47]

The pendulum of change in Defoe's life can perhaps serve as a parallel to the content of the propaganda that Defoe wrote in unsigned tracts and for the government in the *Review*. He continued to defend revolutionary principles and to intone the language of consent and compact. England's coronation oath was still equated with the original contract, but when that oath was broken, kings "cease to be the Lord's Anointed any longer."[48] Many of Defoe's essays and pamphlets counter the divine right theorists on their own linguistic terrain, for we find his discussions ignoring the historical and legal justification for the Revolution of 1688. More and more that Revolution becomes providential, "the immediate Effect of the ever-ruling Hand of GOD; his all-powerful Arm was most visibly seen in that Transaction, above and beyond the Expectation of the Wisest of Man . . . It was GOD's immediate Hand, therefore it will stand, and the Gates of Hell shall never be able to over-turn it."[49] To the High Churchmen who preached divine right, "giving a Soveraignty, to this or that Person by Line, superseding all humane Authority," he answered:

'Tis known to all the World, and was never intended to be conceal'd, That let Her Majesty's Title to the Crown be never so just by Inheritance, or the Descent of it, *as one would fain prove*, be never so Ancient; Nay, even from *Noah* if it were possible, the present Establishment, Grants Her Majesty to be Queen of *England*; by Vertue of Parliamentary Settlement, only built on Revolution Principles, even upon the same foot *and no other*, as the late King *William* Enjoy'd the Crown.[50]

Yet that very same year, when he read of the proprietary governors of the Carolinas running roughshod over their subjects like English parliaments of the recent past, Defoe observed that

they never *learnt to be Kings*, they have not taken in the Hint of *Pater Patriae*, they don't know, that a King must be the *Father of his People*; and that there is a sort of Patriarchial Affection, as well as Obligation, between a King on the Throne, and the People He Governs, which obliges them to treat them with Gentleness, listen to their Complaints, and redress the Grievance; they need have gone no farther, than to their own Sovereign, to have seen a Pattern of this Pious Care, and have reflected, how Sollicitous Her Majesty appears for the General Good; how pleas'd and thankful, when Prosperity Crowns their Affairs, . . . Whence does this proceed? God Almighty, for the Good of Nations, furnishes Princes, born to Crowns and Kingdoms, with the suited Affections for these Circumstances of Government, and thereby fulfills the promise of making them Nursing Fathers, and Nursing Mothers.[51]

[47] Downie, *Robert Harley*, p. 63.
[48] *A New Test of the Church of England's Loyalty* (London, 1702), p. 16.
[49] *Moderation Maintain'd* (London, 1704), pp. 22–23.
[50] *Review*, II, 79 (4 Sept. 1705).
[51] *Party-Tyranny* (London, 1705), pp. 10–11 (misnumbered p. 13).

These observations, while they continue to reveal the sustained eclecticism of Defoe's political thought, also point to his somewhat enigmatic considerations on the nature of government and politics. The bedrock of his political imagination, however, is revealed in the memorandum that he wrote to Harley in the summer of 1704, that was endorsed then and has continued to be seen as only "A Scheme of General Intelligence etc."

That Defoe, whom we have seen hurrying to Monmouth in the west country in 1685, proclaiming the glory of his Dutch hero-prince since 1688, and with apparent sincerity seeking a positive determination of the younger Monmouth's right to the English throne in 1701, now, some two years following William's death, should turn his allegiance and attach himself to the Queen's Secretary of State should occasion no surprise. After all, Harley was a "comer," his talents recognized early, his prominence seemingly assured. Defoe and Harley were about the same age, and, more importantly, shared a dissenting religious heritage. Defoe was indebted to Harley for his release from jail and the employment, gainful or otherwise, that followed. Nor can the incompetence of the Queen's consort, Prince George, be ignored.

During the debates on the Act of Settlement the motion that he share the royal dignity and be titled king upon his wife's accession to the throne had been rejected. The Dutch had obstinately refused to name him their captain-general following William's death. As generalissimo of England's armies and as Lord High Admiral, George is a performer out of *opéra bouffe*. Defoe has virtually nothing of significance to say about the husband of his queen. Perhaps having such an indolent and useless surrogate for monarchy in the council of the queen propelled his search for a vital male figure to take firm hold of the reins of political power.[52]

But that Defoe should now hitch his political ideology, his freedom and his financial future, to the leader of the "Country" opposition, to whom he had presented the unsettling *Legion's Memorial* in May 1701, forces a respect for Defoe's intuition and judgment of character. Much has been written of Harley's shrewd measure of Defoe. But Defoe had chosen to form a deep allegiance and began a lifetime of loyalty with a statesman with whose political ideas he could not have been more compatible. Defoe, like Harley, "was never captivated by the party system of the early eighteenth century. [Theirs] was an anachronistic ideology stemming from the political world of [their] earlier and much younger days."[53] Both had discovered early that party was only a synonym for faction and divisiveness; it was self-serving in

---

[52] For Prince George see Green, *Queen Anne*, pp. 35, 55, 73, 77, 116; and Winston Churchill, *Marlborough, His Life and Times*, 2 vols. (London: Harrap, 1947) I, 168–69. Defoe notes the Prince's death in *Review*, V, 103 (23 Nov. 1708). Significantly, before he comments at length about the marital happiness of the royal pair, he devotes a paragraph to George's one martial act at the Battle of the Boyne: "this I need not mention, but to acquaint these People that would notice his not appearing in the Field of War."

[53] Downie, *Robert Harley*, p. 23.

nature and in practice destructive of the foundations of government. "As for Parties in generall," Harley wrote, in what was repeated many times over in Defoe's essays and *Reviews*, "it hath long been my opinion, that Parties in the State is Knavery and Parties in Religion is Hypocrisy."[54] If Harley did attach himself obliquely to party politics in Anne's reign, Keith Feiling has concluded that his "chequered course as a party man is not entirely to his discredit, for his inconstancy was rooted in something like principle. He disbelieved in the whole scheme of party, and would not frame a rigid programme."[55] Much the very same thing has been written about Defoe to explain the ambiguities and inconsistencies of his writings on politics during the *Review* years and of his journalism for successive Hanoverian ministries. That Harley was the least of the three leaders in the Queen's new government in 1704 reflects on Defoe's insights and his correct measure of one who was later to be Anne's most influential minister.

Yet indebtedness, an ideological affinity, and the need to align with a personality embodying those virtues of political leadership Defoe deemed essential – "CAPACITY, INTEGRITY, COURAGE and APPLICATION"[56] – will go only a little way to explain the content of Defoe's audacious proposal to Harley in the summer of 1704. His and Harley's shared distrust of party politics calls to mind Keith Feiling's telling insight that "non-party government has, as its commonest corollary, one-man rule."[57] Defoe's policy paper written for Harley's private understanding reveals that the Secretary of State had been selected for the role of unitary sovereign in the new monarchy unfitly superintended by an incapacitated queen.

Defoe's private agenda for making Harley "a Supreme Ministry," that is, the Prime Minister, with the bland assurance that "The Nation May Easily be Reconcil'd to it," was conceived and formulated by Defoe following his intense reading of Jean Le Clerc's *Life of the famous Cardinal-Duke De Richlieu, Principal Minister of State to Lewis XIII. King of France and Navarr* (trans. 1665).[58] Four months before his memorandum to Harley, Defoe had concluded that "this great Minister made the Reign of a weak Prince exceedingly glorious."[59] At a time when Defoe was *publicly* consigning Richelieu to Milton's Pandemonium for crimes aganst the people and for supporting tyranny, *privately* Defoe was presenting the Duke to Harley as the master military tactician, the cunning diplomat, and "the true Author of the present

---

54 Sheila Biddle, *Bolingbroke and Harley* (New York: Alfred A Knopf, 1974), p. 101.

55 *A History of the Tory Party, 1640–1714* (Oxford: Clarendon, 1924), p. 334.

56 *Rogues on Both Sides* (London, 1711), p. 30. For Harley's courage see Rubini, *Court and Country*, pp. 210–11.

57 *A History of the Tory Party*, p. 451.

58 The text is in *The Letters of Daniel Defoe*, pp. 29–50. Cited is p. 29. Further citations will be incorporated in the text. For his reading see *Review*, I, 34 (1 July 1704).

59 *Review*, I, 2 (26 Feb. 1704). In Edinburgh, three years later, Defoe "act[ed] the Old part of Cardinal Richlieu," as Harley's premier spy orchestrating the debates over the union of Scotland and England (Healey, *Letters*, p. 211).

French Greatness.''[60] Fashioning an English Richelieu for an indulgent queen, Defoe proposed to make Harley the master strategist of English politics.

Defoe had begun his *Weekly Review of the Affairs of France* in February 1704 by treating "of the Present Greatness of the *French* Nation," the reasons for her hegemonic ascendancy on the continent, and the threat she now posed in the European wars. This "Bold, Adventurous, Wise, Politick, and Martial People," Defoe maintained, outdid the English in the following particulars:

I   In the Unanimity and Policy of their Councils.
II   In the Exactness and Punctual Exercise of their Orders.
III   In the Swiftness of their Motion.
IV   In the Fidelity of their Officers.[61]

With France as his standard, Richelieu as his model, and Harley as his pupil, Daniel Defoe, literary *eminence grise*, fashioned a scenario that would duplicate some of the attractions of French absolutism on English shores. His program would enable Harley to "Make your Self Prime Minister of State, Unenvy'd and Unmolested, be Neither Address'd Against by Parliament, Intreagu'd Against by Partyes, or Murmur'd at by the Mob" (p. 31), in a word, to become the "Supreme Ministry" of England. The process outlined by Defoe would enable Harley to secure in his hands, or in his controlled Department of State, the essential direction and conduct of the government.[62]

To state so baldly the implicit impetus of Defoe's plan for ministerial supremacy, to argue that its tendency is to subvert the development of cabinet government that had begun in William's reign, is to open up the reactionary irregularity of Defoe's project.[63] Essentially, Harley's success would depend upon three elements. First he was to become "The Peoples Darling" (p. 32), to attain the complete love and trust of the population. Second, he was "to Make the Office of Secretary of State an Inner Cabinett,

---

[60] For Richelieu in Pandemonium see *Jure Divino*, VII, 15; *Review*, I, 29 (13 June 1704).

[61] *Review*, I, 2 (26 Feb. 1704). Perceptively, Peter Earle has written that Defoe "had in fact a certain admiration for the benefits of absolutism" (*The World of Defoe*, p. 21).

[62] Healey (*Letters*, p. 35n) asks for a comparison between Defoe's ideal cabinet and one proposed by Sunderland. A more revealing comparison would be with Harley's Plan of Administration written in 1710, in which it is "the Queen who remains the superior, upon whom all are dependent" (*Miscellaneous State Papers from 1501 to 1726*, 2 vols. (London, 1778), II, 485–88). Cf. Henry L. Snyder, "The Formulation of Foreign and Domestic Policy in the Reign of Queen Anne: Memoranda by Lord Chancellor Cowper of Conversations with Lord Treasurer Godolphin," *Historical Journal*, 11 (1968), 144–60.

[63] See the following: Jennifer Carter, "Cabinet Records for the Reign of William III," *English Historical Review*, 78 (1963), 95–114; Horwitz, *Parliament, Policy, and Politics*, pp. 91–93, 204–07; J. H. Plumb, "The Organization of the Cabinet in the Reign of Queen Anne," *Transactions of the Royal Historical Society*, 5th ser., vol. 7 (1957), 137–57. There are two earlier and confusing studies by Edward Raymond Turner: *The Privy Council in England in the Seventeenth and Eighteenth Centuries, 1603–1784*, 2 vols. (Baltimore: Johns Hopkins University Press, 1927–28), and *The Cabinet Council in England in the Seventeenth and Eighteenth Centuries, 1622–1784*, 2 vols. (Baltimore: Johns Hopkins University Press, 1930–32).

and Execute Necessary Parts of Private affaires without the Intervention of
the Privy Council and yet have Their Concurrence as farr as the Law
Requires" (p. 34). Third, the *sine qua non* of popular success and Harley's
direction of government business in a truncated cabinet council, Defoe was
to create for Harley a fully thought through, co-ordinated system of domestic
and continental intelligence, a network of geographical, financial, social, and
political fact-gathering, a spy organization of such breadth and depth and
secrecy that, in Defoe's projecting imagination, it rivals the command of
information that is the ideal of the most totalitarian communities.

One has to be careful determining what was "intended" in this program
through which Defoe's Secretary of State would become the "Peoples Darling" and the "Popular States Man" of "the Common People" (p. 34). One
of the conditions of the unexpectedly harsh sentence meted out to Defoe
following his trial in 1703 was that he find sureties to be of good behavior for
seven years. Defoe could never forget that Harley was the ex-Speaker of the
House of Commons to whom he had delivered the scandalous *Legion's
Memorial* in 1701. And Harley himself would have realized that the recipes for
the gaining of popularity are clichéd echoes of the maxims that were to be
found in the Renaissance and seventeenth-century tracts that were written for
the education of princes: Be generous, reward the lowly and the worthy,
cultivate a merciful image (as Cardinal Richelieu did), and "Let Others have
the Mannagement of Offences, and the Distribution of Justice" (p. 34).
Machiavellian or not, Defoe's plan for political popularity is the classic one
of steering "between the *Scylla* and *Charibdis* of Partyes; So as to Obtain from
Them all a generall Esteem" (p. 42). it was, as Defoe well knew, what
advisers to princes throughout history had openly deemed it to be,
"Dissimulation . . . which is Not Unlike what the Apostle Sayes of himself;
becoming all Things to all Men, that he might Gain Some. This Hypocrise
is a Vertue, and by This Conduct you Shall Make your Self Popular, you shall
be Faithful and Usefull to the Soveraign and belov'd by The People" (p. 43).

Yet beyond these inoffensive commonplaces, Defoe's agenda by which
Harley would dominate the business of government derives from the creation of
an Inner Cabinet to the Queen which would, it bears repeating, "Excecute
Necessary Parts of Private affaires without the Intervention of the Privy Coun-
cil" (p. 34). It was to be fed by an information network that had the potential for
blackmail. Richelieu, with his own French network, "had his Fingers in all the
Actions of *Europe*, was inform'd of every Motion, insinuated himself into every
Cabinet, and in short manag'd all *Europe*."[64] Harley, whom Defoe was to make
"a finished Statesman," would also have at his fingertips the equivalent of
Richelieu's "certain and exact Intelligence in all Parts of the World." And in
England Harley would have

---

[64] *Review*, IV, 118 (13 Nov. 1707).

1st   A Perfect List of all the Gentry and Familys of Rank in England, Their Residence, Characters, and Intrest in the Respective Countyes.

2   Of all the Clergy of England, their Benefices, Their Character, and Moralls, and the like of the Dissenters.

3   Of all the Leading Men in the Cittyes and Burroughs, with the Partyes they Espouse.   (p. 36)

Nothing escaped Defoe's political almanac, this compendious *omnium gatherum* of the whole social, economic, and political structure of England: "a Table of Partyes, and Proper Callculations of their Strength in Every Respective Part," election results, "Men of Great Personall Estates," "the speciall Characters of all the Justices of the Peace, and Men of Note in Every County," enabling "The Secretaryes Office [to] be an Abrigem[en]t of all Europe," and of England too (pp. 36, 37).

From Cardinal Richelieu, who "was the Greatest Master of This Vertue" (p. 39), Defoe had learned the necessity of secrecy. Thus Harley's intelligence service was to be maintained "Under a Secret Management," with "Secret Heads [who] Need Not Correspond" with one another (p. 43), but who would be completely loyal and subservient to the Statesman of the People. And

From This fund of Advice all Things Needfull to be Concerted for the Occasions of State, May be Form'd into schemes, and Come Out Perfect. The Proposalls Made by the Secretarys Shall No More be Embrios, and be brought before the Council to be Argued, and Amended, but shall be born at Once, and Come before them wholl and Compleat, and the Council have Little to do but to Approve a thing as it is Proposed.

If all the Proposalls Relateing to Publick Matters were Thus Digested, her Majtie would find There was a Secret Sufficiency Some where in her Secretarys Office, that in Time would bring both her Self and Council To Depend upon the Secretarys of State, for all the Modells of Action, as well as the Mannagement, and Thus Sir I have brought Out what I Affirm'd at First, That the Secretary of State Must of Course be Prime Minister.   (pp. 43–44)

It is easy to overestimate the degree of control that is reflected in Defoe's plan for a Supreme Minister. But it must be recalled that Defoe was challenging a long-standing national antipathy to a "prime minister," a term that continued to be used in a derogatory sense long past his time.[65] Carried away by his vision of a government harmonized by an English Richelieu, "a Noble and Wise Statesman," who would implement the French virtues of Silence, Secrecy, Unanimity, Policy, Exactness, and Punctual Execution carried to his English shore, Defoe's rhetoric has spawned an apparatus of control that has no counterpart in English history. Perhaps he never considered that with the collective power of a satisfied people, the acquiescence of a pliable and secretly managed parliament, and the support of a fawning

---

[65] Robert A. Smith, *Eighteenth-Century Politics: Patrons and Place-hunters* (New York: Holt, Rinehart and Winston, 1972), pp. 163–75. But cf. Williams, *The Eighteenth-Century Constitution*, p. 125.

queen, he had given Harley a mandate for absolute domination of "All Publick Business." Perhaps he can be excused for opening the door to a ministerial tyranny as complete and as total as any legislative or monarchical tyranny that he had lived under. But he cannot be found innocent of what he knew to be political heresy, subversive of English law. For the Act of Settlement had prescribed that "all matters and things relating to the well governing of this kingdom, which are properly cognizable in the privy council by the laws and customs of this realm, shall be transacted there; and all resolutions taken thereupon shall be signed by such of the privy council as shall advise and consent to the same."[66] Defoe surely knew that providing Harley with an Inner Cabinet that would be "the Moveing Springs of the State," to "Execute Necessary Parts of Private affaires without the Intervention of the Privy Council," that would with the Supreme Minister's leadership and concurrence define what was "Legall" and "Really for the Publick Good," was to go against a long-standing parliamentary criticism of executive absolutism. He may even have been aware of a 1692 debate of a Grand Committee of Parliament investigating the flawed execution of naval orders and the failure of English intelligence – one of his interests in this 1704 memorandum to Harley. " 'Cabinet-Council,' Mr. Waller responded in that debate, 'is not a word to be found in our Law-books. . . Nothing can fall out more unhappily than to have a distinction made of the 'Cabinet' and 'Privy Council'."[67] To Defoe's proposal of 1704 Goodwin Wharton could have responded as he had earlier to what he foresaw as fundamental changes in the management of his government: "The method of this Cabinet is not the method nor the practice of *England*."[68] This exchange in 1692 occurred in a parliament that was registering its antagonism to the creation of any intermediary between itself and the Crown. It was an affirmative response to the question proposed, "That the King be advised, that all matters of State be advised on in the Privy Council, and that the management by them by a Cabal is dangerous."[69] And whether or not Defoe had any hand in the writing of King William's last speech to parliament in December 1701, as Frank Bastian believes, he did refer to it an inordinate number of times in later years.[70] He may then have been aware of the ardent Whig response of the Third Earl of Shaftesbury to

---

[66] *Select Documents of English Constitutional History*, ed. George B. Adams and H. Morse Stephens (New York: Macmillan, 1919), p. 478. This clause, with others, was repealed by the Regency Act (1706).

[67] Anchitell Grey, *Debates of the House of Commons, from the Year 1667 to the Year 1694*, 10 vols. (London, 1763), X, 276. Cf. J. R. Jones, *Country and Court: England, 1658–1714* (Cambridge, MA: Harvard University Press, 1978), p. 266.

[68] Grey, X, 279. Wharton's criticism is a proleptic indictment of Defoe's program: "things are concerted in the Cabinet, and then brought to the Council; such a thing resolved in the Cabinet, and brought and put upon them, for their Assent, without showing any of the Reasons. That has not been the Method of *England*" (X, 279).

[69] Grey, X, 277.

[70] Bastian, *Defoe's Early Life*, p. 264.

the monarch's "Princely, Pious, and most Gracious Speech." Shaftesbury foresaw a country unified by and geared for war, devoid of factions and divisions, and with its liberty guarded by a legislative trinity: the Treason Bill, the Triennial Bill, and the Act of Settlement, which ruled for "the transacting of State Matters in the privy Council."[71]

The education of princes genre gave recipes for the moral development of the sovereign and for the preservation of the kingdom. But Defoe's memorandum is no recapitulation of those models of action. In his there are no maxims of state, no learned and pithy aphorisms distilling the lessons of history. Neither is Defoe elucidating a program that is intended for the moral elevation of his patron. And, finally, Defoe is far from detailing the necessary qualities of the statesman who is serving his monarch for the good of the country. While he begins his memorandum to Harley with talk about the virtues and generosity of the good man, his developing commentary as he moves to his real interest – and that interest is power – lays out a program of control divorced from any theological or moral considerations. Those earlier political treatises limning the loyal adviser to the monarch asked that he be a model of subordination, that he maintain a subservient devotion to the reigning prince. Such is the hallmark of his role as good counselor. In Defoe's treatise virtues are subordinated to action, philosophy to the practical politics of secret service dossiers. If there were a body of secret police able to be developed in Queen Anne's England, Defoe very likely would have found use for it. If the previous treatises were to "frame a Minister of State, and a prudent Courtier," Defoe innovatively arranges an agenda for coupling popularity and control in order to guarantee the rule of the realm by the Queen's first minister.[72]

If, then, Defoe's memorandum is an agenda only for ministerial magnipotence, it is a magnipotence that renders the Queen a cypher. She may hold the scepter and wear the crown, but she "ruleth not though she raign over realms."[73] Her privy council, her parliament, and her people all have become mere accessories to the decisions made in private by the Prime Minister at the head of a Cabinet Council that he completely dominates with the data of the nation. His power is equal to that oppressive irregulated power that the "Lords States General" of the Commonwealth had had, "that of even initiating legislation by drawing up bills to present to Parliament."[74]

---

[71] *Paradoxes of State* (London, 1702), p. 2. See Robert Voitle, *The Third Earl of Shaftesbury, 1671–1713* (Baton Rouge: Louisiana State University Press, 1984), pp. 207–08.

[72] Cf., for example, Sir Walter Raleigh, *The Cabinet-Council* (London, 1658); Raleigh, *Maxims of State* (1751 ed.), I, 1–38, 62–115; J. de Silhon, *The Minister of State*, trans. H. Herbert, Part I (London, 1658), Part II (London, 1663); Nicolai Machiavelli, *The Prince*, in *Works* (London, 1680), esp. pp. 231–32. I quote from Saavedra Faxada, *The Royal Politician in One Hundred Emblems*, trans. James Astry (London, 1701), p. A4v.

[73] *Tottel's Miscellany* (1557–1587), ed. Hyder Edward Rollins, 2 vols. (Cambridge, MA: Harvard University Press, 1928), I, 212.

[74] *The Writings and Speeches of Oliver Cromwell*, ed. Wilbur Cortez Abbott, 4 vols. (Cambridge, MA: Harvard University Press, 1939), II, 33.

The organs of government and the voices of the community resemble nothing so much as rubber stamps; the repository and cause of all legislative direction, procedure, and authority is the Prime Minister. Presented as an intermediate body seemingly headed by a first minister and mediating between the queen and the parliament, Harley's Cabinet Council, as it maintains control over every area of society and government, would make Defoe's new mentor, in effect, master of queen and parliament. Anne would become a ceremonial monarch, left to preside over symbolic functions only.

It surprises us to discover Daniel Defoe, defender of the power of the people, versifier of "Lockean principles," engaging in a program of administrative reform that concludes in what Shaftesbury most feared, "the monarchy of one," installed in the office of the new Secretary of State.[75] Yet the models available to Defoe that could provoke his ideal of "greatness" in government were few. How was England to avoid "Our Confusions in Council, Our Errors in Execcuting and Unwaryness in Directing from the Multitude and bad Conduct of Ministers?" "the Delay, the Hesitations, the Ignorance, or Something worse of Privy Councelors"? How could "Att home Partyes . . . be Suppresst, Furious Tempers on all sides Check't and Discountenanc't, Peace Promoted and Union Obtain'd"? Finally, how would a simple and weak queen, ill-educated and unprepared for the masculine endeavors that were now the province of her throne, find that "Secret Sufficiency . . . that in Time would bring both her Self and [Privy] Council To Depend upon the Secretarys of State, for all the Modells of Action, as well as the Mannagement . . . of All the Great Actions of State"? Questions similar to these Defoe himself had posed upon the death of his beloved king:

> Who shall the jarring Generals unite;
> First teach them to agree, and then to fight?
> Who shall renew'd Alliances contrive,
> And keep the vast Confederacies alive?
> Who shall the growing Gallick Force subdue?[76]

Defoe's remarkable memorandum to Harley provides one answer to the questions posed. For Defoe it was a prime minister of state, an *imperium in imperio*, who had absorbed in his totality of understanding and domination all the other officers of state. There is no messianic leader in Defoe's Harley, no champion on horseback leading well-formed armies into Europe's battles to rescue English Protestantism from the threat of extinction posed by the Romish France of Louis XIV. Defoe's answer for now was a benevolent ministerial despot. He would be, like Cardinal Richelieu, "an abridgment of all Europe," even of England herself. Thus far had Defoe come from his earlier faith in the mystic union and tension-in-equilibrium of his country's constitutional grandeur:

[75] Voitle, *The Third Earl of Shaftesbury*, p. 207.
[76] *Mock-Mourners, POAS*, VI, 393.

And as the several parts of our Government have such a mutual dependance one upon the other, so they have the same opportunities of reciprocally endearing and obliging one another: So that I have often thought, with reverence be it spoke, that we have a kind of *Trinity* in our Government, as well as in our Faith.[77]

Such had been Defoe's beliefs in 1689 in his *Reflections upon the Late Great Revolution*. Fifteen years after, in this "Scheme of Generall Intelligence etc." for Harley's eyes only, Defoe appears to have abandoned his faith in the triune and subjoined glory of England's balanced constitution.

If we can believe Defoe, all during those tumultuous years following the death of William, in prison and out, and during his journeys through England while he performed as Harley's secret agent and one-man intelligence system, he had been composing his magnum opus, *Jure Divino. A Satyr. In Twelve Books. By the Author of the True-Born-Englishman*.[78] Carefully printed, generously subscribed, with its frontispiece carrying a new, engraved portrait of Defoe, this folio volume of more than seven thousand, six hundred couplets immediately suggests that Defoe has entered the lists with *Paradise Lost*. Carried on by Defoe with unimaginable dedication under the most exacting conditions of traveling and penury, it asks that we take its author seriously as a poet, satirist, and political philosopher. Not many have, and for good reasons. Its repetitiousness Defoe himself admitted: *"too often, we the Strain repeat."*[79] At times it seems to be nothing more than incessant recapitulation, and in atrocious verse, of Defoe's prose and poetic effusions, from the *Reflections Upon the Late Great Revolution* to *A New Test of the Church of England's Loyalty*. Self-quotations, from *The True-Born Englishman* and *The History of the Kentish Petition*, abound. It versifies, paraphrases, and quotes voluminously from a wide range of classical and contemporary sources, revealing, if not a mind that has read well, then at least one that had plundered widely. (For this self-education Defoe has never received the credit or the acknowledgment he deserves.)[80] When *Jure Divino* has been read for its political ideas, it has simply been found to exhibit "Lockean themes" or has been held to be a "vindication of Whig doctrine."[81] Given its hodge-podge of jingling couplets, with supporting footnotes, quotations, and prose exegeses, it is a disorderly assemblage of

---

[77] *Reflections*, p. 37.

[78] *Jure Divino*, pp. xxv, xxvii; *Letters*, p. 63; Moore, *Daniel Defoe*, pp. 58, 236–38; *Review*, I, 59 (26 Sept. 1704).

[79] *Jure Divino*, VI, 7.

[80] Kenyon dismisses Defoe as the possible author of *Vox Populi Vox Dei*, "a remarkably competent and concise piece of work," because "it is to be doubted if he had the necessary legal or historical knowledge" ("The Revolution of 1688," pp. 62, 63n.). But cf. Ashcraft and Goldsmith, "Locke, Republican Principles, and the Foundations of Whig Ideology," who consider Defoe as a prime suspect for its authorship (pp. 786–800).

[81] Moore, *Daniel Defoe*, p. 291; Kramnick, *Politics of Nostalgia*, p. 190. For the most recent and most elaborate reading of *Jure Divino* as a versification of the *Second Treatise* see Paula Backscheider, "The Verse Essay, John Locke, and Defoe's *Jure Divino*," *ELH*, 55 (1988), 99–124.

political commonplaces. But, as with most of Defoe's political tracts in which
he grappled with the political upheavals of his day, it also has its salutary
consistency.

Leonard Krieger, in a study of the shifting course of political thought in the
century following the Revolution of 1689, theorized about the "anomalous
mixture of hierarchy and equality," of the varied contradictory and antithetical ideas that permeate the writings of nearly all of the thinkers of the
age. Some "attempted to combine natural law with divine right or natural law
with historical situations." Krieger argues that no coherent political
philosophy was concocted that had a significant effect, dominated as each was
with an "inchoate quality of political thinking." Many of the writers were
Defoe's contemporaries, like "Archbishop Fenelon (1651–1715), who recommended a melange of royal absolutism, popular reforms, and the restoration
of the French aristocratic constitution; Jean Jacques Burlamaqui
(1694–1748), who put a bewildering amalgam of individual rights, sovereign
authority, and corporate privilege into the deceptive format of a legal system;
and Christian Thomasius (1655–1728), who tried to bring rationalism and
German Pietism together in an unstable alliance of natural law and divine
right."[82]

Krieger's insights indicate that it was an age of strange contradictions and
stranger attempts to reconcile political languages that were hostile to one
another. To reject, then, the republican, populist, or whiggish tenets in *Jure
Divino* is, of course, to falsify the many-sided Defoe. But to be asked to consider Defoe's king as God's vicegerent on earth should not immediately excite
laughter.[83] To suggest a royalist strain in Defoe's political thought is to
challenge a critical hermeticism that has obscured some important discon-
tinuities in that thought that came about from his growing preoccupation with
kingship and war. That challenge gains some support when one examines the
paradigm that Defoe made his own from his readings in the Old Testament.
Defoe's *magnum opus* attempts to resolve nature and providence, the secular
and the spiritual, the holy and the profane, the biblical and the historical, the
military and the civil, and God and the people in the interests of a complete
theory of monarchy and government.

Before my reading of *Jure Divino*, I wish to focus on two constituent
elements of Defoe's political vocabulary as we have seen them developing
since the Revolution. Like "magnipotent," Defoe has made them his own.

[82] *Kings and Philosophers*, pp. 11–12. For a fascinating account of more modern political contradictions see Terge I. Leiren, "The Role of Kingship in the Monarchist – Republican
Debate in Norway, 1905," *The Historian: A Journal of History*, 48 (1986), 268–78.

[83] A paraphrase of David Hume; see *Essays* (World's Classics), p. 52, cited in C. B. Hill,
"Reason and Reasonableness in Seventeenth-Century England," *British Journal of Sociology*, 20
(1969), 237. Henry Fielding may have mocked those of his nation who proclaimed, "I am a
Jacobite upon republican principles," but the ideological eclecticism of the Tory-Jacobite is
one of the themes in Linda Colley, *In Defiance of Oligarchy: The Tory Party, 1714–60* (Cambridge:
Cambridge University Press, 1982), pp. 28, 29, 308n 10. Fielding is quoted on p. 102.

By 1706 they have become constants and have stabilized in his political imagination. They are the recurring image of Saul and Sauline monarchy as explicated in the First Book of Samuel, and the linked and ordered metonyms of the monarch: crown, sword, and scepter.

In his *Reflections* we saw Defoe validating the argument of compact and the institution of monarchy by drawing on the narrative of Samuel and Saul. In Defoe's first use of the myth, God complied with the people and set a king over them. "*That the Kings of Israel and Judah did owe their crowns at the first to the Peoples Importunity*, is, I think, so evident, by what I have already cited out of *Samuel*, that I shall suppose it needless to repeat it here; for although God did comply with the Peoples Request, yet we cannot say he approved it, but barely permitted it." Defoe is unambiguous in his first reading of the biblical story; " 'tis from the People that [kings] immediately receive their Power." The Samuel – Saul narrative illustrates the origin of monarchy, from which we learn that "Kings must be contented to owe their Power as well as Birth to be of humane extraction." But, with a disclaimer that will be more pronounced as events overtake William's monarchy, Defoe concludes that "although I there deny its first Institution to be by God's immediate Appointment and Direction; yet I would not be understood so, as if I meant to exclude God from having any thing to do in the setting up or making of Kings."[84] In the standing army debate Defoe read the Saul narrative as justification for the executive's control over the armed forces of England. 1 Samuel 8–11, which whiggish writers had generally explicated as the type of kingly despotism, Defoe associated honorifically with the crown and the sword: "God himself, when the Israelites would have a King, told them this would be the Consequence; as if it might be inferr'd, as of absolute necessity, that a Military Power must be made use of with a Regal Power; and as it may follow *No King, no Army*, so it may as well follow, *no Army, no King.*"[85]

In his most important pamphlets, or at the most dramatic moments of his country's history, Defoe turned to the biblical story. Dedicating *The Original Power of the Collective Body of the People of England* to King William, Defoe proclaimed that "God himself appointed, the Prophet exclaimed, but the Peoples assent was the finishing the Royal Authority of the first King of Israel."[86] His sermon commemorating the birthday of William in 1709, as we have seen, had as its text the lament of David for the anointed king of Israel who had fallen in battle. His first tract following George I's entry into London in 1714 implored his English readers to behave "like good Subjects" to their new sovereign "whom God and the Laws have set over them, to Rule them not as a King only with Authority and Justice, but as a Father of his Country, and of his People, with Tenderness and Affection." But it was not Defoe's

---

84 Pp. 12, 54, 53.
85 *Some Reflections on a Pamphlet Lately Published*, p. 5.
86 P. Alr.

but the voice of the old King of Israel that concluded the plea for peace and reconciliation: *"And* SAUL *said,* there should not a *Man be put to Death this Day, for to Day the* LORD *hath wrought Salvation in* Israel.*"*[87] Two years later, in a dialogue with a Jacobite defending the harsh justice meted out to the leaders of the rebellion against the new king, Defoe again recast the language of the *Reflections* that he had written a quarter of a century earlier. Again citing the Old Testament, Defoe retorted that

You can't prove, nor all the *Jacobites* on Earth, that God has appointed any one particular Species of Government, as what he would have obtain universally and in every Nation: Much less has he fix'd the Right, the Manner, and Order of Succession. The Jews indeed, were put under Kingly Government, at their own foolish and sinful request (after they grew weary of the Theocracy) and against the Remonstrances of God and the Prophet. Their first King (Saul) had a divine Right, being chosen immediately by God, as well as the People; and yet this was so far from being indefeasible and hereditary, that he forfeited the Crown by his Male-administration, was rejected of God, and his Posterity depriv'd of the Succession.[88]

Yet once again the turn to language that desacralizes kingship forces Defoe to return to countering language that reaffirms the immediacy of God in the selection of kings and the holy nature of kingship. For "God chose a King for his People the *Jews*" and "*Saul* had a more divine Right" than any of the Stuart pretenders.[89]

We must not be put off by these hesitations and contradictions to overlook the essential truth, that Defoe's imagination instinctively and continually collocated his arguments of monarchy with 1 Samuel 8–11. What Defoe appears to have been captivated by is the most significant proof text of political argument in the seventeenth century, which also became an almost ubiquitous component of the language of political debate in the Glorious Revolution. Sauline kingship was as pivotal an issue in that English constitutional debate as it was for the biblical scribes and canonists of the church. But before we can fully appreciate Defoe's idiosyncratic manipulation of the biblical narrative, we must first see how Filmer, Locke, Sidney, and Leslie, republicans, Stuart apologists, and divine right controversialists, read what the Old Testament story had become, the *locus classicus* of political leadership and divine sanctions.

In the narrative of Saul's ascension to the throne of Israel the prophetic scribes grappled with the contrast between a divinely chosen king *de jure*, the vicegerent of God, and a king *de facto*, finally and of necessity chosen by the

[87] *Advice to the People of Great Britain* (London, 1714), pp. 25–26, 40.
[88] *A Dialogue Between a Whig and a Jacobite Upon the Subject of the Late Rebellion* (London, 1716), p. 8.
[89] *Ibid.*, p. 9.

community. Medieval canonists and popes noted its contradictions.[90] Its prominence in seventeenth-century political debate derives from the uses to which it was put by the author of the *Vindiciae contra tyrannos*, the influential Huguenot defense of religious freedom and of resistance to despotic kings, who attempted a reconciliation of the Old Testament's inconsistencies. The resulting ambivalence of the *Vindiciae* is characteristic of the polemics of royalists and republicans in the century. If, as the author of the *Vindiciae* admits, "we have shewed before that it is God that does appoint kings, who chooses them, who gives the kingdom to them; now we say that the people establish kings, puts the sceptre into their hands, and who with their suffrages, approves the election." Or, as he concluded, "the election of the king is attributed to God, the establishment to the people."[91] In language that was to be repeated, redefined, and finally reversed in the rush of debate in 1689, the *Vindiciae* clarified the pattern of activity in the choosing of Israel's first king: God appointed and chose kings; God chose Saul for the governor of his people; but the people established him as a monarch. Saul is established king by the suffrages of the people. By one commandment of God Saul is chosen, by a second commandment of the people Saul is elected, king.

> . . . Reges eligere. Dicimusiam, Populum Reges
> constituere, Regna tradere, electionem suo
> suffragio comprobare.
> Hic vides electionem Regis tribui Deo, constitutionem Populo . . .
> . . . ait Moses tu dices, Constituam Regem super me,
> ut caeterae gentes, quae sunt in circuitu: tum vero
> eum Rege[m] constitues, quem Dominus tuus
> elegerit e medio fratrum tuo rum . . . [92]

Political and religious developments in England, following the religious wars of the sixteenth century that produced the *Vindiciae*, turned scores of commentators to the Saul narrative. As a result, that complex tale was made to yield two simple, unequivocal, and finally antithetical messages. The explications of James I and Philip Hunton can stand for the two competing

[90] See Brian Tierney, *Religion, Law, and the Growth of Constitutional Thought, 1150–1650* (Cambridge: Cambridge University Press, 1982), pp. 34–35; also Tierney, *The Crisis of Church and State, 1050–1300* (Englewood Cliffs, NJ: Prentice-Hall, 1964), p. 155. I would like to thank Professor Tierney for bibliographical advice. See also Michael Wilks, *The Problem of Sovereignty in the Later Middle Ages: The Papal Monarchy with Augustinus Triumphus and the Publicists* (Cambridge: Cambridge University Press, 1963), p. 541n. For Aquinas, see *Summa Theologiae*, vol. 29, *The Old Law*, ed. David Bourke and Arthur Littledale (London: Eyre & Spottiswoode, 1969), pp. 269, 271.

[91] *A Defence of Liberty. A Translation of the Vindiciae Contra Tyrannos by Junius Brutus*, intro. Harold J. Laski (1924; rpt., Gloucester, MA: Peter Smith, 1963), pp. 118–19. The text is the English translation of 1689. It should be noted that Saul is never on the list of good kings; see pp. 69, 72, 84, 94, 106.

[92] *Vindiciae* (Edimburgi [Basle?], 1580), pp. 67–68. It is a long way from a Huguenot of the sixteenth century to a New Yorker of the twentieth but . . . cf. Mayor Edward Koch, who said, "I believe that everything that happens on this earth is preordained by God, and I believe that, while it was the people who elected me, it was God that selected me." Andy Logan, "Around City Hall," *The New Yorker*, 6 May 1985, p. 138.

ideologies. The former, intent upon asserting the independence, if not the superiority of the monarch in his relations with the papacy, found confirmation in the First Book of Samuel. James vehemently denied that prophets like Samuel or prelates of the church could ever depose a monarch. He refuted Cardinal Bellarmine by asserting that King Saul himself could never have been deposed by a prophet because he had never been made a "private person." Like David, Saul was a king "by Gods promise, and by precedent unction." Like Saul, then, he and the Stuart dynasty that was to follow were "a testimony of the choice of God."[93] Hunton, in his *Treatise of Monarchy*, provided the other contour of evaluation that was taken up by the polemicists of the Revolution in 1689. He conceded the divinity of the crown, yet he sought to make the consent of the people necessary to institute moral and legitimate government. Thus, while Saul was truly an anointed king, "as it were by God's own hand, . . . yet [he was] not thereby actually endowed with Kingly power, but remained as a private [man], till the peoples choice put [him] in actual possession of that power . . ." Approximating Calvin's traditionalist view that prophets and kings, like Samuel and Saul, were singled out by God "in order that the people might receive them with greater reverence," Hunton nevertheless considered the approval of the nation necessary to confirm the crown. "That unction was a manifestation of the appointment of God, and when it was made known to the people, I think it had the power of precept, to restrain the peoples choice to that person; which if they had not done, they had resisted God's ordinance. Yet they were not thereby actually endowed with Kingly power, but remained as private Men, till the peoples choice put them in actual possession of that power. . ."[94]

That diverse English writers felt it necessary to confront, refute, or reaffirm the radical reading of the *Vindiciae* is disclosed to us when we examine the arguments of Filmer, Locke, and Algernon Sidney. *Patriarcha* anticipates the language of royalists who were hostile to William's claim to the throne on a foundation of parliament's settlement. In it Filmer went beyond the refinement of language that we have noticed in the *Vindiciae*:

But it is vain to argue against the liberty of the people in the election of Kings as long as men are persuaded that examples are to be found of it in Scripture. It is fit, therefore, to discover the grounds of this error. It is plain by an evident text that it is one thing to choose a King, and another thing to set a King over the people. This latter power the children of Israel had, but not the former. This distinction is found most evident in Deuteronomy xvii. 15, where the law of God saith: 'Him shalt thou

93 *The Political Works of James I*, ed. Charles H. McIlwain (Cambridge, MA: Harvard University Press, 1918), pp. 213, 214.
94 London, 1689, pp. 19, 20. I quote from the Smith-Taylor edition. The book was first published in 1643. For the response of a royalist see Michael Hudson, *The Divine Right of Government Natural and Politique* (London, 1647), pp. 108–11.

set King over thee whom the Lord shall choose.' So God must *eligere*, and the people only do *constituere*.[95]

Locke, whose *First Treatise* was written to detect and overthrow the false principles of Filmer's doctrine of monarchy by inheritance, whether it be from Adam or the first "Lawful Ruler," was willing to concede that God gave "*Rule* and *Dominion*" to Saul, "who received his Crown from the immediate Appointment of God. . ." But his concession held little danger, "for the same Authority, that made the first a Lawful *Ruler*, must make the Second too, and so give Right of Succession." Thus Locke can readily accept Saul's "immediate Appointment" because subsequent events – the exclusion of Jonathan and the succession of Solomon – destroy any argument for primogeniture or indefeasible hereditary right derived from God's word in the First Book of Samuel.[96] Considering the same texts as Filmer and Locke, Sidney concluded that "God never Instituted any such Kings as had their commission only from him; for even those very Kings which he himself Named, as *Saul*, etc. were made Kings, and set up by the People under certain conditions . . . It is yet clearer, that the People Created *Saul* King, from *I Sam*. 11. 15. *And all the People went to* Gilgal, *and* there they made *Saul* King before the *Lord* in Gilgal."[97]

In addition to these explications by engaged political propagandists, the pamphleteers of 1689 were markedly influenced in their reading of the First Book of Samuel by the commentaries and annotations of the English clergy. These explications were determined by the winds of prevailing orthodoxies and the tenor of the political moment. The English Bible of 1560, "a manifesto of the Calvinists," translated at Geneva by English reformers who had found asylum there, echoes the commentaries of Calvin, for whom Saul had been singled out by God as prophet and holy warrior. These radicals in exile did not equivocate about their providential liberator, their godly prince. In their text, the Holy Ghost anoints, God appoints. It is God who "gave [Saul] such vertues as were mete for a King, God who gave him the spirit of strength & courage. . ." Theirs is a passive universe in which only God acts; thus through Saul's battle victories, "the Lord wone the hearts of the People" to Saul," who then became Israel's king "annointed by the comandment of the Lord."[98] More than a century later, Rev. Matthew

---

[95] *Patriarcha and Other Political Works*, ed. Peter Laslett (Oxford: Basil Blackwell, 1949), p. 83. Cf. Richard Hooker, *Of the Laws of Ecclesiastical Polity, Books VI, VII, VIII*, ed. P. G. Stanwood (Cambridge, MA: Harvard University Press, 1981), p. 337 (Book VIII, chap. 3.2). The Deuteronomic text is the proleptic citation used by all who commented on 1 Samuel.

[96] *Two Treatises*, ed. Laslett, I, 95, 94 (p. 229). For Locke's earlier view see *Two Tracts on Government*, ed. Philip Abrams (Cambridge: Cambridge University Press, 1967), p. 231. Cf. his *Essays on the Law of Nature*, ed. W. von Leyden (Oxford: Clarendon Press, 1954), p. 26.

[97] *Sidney Redivivus: Or the Opinion of the Late Honourable Collonel Sidney, As to Civil Government* (London, 1689), p. 11. Cf. his *Discourses Concerning Government* (London, 1763), p. 85.

[98] The English Bible (1560), p. 125. For further commentary on the 1560 Bible, see A. S. Herbert, *Historical Catalogue of Printed Editions of the English Bible, 1525–1961* (London: British & Foreign Bible Society, 1968), p. 61.

Poole's influential *Annotations* endorsed the language of the Anglican reformers. His exegesis of the First Book of Samuel, published at the height of the Stuart repression, could serve as a handbook for Stuart royalism, passive obedience, and the divinity of kings.[99]

At the other extreme, commentators who published during the Commonwealth and Protectorate stressed the elective nature of Saul's monarchy. Though he was accepted as the anointed prophet of God, popular ratification, a public ceremony, was necessary, during which he was installed by the people and invested into the kingdom. In these texts, ecclesiology and divinity are complemented by essential human activities empirically recognized, responded to, and rewarded by the political community. The people proceed to "the election of [Saul]," yet "his election is nevertheless not yet independent of the spirit that God has settled upon him, for he was called thereunto by Gods immediate and free choyce." The constitution drawn up by Samuel reveals "as it ought to be in a lawful and free monarchy, appointed by God himself, according to the fundamental laws of the kingdom." Deuteronomy and 1 Samuel once again prove that Saul was an "elected king, yet he was not crowned, nor received generally by all the people as their Soveraign . . . And this was no disparagement to his royal dignity, seeing it hath been the practice of many great Potentates, as divers of the Consuls, Dictators, and Emperors of Rome, yea of David himself. . ." Saul's public election follows his receipt, "not [of] the Spirit of regeneration and sanctification, but of fortitude and princely prudence . . . an heroical spirit of courage and strength, fit for a king and Captain, moving him to go out as General of the Lords people to fight against this cruel tyrant, for propounding such dishonorable and insolent conditions." At Gilgal, then, "they anoynted him King publiquely, as Samuel had before done privately; Whereof it is, that Samuel afterward giveth unto him the title of the Lords anoynted . . . For though he was elected before; yet they now meet again to confirm him in his Kingdome, and to prevent all future rebellion, by giving their universall consent. . ."[100]

Such is the resonance of discourse that followed from the seventeenth-century's confrontation with the challenge of the First Book of Samuel and the narrative of Saul. It now remains to examine the languages of Whig and Tory as they construed the tale to suit their ideological needs in the changed context of 1689. Then we shall be in a position to evaluate Defoe's redaction of Sauline monarchy in *Jure Divino*.

Inside the Convention, in the first month of 1689, some Englishmen turned to the Saul narrative to solve the crisis of military leadership that had

---

[99] *A Commentary on the Holy Bible*, 2 vols. (London: Banner of Truth Trust, 1962), I, 531–39; also I, 370, 816, 883. The work was originally published as *Annotations on the Holy Bible*, vol. I (London, 1683), vol. II (London, 1685).

[100] John Downame, *Annotations Upon All the Books of the Old and New Testament: This Second Edition So Englarged, As They Make an Entire Commentary on the Sacred Scripture* (London, 1651), 1 Samuel 10.17, 19, 25; 11.3–14. Cf. *Mercurius Politicus* no. 98 (15–22 April 1652).

overtaken the nation with the flight of King James. The confused Williamite Whig, Hugh Boscawen, speaking against a regency or the placement of Princess Mary *sole* on the throne, observed: "I think we have a great deal of reason to declare the Throne is void. I'm sure France has long entangled us, & is now like to make open war against us, & wee have reason to make use of our best weapon, to chuse a King to go before us & to fight our battells, (which was the first occasion of Kingly government) & that a Woman cannot so well do."[101] Some minutes before, Sir Robert Sawyer, fighting the populist drift of Convention debate, phrased Tory political theory with those distinctions that we have read in Filmer and other royalist polemicists: "The People cannot decide, they may indeed Declare who is King."[102]

But it is without the doors of the 1689 Convention that we hear more clearly the uses to which the narrative of Saul was put. If, as William III declared, Boscawen was a "blockhead," and unable to think for himself, he might have picked up his tag from 1 Samuel 8.20 from a publication of the moment. The writer of *Four Questions Debated*, which was in print before the debates in the Convention, had already noted that "a Princess not so able to make War, the great end of Israels choosing a King was to fight their Battles, which a Woman can't do."[103] In January also, *Some Short Considerations relating to the Settling of the Government, humbly offered to the Lords and Commons of England now assembled at Westminster*, was published. Its first proposition offered the commonplace that "All power is from God, as the foundation and original." It continued:

2.   The designation of the persons, and the form of government, is either, first, immediately from God, as in the case of Saul and David, and the government of the Jews; or, secondly, from the community chusing some form of government, and subjecting themselves to it. But it must be noted, that though Saul and David had a divine designation, yet the people assembled, and in a general assembly, by their votes, freely chose them; which proves that there can be no orderly or lasting government without consent of the people tacit or expressed; and God himself would not put men under a governor without their consent.[104]

In many other tracts of that remarkable year Saul figures prominently and the same distinctions occur. One writer, tracing the evolution of society from patriarchy to Nimrodian tyranny to compact, concluded: "Thus all Governments in the same degrees that they differ from Patriarchal and Tyrannical must derive their Originals from Compact, and the Governour must necessarily derive his Power from and by, the mutual Consent of the People he governs; unless God does himself immediately appoint a Magistrate,

---

[101] Lois Schwoerer, " 'A Jornal of the Convention at Westminster begun the 22 of January 1688/9'," *Bulletin of the Institute of Historical Research* 49 (1976), 255.

[102] Schwoerer, " 'A Jornal', " p. 254.

[103] P. 5. The sentence was reprinted in *Some Remarks Upon Government, and particularly upon the Establishment of the English Monarchy, relating to this Present Juncture* (London, 1689), p. 7. For Boscawen as "blockhead" see the *Dictionary of National Biography*.

[104] In *Somers Tracts*, X, 274. Note again the rhetoric of Hooker.

and even then the People have usually confirm'd as in the case of Saul [.]
I *Sam.* 10.11.''[105] William Denton's *Jus Regiminis*, unable to find a printer in
the repressive years of James's reign, was published in June 1689. For Denton, "Saul was not *King* so absolutely and so immediately from *God*, that it
excluded all Election of the People, but was afterwards chosen by Lot *by all
the People at Mizpeh.* And all the People shouted, and said *God Save the
King.*''[106] Allegiance pamphleteers like Samuel Masters and Thomas
Long, moderate Whig and moderate Tory respectively, continued the
delicate balance. For the former, Saul, though he was an absolute monarch,
was elected by the people; for the latter – modifying somewhat his divine
right language of 1685 and now rejecting Filmer's patriarchal absolutism –
"it is not the People that confer this power but God . . . The People are only
a *Medium* of conveying This power of the Magistrate to a particular person.
God is the Author of the Magistrates Power. . .''[107] In the late spring of
1689 a knowledgeable pamphleteer of the day responded to a private letter
that sought to defend *jure divino* kingship and passive obedience. The first of
the thirty-four propositions that make up the ideological baggage of his fervent Tory antagonist is the following: "By the Word of God it appears, That
Monarchy is the Government which God hath chosen above all others, and
that the People were always obliged to accept that form of Government which
God had chosen for them, before they did actually bind themselves." The
substantiating chapter and verse is 1 Samuel 10.24: "See him, said Samuel
to all the People, whom the Lord (not you) hath chosen.''[108]

Election and contract language defending the Revolution became more
pronounced in the wake of William's parliamentary elevation to the throne.
As a result, conservative Anglicans resorted to the narrative of Saul and the
Old Testament text to rationalize their allegiance to the new regime, for from
it they were able to justify William's right to rule from the arguments of Providence and conquest. The sermon of William Lloyd, Bishop of Asaph,
preached before the King and Queen on 5 November 1690 reveals the pattern
of that rhetoric. A zealous defender of the king, Lloyd resorted to the most
orthodox authorities to validate William's title as "Restorer and Deliverer"
of the nation. He claimed in his introduction to the sermon that "it will appear
that I have deliver'd no other Doctrine then that which has been receiv'd and
past for current in the Church of England, ever since the Reformation." But
whatever erudition is anticipated is displaced by voluminous evidence from
the Scripture of God's divine activity in the ordering of societies and governments. Disruptions in the hereditary transmission of a crown, the cessation

---

[105] *Some Remarks Upon Government*, p. 8.
[106] Pp. 21–22.
[107] Masters, *The Case of Allegiance Considered*, p. 25; Long, *A Resolution of Certain Queries*, p. 4.
[108] *The Letter Which Was Sent to the Author of the Doctrine of Passive Obedience and Jure Divino disprov'd,
etc. answered and refuted*, p. 2. For the importance of this pamphlet see Ashcraft and Goldsmith,
"Locke, Revolution Principles, and the Formation of Whig Ideology," pp. 790–800.

of familial lines through sudden deaths, just wars that make for just conquests – all are determined by God. Thus in the beginning it was God who chose Saul. Lloyd observed that "God was pleas'd so far to grant his Peoples Request, that they should be an Hereditary Kingdom: But for the first King of the reigning Line, God would have the chusing of him himself. And accordingly, first he chose Saul, whose Kingdom should have been Hereditary, if he had not hindred it by his Disobedience to God." In elevating his chosen immediately to the throne, God does not distinguish between a Nimrod or a Saul, for "those Persons Title to the Government was either Patriarchal, or by Divine Nomination: Both which ways of coming into Power were so wholly of God, that the People had nothing to do, but to accept the Choice of God, and to submit to it."[109]

Orthodoxy continued to insist upon Saul's divine kingship, to view him as one who had been raised to the throne by God's immediate and wonderful Providence. But factors were already in motion that were to force Whig and Tory to rediagnose the legend of King Saul. The argument from conquest, as we have noted, was proscribed in 1693. Moderate Tories became estranged from William's camp following the death of Queen Mary in 1694. "The cult of divine right monarchy" was significantly renewed in the fast-day sermons on the anniversary of Charles I's martyrdom.[110] The succession debates of 1701 and Anne Stuart's accession to the throne emboldened the traditionalist Tory-Jacobite defenders of a Stuart restoration legitimated by Old Testament principle and practice. As a result, Whig ideologues decided to give King Saul over to their enemies while they returned to the theme of Saul's apostasy from God and the wishes of his people as a justification for resistance. In addition, they claimed that kings like him were instituted by God as punishment for the nation's sins. Their denunciations echoed the judgment that James Harrington had pronounced a half-century earlier, that Saul, like Nimrod, "had broken the balance and brought in a reign impotent and perverse."[111] Following the discovery in 1696 of the assassination plot against the king, one patriotic Whig remembered Saul as a jealous tyrant and unsuccessful "killer of Israel's great king."[112] In 1699 Richard Kingston, one of the most vociferous voices for the king, admitted that "*Saul* was an Anointed *King*, and yet *David* had commission from God Almighty to make War against him when he transgressed the bounds that God had set

---

[109] *A Discourse of God's Ways of Disposing of Kingdoms. Part I* (London, 1691), pp. 67, 10.

[110] See Kenyon, *Revolution Principles*, pp. 61–82.

[111] *The Political Works of James Harrington*, ed. J. G. A. Pocock (Cambridge: Cambridge University Press, 1977), pp. 642 and 81.

[112] *A Poem Occasioned by the Happy Discovery of the Horrid and Blasphemous Conspiracy to Assassinate his Most Sacred Majesty and to Incourage an Invasion from France*, p. 2. Cf. the verse attack on Danby (1690), cited in Mark Goldie, "The Roots of True Whiggism, 1688–94," *History of Political Thought*, I (1980), 222n. Also *The Golden Speech of Queen Elizabeth to her Last Parliament November 30, Anno Domini, 1601. With Observations Adapted to these Times*, p. 9.

him.''[113] By the time of Defoe's *Jure Divino* the fine-tuned Whig position concerning the Saul narrative can be most clearly seen in two publications. The
first is *An Antidote against Rebellion . . . To which is added A Letter to the Nonjuring
Party* (1704). The second is Benjamin Hoadly's establishment sermon preached
at the Assizes at Hertford on 22 March 1708. For both, Israel's demand
for a king and Saul's accession is a scourge from God. The glorious Whig
value of resistance was denied under Saul, for the subject was obliged to obey.
''1. *Because it was their own evil Inclination and Desire to be govern'd by Kings, rather
than by God.* 2. Because then Kings were Persons appointed, anointed, and
directed by God.''[114] Hoadly's Whig sermon took as its scriptural text
1 Samuel 8.9: ''*Now therefore, hearken unto their Voice: Howbeit, yet protest solemnly
unto them, and shew them the manner of the King that shall reign over them.*''
Elucidating the text, Hoadly's Saul comes as ''an absolute Monarch Governing by his single Will, without the restraint of any Coordinate Legislative
Powers.'' For Hoadly, as for his predecessor, the occasion was ''sad and
lamentable.'' God's ''Original and immediate Appointment . . . may be all
summ'd up in one Comprehensive Word, and that is Slavery.'' But Saul,
slavery, non-resistance and Tory-Jacobite notions of hereditary right have a
bearing no longer for ''certainly Mankind in this Age are no more oblig'd to
submit to the same Laws of Non-Resistance, than to the same Form of
Government.'' Saul and the kings of Israel ''were oblig'd by no other Laws
but the Laws of God; but 'tis not so now; they receive their Kingdoms upon
Conditions from the Hands of the People now, and they did not then.''[115]

Thus, the Whigs had finally jettisoned God and Saul and conquest by the
sword from their political vocabulary. But throughout William's reign, those
who continued to hold that kings received their crowns from God retained and
reaffirmed that belief through more dogmatic and unequivocal readings of the
First Book of Samuel. Theirs was the descending conception of society and
government defined by Walter Ullmann. In it, ''governmental authority and
law-creating competency descend from one supreme organ: power is
distributed 'downwards' . . . This one supreme organ, in whom all power is
located and who hands it 'downwards', is God Himself who has appointed a
vice-gerent on earth: in actual fact it is the vice-gerent who possesses the sum
total of power, having himself derived it from God.''[116] Vicegerents, kings
like these, enjoyed absolute political power and thus the freedom to impose
any law they liked upon the community. Such was the ideology of the

---

[113] *Tyranny Detected; And the Late Revolution Justify'd, By the Laws of God, the Law of Nature, and the
Practice of all Nations*, p. 76. Elegies on William's death, equating him with David, generally
depicted Saul as his tyrant-adversary; see, e.g., Deuel Pead, *Greatness and Goodness Reprieve Not
From Death. A Sermon Occasion'd by the Death of that Glorious Monarch, William the Third* (London,
1702), p. 5.

[114] *An Antidote*, pp. 40–41.

[115] *The Happiness of the Present Establishment, and the Unhappiness of Absolute Monarchy* (London,
1708), pp. 3, 4.

[116] *Principles of Government and Politics in the Middle Ages* (London: Methuen, 1961), pp. 20–21.

extreme royalists throughout the seventeenth century, substantiated by their reading of the First Book of Samuel. That voice in 1689 proclaimed that "Monarchy is the Government which God hath chosen above all others." In 1699 there was republished an exhaustive and detailed condemnation of the republican and democratic writings that had appeared in print as a result of the Exclusion controversy. Saul was represented as an absolute monarch forewarned and anointed by the prophet of God. The writer informed his readers of *"Samuel's* frightful Description of an Arbitrary Prince, . . . yet even *this* after he was by the same Prophet anointed, and endowed with all that formidable Power, he so fearfully represented, we don't find even *him* [Saul] reproach'd for a Tyrant, or upbraided for violating the *Laws*, or any breach of Trust."[117] In 1701 an anonymous writer, responding to Defoe's request of parliament that it re-examine the Earl of Dalkeith's claim to the English throne, first found it was necessary to correct Defoe's mistaken inference that the people "originally" had the power of declaring kings. "Since Saul, who was the first of Kings, was Representatively Chosen by the People of *Israel*, in the Person of *Samuel* who was their Judge and Ruler before him. It must be confess'd that they were earnest for a King, but they never Murmur'd against God's Providence for the Son of Kish. Any individual amongst the twelve Tribes had pleas'd 'em under that Denomination, and as soon as *Samuel* told 'em God had nam'd *Saul* to sit upon the Throne of *Israel*; they receiv'd him without demanding a Poll; or insisting upon one of their own Choice. Which is an Evidence, that Kings were not originally chosen by the Collective body of the People, but were instituted and ordained by God, th[r]o' the intermediate Assistance of his Holy Prophet."[118]

As we would expect, the most strident promulgator of the Tory-High Church doctrine that Saul was a king by divine appointment who had received his crown from God without the consent or approbation of the people was Charles Leslie. Following the Revolution Leslie had begun to attack the new fashioners in morality, ethics, and religion who were undermining God's holy word as it was found fixed and final in the Old Testament. Sherlock, Quakers, Whig divines, and anti-sacramentalists felt his scorn and wit, though he was not "so preoccupied with the quaker as to neglect the deist and the Jew," as his biographer dryly observed.[119] But in 1704, with the accession of Anne, the High Church revival, and the consequential re-emergence of resolute arguments for indefeasible hereditary right, Leslie turned his ebullience and intellectual energies to a new enemy. These were "Modern Whigs and Fanatics [who are prepared] to undermine and blow-up the present Church

---

117 *Remarks Upon the Most Eminent of our Antimonarchical Authors and Their Writings* (London, 1699), p. 522.

118 *Animadversions on the Succession to the Crown of England Consider'd. Publish'd by Captain D—by* (London, 1701), p. 9.

119 Dictionary of National Biography. See Daly, *Sir Robert Filmer and English Political Thought*, pp. 133–39.

and Government.''[120] Like his Stuart counterparts, Leslie attacked those
''Republican Schemes'' of government that asserted that power was originally
in the people. And like them he turned to the First Book of Samuel to prove that
all power is anchored in divinity and that kings are vicegerents of God. Dismiss-
ing all whiggish and republican arguments for contract and consent, he concluded that ''here is no Foundation for the *Election* of the *People*, but the Direct
Contrary. *Saul* first Chosen by *God*, Then *Reveal'd* to Samuel, and by him
Anointed. Thus shew'd to the *People* by him . . . [Thus] it was by Gods express
ordering, without any *Election* of the *People*, as to the *Person*.''[121]

The *Tragedy of King Saul*, a whiggish play that was denied production by
''persons that have the Government of the Stage,'' was published in 1703. It
clearly reveals the mutually exclusive categories by which royalists and constitutionalists, Tories and Whigs, Stuart proponents of passive resistance and
whiggish justifiers of rebellion, even regicide, responded to the Saul story.
From the Prologue, spoken by Jonathan, to the death of Saul, Saul's tyrant
passion and his unregulated hatred for David inform the action. Surrounded
by evil subordinates, jealous of the Deliverer of Israel, cruel and despotic as
a father, murdering temple priests, Saul is little more than a monstrous God-
appointed king who should have been anathema to even the most immoderate
Tories of the time. Yet the tenor of the action is contradicted by what appears
to be the contemporary introduction of the preface writer. Saul is one for
whom sympathy is invoked, for we see a prince ''struggling with Misfortunes
at the same time as He is under a Perfect Resignation to the Will of Him that
sent 'em;'' and this dogmatic admirer of kings concludes to stress the just
punishment of the Amalekite, ''for lifting up his Hand against the Lord's
Anointed,'' and to castigate the ''Calves Head Assemblies, [that] keep Feasts
for that Royal Blood the Nation can never do enough Penance for.''[122]

That Defoe was infatuated with the warlike endeavors of the biblical Saul
is beyond dispute. That he knew of the contrasting and mutually exclusive
interpretations of the First Book of Samuel that prevailed in his time is also
beyond dispute, given his understanding, production, and domination of the
literature of political debate in Anne's reign.[123] That he had read Leslie
closely is evidenced by his pamphlet war with one of the ablest of controversialists for the Tory-Jacobite position, which he began almost immediately
upon his release from the pillory.[124] Leslie's Saul was one to whom God had

---

[120] *Cassandra (But I Hope Not)* (London, 1704), p. 4.
[121] *Cassandra*, p. 5.
[122] London, 1703, pp. A3–A3r. The Folger Library attributes the play to either Roger Boyle
(d. 1679) or Joseph Trapp (1679–1747). If the former, the play becomes a remarkable contribution to the Exclusion Controversy. But in either case it still serves my critical test. I would
like to thank Vincent Carretta for making it available to me.
[123] See *POAS*, VI, xxxi–xxxii; VII, xxxv–xxxvi.
[124] See *The Dissenters Answer to the High-Church Challenge* (London, 1704); and under ''Leslie'' and
''Rehearsal'' in William C. Payne, *Index to Defoe's Review* (New York: Columbia University
Press, 1948).

given "the *Spirit of Government* that he might be capable of that great office," but one who, like David and Solomon, was a "*King by Divine Appointment, without the Consent and Approbation of the* People."[125] He it was whom God alone had invested with the regal majesty and authority. By the time Defoe was writing *Jure Divino* Saul had been appropriated by absolutists of monarchy; thus, he was tainted as the paradigm in Defoe's myth of the evolution of society and the origins of kingship. Yet in Saul Defoe had discovered the model king in whom was delineated his William III. Consequently it was necessary for Defoe to reconstruct the Sauline monarchy for his own ideological purposes. In *Jure Divino*, his political imagination is once again at work, bridging two worlds, with one span resting in the First Book of Samuel and the other in the constitutional reforms of the late seventeenth century.

---

[125] Luke Milbourne, *The People Not the Original of Civil Power* (London, 1707), p. 6; *High-Church Politics: Or the Abuse of the 30th of January Consider'd* (London, 1710), p. 7.

5

Jure Divino

Perhaps it has been the obviousness of the satire in *Jure Divino* of those who believe in the divine right of hereditary succession that has denied it serious consideration. Perhaps the clarity of Defoe's prose notes has turned many to dismiss the "unreadable" poetry. After all, Defoe unequivocally stated that "[n]othing in this Book is design'd, or can be construed to Decry or Expose Monarchy, or the Sovereignty of Government by Kings; but to prove that they have no Powers immediately Deputed from Heaven superiour and unsubjected to the Good of those they govern; and that when they assume such a Right, they become Tyrants, Invaders of Right, and may be Deposed by the People they Govern" (II, 2). Nevertheless, despite its momentarily digressive populist and "Lockean" overtones, it is in *Jure Divino* that Defoe's scriptural and martial imagination disposed to the Book and the Sword orders his myth of the origins of government and kings.

Before he illuminated the pattern of right monarchy from scriptural foundations in Book II of *Jure Divino*, Defoe explored in Book I the creation and the development of tyranny, to rehearse "The Crimes of Men, and Crimes of *Gods*" (I, 1). Invoking his muse of Satyr, Defoe shapes a negative, critical, and castigating record of man, politics, and government. Satyr's purpose is to "Trace the first Tyrants to their fancy'd Thrones" (I, 6). Defoe's euhemeristic enumeration of the gods and goddesses of the classical pantheon begins with Nimrod, "call'd in Scripture a *mighty Hunter*, [who] was the first Man that Usurp'd Superiority of Power, and form'd Men into Governments, under his absolute Rule; all Histories agree him to be a Tyrant, and to Erect this Government against, and in opposition to the Divine Power" (I, 3; also 5). Opening with Nimrod, this "paragon" of the tyrant, Defoe can look forward and back, in space and time, to all continents and nations, and catalog western man's history. The 800-odd lines of Book I reveal a civilization that has gone berserk. Individuals lost to lust and pride have been established on national thrones and have brought on universal holocausts and world conflagrations. In his roll call of the deities from Homer, Virgil, and Horace, Defoe not only impugns a whole classical culture but indicts those poets who have made heroes of monsters who have caused the blood of millions to flow.

Fueled by a Hobbesian vision of natural man, Defoe construes the human personality driven by a will to power and domination; man "aims at general Tyranny" (Intro., iii). In a proleptic note, Defoe defines it as base tyranny of the sword, devoid of the crown and the scepter (I, 2). The former, Defoe will explain later, is God's metonymic free gift affirming the king, the latter the iconic affirmation of the free allegiance of the people. Absent the crown of God and absent the scepter of the people, the model tyrant is one who can "Hew his Crown out, by his Lawless Sword" (I, 4). Crowned monsters, base power, and tyrannies are the substance of the political hell that is the theme of Book I.

Given the perversities of evil monarchy, corrupt power, and despotic succession with which he had begun Book I, Defoe was now obligated to account for the origins of government that would be right by nature and right in the eyes of God. The monarch must be made divine, legitimate. Since Book I has begun in *media res*, Defoe in Book II moves backward in time to sketch embryonic monarchy in the patriarchal beginnings of the world superintended by Adam, "The first Majestick Father of Mankind" (II, 2). Defoe's theme echoes the commonplace of the Golden Age but it is rendered, not in the bucolic pastoral strains that he despised, but in the triad of substantives that had already become his trademark:

> No Sword was drawn to make his Power be known,
> *Age* was his *Scepter*, and *Grey Hairs* his *Crown*.   (II, 7; also VII, 11)

But a patriarchal society only functioned well when "Men [were] untainted, and their Number few" (II, 4). Moral degeneration and a population explosion led to the disruption of the political innocence of that earthly paradise. A "sham-Power," a "Tyrannic Power," function as apposites for the conquest that shook the patriarchal crown, "And *Right by Power*, pull'd *Right by Nature* down" (II, 7). In Defoe's evolutionary myth of societal development, even in its most tyrannical manifestations, conquest becomes the occasion for man's progress beyond the primitive, almost static condition of patriarchal innocence.

Patriarchal power was divine whereas political power carried both a psychological and a cosmic malaise. And if such power was tainted, and if it was synonymous with conquest, the handmark of tyranny, as is clear from Book I, so too is the wielder of power, the war leader, the conquering captain of scriptural myth. How does one reconcile the battlefield king who yet, in the wake of war, is responsible for progress and civilization, as Defoe argued in his *Essay Upon Projects* a decade earlier? It is this paradox of power that invites Defoe's most careful elaboration, and his grappling with it is evidenced by the lengthy rationalization that is central to Book II:

> Thus *Power by Conquest* was at first begun,
> And by Oppression has been handed down;

> The Crown at first upon the Sword depends,
> And what the Sword *set up*, the Sword *Defends*;
> Nor does it sink the Value of the Crown,
> Only it pulls *the Mask of Sacred* Down:
> For Conquest is a Title Heaven permits,
> And few Crown'd Heads can boast of better Rights.
>
> But this does personal Sanction all confound,
> Where Conquest Reigns *Divinity's a-ground*:
> *Title* and *Right'*s an empty formal Word;
> And all the *Jus Divinum'*s in the Sword;
> The Crown's a *Hieroglyphick* to the Steel,
> Subjects may *think of This*, but *That they Feel*:
> 'Tis Force supports the High Tyrannick Jest,
> And Men Obey, *because they can't Resist*:
> So Heaven it self, as Learned Men have said,
> Wou'd have no Subject, *if the Dev'l were dead*;
> Religion may in some few things appear,
> *But all Submission is produc'd by Fear*;
> The High Pretences may perhaps be Great,
> But 'tis Subjection makes a Law compleat,
> *And Sense of Punishment preserves a State*:
> 'Tis Power alone which keeps the World in awe,
> As *'tis the Penalty supports the Law*;
> Without it, 'twou'd be but an empty Sound,
> A Cloud in which no Thunderbolt is found:
> Rule without Power's an empty senseless Word,
> *And Justice Nonsense is without the Sword.*   (II, 22)

The problem expressed in this lengthy quotation is central to Defoe's political concerns, and it would be difficult to overestimate its importance for Defoe's myth. After all, he had begun with the corruption of power; an oedipal conflict between father and son had been presented as the pattern for all endeavors, heavenly and earthly, familial and political. So far the content and theme of *Jure Divino* has been lawless swords, tainted crowns, and absent scepters. Defoe has based his dismal picture of human development on the witness of history and the effusions of obsequious poets, who had been misled by false custom and impoverished traditions. For almost two books the linkage has been Satan-tyrants-slaves. Since, of course, Satan cannot privilege what God has founded, how can Defoe move to the positive opposite, of God-kings-people? From an unideal world of slavery and despotism to a politically beneficent one of constitutional order and social harmony?

Defoe's answer once again lay in the authority of Scripture, specifically the advent of God's model king as it was choreographed in the relevant chapters of the First Book of Samuel. Rejecting the whiggish and anti-monarchical line of his moderate contemporaries, Defoe paraphrased the Jews' request for a king in a positive light. An angry but understanding God elects to hear his people's prayers for a leader fit for the special conditions of the times. The divine sanction of Defoe's narration strengthens the concept of Saul's appointment by God's will, rather than popular acclamation:

> Himself chose out the King, and plac'd him there;
> Disown'd the Pop'lar Right and fix'd the Choice
> In Providence, and not the Peoples Voice;
> From whence the Claim of Right by Regal Line,
> Made *Israel's* Kings be Kings by Right Divine.   (II, 24)

"*Thus* Saul *was King* by Heaven's immediate Hand" (II, 24). But special "Conditions" and "*Needful* steps" become necessary before the young prince can morally and perfectly attain his crown. As we have come to expect from the writer of the *Reflections*, "*the Manner of the Kingdom*" that was told to the people by the prophet and written up in a book and laid before the Lord is the equivalent of the coronation oath, the constitution, and the compact that legitimately link sovereign with subjects. But it is not enough. Neither is "*Samuel's Ointment*," nor the condition of "God's Singling him out by Lot" (II, 26, 27). No king is fully and completely a king whose valor has not been tested, who does not reveal his vitally distinctive gift for leadership in martial combat.

> *Is this the Monarch shall our Foes destroy,*
> *Does Heaven design to rule us* by a Boy?
> The floating *Rabbies* Cry, *we scorn to own,*
> *A Man that* has not Merit *for a Crown,*
> *Give us a better King, or give us None.*
> *Is this the Tyrant whom you bid us Fear?*
> *Is that* young Cowardly Boy *to Govern here?*
> *Is he the Man shall* Judah's Scepter *Sway?*
> *And are we mad enough, d'ye think, t'Obey?*
> Our King *must lead the Glorious Tribes to Fight,*
> *And chase the Thousands of the* Ammonite;
> *From* Israel's *Chains* release her, *and defy,*
> *The mighty Chariots of the Enemy;*
> His personal Valour *must our Triumphs bring,*
> *'Tis such a Man we want, and such a King.*   (II, 27)

Given God's anger earlier at his people's rejection of his leadership and their scornful disdain of his prophet's warnings for the future, one could expect the Lord to be angry once more at their revealed contempt for his chosen king. But here, in a sense greater than anywhere else in Defoe's canon, *vox populi, vox Dei*. Both the Lord and his prophet acquiesce to the Israelites' request. The reason for this is that it not only is Nature's Law "that *Men should Choose* their Kings" (II, 28); but, as Defoe explains in prose, "It seem'd as if God had own'd there was some Appearance of Reason in the Peoples dislike of their new King; and therefore he was not pleased to express any

Anger at the Contempt: their rejecting *Saul*, put upon the Divine Designation, as it were owning that a King ought to have Personal Merit to recommend him; and therefore directs his Providence to work upon the Peoples Judgments, and even by a Miracle gives *Saul* that Merit which he knew would obtain upon the People's good liking'' (II, 28). Since God's ''Miracle,'' Saul's ''Merit,'' and the People's ''good liking'' have conjoined earlier in *Jure Divino* and will continue throughout Defoe's developing myth in the figures of the crown, sword, and scepter, Defoe might have found it superfluous at this moment in the narrative to make explicit the triad of heaven-ordained kingship that connects ''the things above, and things below'' (II, 29). But all fuse on the field of war with the attack of the Ammonites. And the God who speaks here in response to his people's request for a ''praying and fighting monarch'' is one who supports Defoe's imprimatur on all of his Protestant heroes who have chosen to wear the crown of right rule:

> *I'll Spirit* Saul, *and Arm his Soul for War,*
> *The* Boy *they scorn, shall in the Field appear;*
> *I'll teach the unexperienc'd Youth to fight,*
> *And flesh him with the slaughter'd* Ammonite:
> *The General Suffrage then he'll justly have,*
> *To Rule the People, he knows how to save;*
> *Their Willing Voices all the Tribes will bring,*
> *And make my Chosen Heroe be their King.*   (II, 29)

Thus, to a Saul of whom thricely ''God had arm'd his Soul for War,''

> The willing Tribes their purchas'd Suffrage bring,
> And Universal Voice *Proclaims him King*;
> As if *Heaven's Call* had been *before in vain,*
> Saul from this proper Minute *Dates his Reign.*   (II, 30)

I have already noted Walter Ullmann's ''descending'' conception of government, according to which one was king *dei gratia*. Opposed to this was the ''ascending conception of government and law according to which law-creating power may be ascribed to the community or the *populus* . . . which makes law through the appropriate machinery: power is concentrated in the people itself, so that one can speak of law and governmental power rising or ascending.'' The king or other organs of government remain responsible to the people because the people have been the repositories and the dispensers of political power. And Ullmann realized that ''the one is the reverse of the other,'' that, in fact, they were ''so much opposed that they were exclusive of each other.''[1]

Yet even in Defoe's time there were political imaginations that saw clearly

---

[1] *Principles of Government and Politics in the Middle Ages*, p. 20.

that opposition and contradiction. Throughout Queen Anne's reign Charles Leslie's had been the most insistent voice criticizing Locke and the natural rights of the people. Not only must there be a king in actual possession before any consent of the people can be given, Leslie affirmed, but the king to whom that consent is given, be he Adam or Saul, has been the choice of God. In 1711 Leslie summed up the disagreement that had been raging between himself and Rev. Hoadly, the outspoken proponent of Lockean principles:

> I think it most natural that *Authority* shou'd *Descend*, that is, be *Derived* from a *Superiour* to an *Inferiour*, from *God* to *Fathers* and *Kings*, and from *Kings* and *Fathers* to *Sons* and *Servants*: But Mr. *Hoadly* wou'd have it *Ascend*, from *Sons* to *Fathers*, and from *Subjects* to *Sovereigns*: nay to *God* Himself, whose *Kingship* the Men of the Rights *say*, is *Derived* to *Him* from the *People!*[2]

Once again the divine right theorists and the natural law–natural rights theorists of the period had resolved their problems by embracing rigid and irreconcilable ideological extremes. In this era of "one-track minds," we should come to admire Daniel Defoe's attempt to maintain the activity and integrity of God and men in the origin of political authority and the determination of the king.[3] In his retelling of the legend of Saul and Samuel, Defoe resolved his age's most extreme political contradictions. Anachronistically, his people elect whom God has selected. In his text we remain with the paradox that the people make a king a king.

Throughout the cosmic and earthly episodes of *Jure Divino*, Defoe's consideration has been political power, the instinctive, unjust, unregulated drive in divinities and men for domination channelled into political energy. He was aware, as the *Essay Upon Projects* and his biographies of war leaders indicate, of the enormous power of the state and the unprecedented havoc and destruction that could be wrought as a result of the improvements in the art of war and the tactical and strategic possibilities available to the new warrior-king.[4] His theme is the control of that power. Thus might is rule, but it does not give the right to rule, nor right rule. Natural power is not moral power. But while the power of the sword alone is no heavenly hieroglyph, it is an indispensable ensign of royalty. Justice, *"Nonsense is without the Sword,"* he made insistently clear in *Jure Divino* (II, 22). Denied the imprint of the divine, it yet can both create and support earthly kingship. Defoe's

---

[2] *The Finishing Stroke. Being a Vindication of the Patriarchial Scheme of Government, In Defense of the Rehearsals, Best Answer, and Best of All* (London, 1711), p. 87.

[3] See L. C. Knights, *Public Voices: Literature and Politics with Special Reference to the Seventeenth Century* (Totowa, NJ: Rowman and Littlefield, 1972), pp. 11–29.

[4] See Theodore K. Rabb, *The Struggle for Stability in Early Modern Europe* (New York: Oxford University Press, 1975); Geoffrey Parker, "The 'Military Revolution', 1560–1660 – a Myth?," *Journal of Modern History*, 48 (1976), 195–214; J. V. Polisensky, *War and Society in Europe, 1618–1648* (Cambridge: Cambridge University Press, 1978); *The Thirty Years' War*, ed. Geoffrey Parker (London: Routledge & Kegan Paul, 1984). As late as 1718, Defoe still distinguished between "the Sword of Justice" and "the Sword of Power;" see *Mercurius Politicus*, February 1718, p. 99.

kingly ideal is the sword in the hands of a providential monarch; his crown, immediately derived from God, is a symbol of more than supreme earthly dignity; and his scepter is the gift of a free and compliant people. In his distinctive constitutive vocabulary, the monarch is given his authority by God, assumes that authority by virtue of the sword, and morally exercises that authority by his management of the scepter. God is the moving cause of the king's authority; the sword is the necessary but not sufficient cause; and the people are the final cause.[5] Like Samuel Rutherford and others, Defoe believed that "mere conquest by the sword, without the consent of the people, is not a just title to the crown."[6] But his writings reveal that he simply cannot admit his monarchical ideal to be completely man-made. He too would have exclaimed, as did Tennyson's knight when he saw young Arthur's trial by combat and victory, "Sir and my liege, the fire of God / Descends upon thee in the battlefield: / I know thee for my King!"[7]

Defoe, of course, never had any doubt that moral authority was determined with the consent of the people. But his writings can be understood as a response to a politics that was intent upon degrading the king from a position of special transcendence. If, in the *Reflections Upon the Late Great Revolution*, he had tended to stress the elective nature of monarchy, or the mutuality of the ceremonial act of the coronation, in *Jure Divino* the voice of God undermines the populist emphasis of that earlier tract and challenges the extravagant tendencies of whiggish thought in his day. In *Jure Divino* the election-coronation-compact sequences seem to carry the same weight as they did sixteen years earlier, yet now consecration by the people merely confirms and ratifies an existing condition. Locke and his contemporaries, whether they were speaking generally or about the Saul narrative in particular, repeated the commonplace that "all authority is held to come from God but the nomination and appointment of the persons bearing that power is thought to be made by the people."[8] But for Defoe God was something more than a distant and impersonal "legitimating force."[9] We have remarked Defoe's king as a mediator between parties and factions, between parliament and

---

[5] The singularity and the attributive and ideological significance of Defoe's vocabulary is reinforced when it is compared to the only other pattern I have found that approximates it in the seventeenth century. Edward Gee, a Presbyterian divine hostile to the Cromwell regime, published in 1658 *The Divine Right and Originall of Civil Magistrates from God*. Attacking executive tyranny that is obtained by the sword, Gee distinguished between just and natural, moral and violent, and lawful and illegal government. It is the legislature, Gee wrote, that enforces the moral law, the law of reason, of a community. "It [the legislature] hath the Sword not only in its hand, but in its commission, and the Sword that it hath is not the cause, but the consequent of its superiority. It doth not assume, or hold its authority by vertue of the sword, but it assumes and holds the sword by vertue of it's authority. The Scepter goes before the Sword, and is that which legitimates it" (p. 21).

[6] *Lex Rex* (London, 1644), p. xii.

[7] Alfred Lord Tennyson, "The Coming of Arthur," *The Poems of Tennyson*, ed. Christopher Ricks (London: Longmans, 1969), p. 1473.

[8] John Locke, *Two Tracts on Government*, ed. Philip Abrams, p. 231.

[9] A phrase used by Professor Alexander Bickel of Yale University speaking of the United States Supreme Court.

people. In *Jure Divino* Saul functions in a similar fashion; he is the fulcrum between God and community. But Defoe's triune construct, which he assembled from the contradictory strands of the First Book of Samuel, reintroduces a God of immediate exertions, committed intimately to the creation of a warrior-king. Defoe's seventeenth-century imagination contains "the concept of the *corpus mysticum* of the ruler." In crown, sword, and scepter, "the earthly is joined to the transcendent in a perfect *incorporation* at once mystical and down to earth."[10]

The triune construct of crown-sword-scepter, like "magnipotent" and "Titus," Defoe has made uniquely his own. In his book on the portraiture of English and Scottish monarchs David Piper observed that "the royal portrait can be really little more than a likeness of the throne, crown, scepter and orb."[11] And Shakespeare's Henry V enumerated from England's consecration orders the many ritual objects that invested the sacred person of the king.[12] Nevertheless, the attributes of monarchical authority since the middle ages had coalesced into the triad of crown, sword, and scepter.[13] In her study of the iconographic density of Spenser's *Fairie Queene* Judith Aptekar concluded that "monarchy and justice were almost always pictured . . . as a young and beautiful woman crowned . . . They often had a scepter and a sword."[14] In the most influential emblem book of the seventeenth and eighteenth centuries two emblems, Authority and Potesta-Government of a Commonwealth, generally are helmeted, carrying sword and scepter, the equivalents of the olive and dart symbolizing peace and war, in their hands.[15] Those London citizens who witnessed the coronation of English kings – as did Celia Fiennes for James II, William and Mary, and Anne – appear to have been impressed with these ensigns of royalty because they were more in evidence and functioned more dramatically in the ceremony than the other ritual objects, like the gloves, rings and spurs.[16] In the Coronation Orders of James II and William and Mary, the archbishops, bishops, peers,

[10] A medieval concept voiced by a modern in George Steiner, "The Portage to San Cristobal of A. H.," *Kenyon Review*, n.s., 1 (1979), 88. Cf. Michael Wilks, *The Problem of Sovereignty in the Later Middle Ages*, p. 275.

[11] *Kings & Queens of England and Scotland* (London: Faber and Faber, 1980), p. 7.

[12] *Henry V*, IV.i.260. John Rushworth noticed the swords, maces, crown, and scepter; see *Historical Collections. Third Part* (London, 1692), p. 728. This volume deals with the history of the period 1640–1644.

[13] See Walter Ullmann, *The Growth of Papal Government in the Middle Ages* (London: Methuen, 1955), pp. 311–19; and Ullmann, *A Short History of the Papacy* (London: Methuen, 1972), p. 95. There is a revealing note on the absence of the sword in the coronation orders of a fourteenth-century English queen in Percy Ernst Schramm, *A History of English Coronation Orders*, trans. L. G. Wickham Legg (Oxford: Clarendon, 1937), p. 84.

[14] *Icons of Justice: Iconography and Thematic Imagery in Book V of "The Fairie Queene"* (New York: Columbia University Press, 1969), p. 59.

[15] Caesar Ripa, *Iconogia: Or, Moral Emblems*. I have used the 1709 London edition reprinted by Garland Press (New York, 1976).

[16] *The Journeys of Celia Fiennes*, ed. Christopher Morris (London: Cresset Press, 1947), pp. 296–303.

and heralds are more busy with the crowns, swords, and scepters than they
are with "the Rest of the Regalia."[17] Again, in the most prominent of the
three triumphal arches erected in 1691 to welcome William at the Hague,
there was "represented a balance with two scales, in one of which are several
crowns, and in the other a sword, the sword outweighing the crowns." At
another table there rested "a sceptre and three crowns."[18]

The prominence, if not the dominance, of the sword among the crown and
the scepter is characteristic of the iconography of English monarchy in the
literature of the early seventeenth century.[19] "Sovereignty," as Sir Walter
Raleigh observed in *The Cabinet Council*, "is an absolute and perpetual Power
in every public State; and he is properly and only a Sovereign, that
acknowledgeth no Superiour or Equal nor holdest of any other Prince, Person
or Power, but God and his own Sword."[20] But even as Raleigh was writing
his commonplaces, a disjunction was developing between courtier representatives of an old aristocratic order and civilian spokesmen who were intent
upon glorifying their new unmartial ethos. Thus before the advent of Oliver
Cromwell some disquietude already had surfaced over the coupling of
militarism and monarchy. In his perceptive study of English panegyrics of the
seventeenth century James Garrison tellingly observes that "the traditional
panegyrist, although he may occasionally allude to the classical epics, limits
the monarch in a way that specifically denies him the usual means of heroism,
the sword." At least in England the drift of history was detaching the king
from battlefield activity; "the king's power," Englishmen were concluding,
"has nothing to do with the sword."[21] When the English wrote of the regalia
of kingship during the Interregnum they severed the sword from the crown
and the scepter. J. R. Tanner acutely remarked that "Oliver was Protector
because he had been Lord General."[22] In word and print Cromwell enters

---

17 See Leopold G. W. Legg, *English Coronation Records* (Westminster: Constable & Co., 1901);
    and J. Wickham Legg, *Three Coronation Orders*, Henry Bradshaw Society, vol. 19 (London,
    1900). Also *An Account of the Ceremonial at the Coronation of their Most Excellent Majesties King James
    II. and Queen Mary* (London, 1685); Francis Sandford, *The History of the Coronation of the Most
    High, Most Mighty, and Most Excellent Monarch, James II* (London, 1687); and *The Form of the Pro-
    ceeding to the Coronation of their Majesties King William and Queen Mary* (London, 1689).

18 *A Description of the Most Glorious and Most Magnificent Arches Erected at The Hague, For the Reception
    of William The Third, King of Great Britain* (1691), in *The Harleian Miscellany* (London, 1810), ix,
    556. I have been unable to locate the following, which was advertised in Tutchin's *Observator*,
    no. 16 (13–17 June 1702): *King Williams last Speech to both Houses of Parliament, Printed on a large
    Sheet, and Ruled with Red Lines; Over it is a Pedestal, with the Globe of the World, Crown, Sword, and
    Scepter, . . . and over that King Williams Head . . .* Sold by the Contriver, Samuel Cope.

19 See, for example, Henry Godyere, *The Mirrour of Maiestie* (London, 1619), emblem 2. Also
    Frances Yates, "Queen Elizabeth as Astrea," *Journal of the Warburg and Courtauld Institutes*, 10
    (1947), 41, 55.

20 *The Works of Sir Walter Ralegh, Kt. by Thomas Birch*, 2 vols. I, 42.

21 *Dryden and the Tradition of Panegyric* (Berkeley: University of California Press, 1975), pp. 113,
    114.

22 J. R. Tanner, *English Constitutional Conflicts of the Seventeenth Century, 1603–1689* (Cambridge:
    Cambridge University Press, 1928), p. 201; cf. General Monck's language cited in C. H.
    Firth, *Cromwell's Army* (1902; rpt., London: Methuen, 1962), p. 380.

English history and literature carrying nothing but the sword; he is devoid of crown and scepter.[23] Military strength alone had validated his right to rule. His special providence had "brought forth the government of the sword."[24] That fact was never to be forgotten by Englishmen who chose to participate in a respectable revolution in 1688. John Stephens, when he responded to the proposition that army officers be barred from places in the government in the debate in Richard Cromwell's first parliament in the spring of 1659, could have been speaking as much for them when he rose to declare that he wanted a government "by law and not by the sword." He wished the members of the House of Commons to remember the experience all had lived through, of the "mischief of the sword."[25]

In the literature of the Restoration we read consistently of that absence, or of an opposition. For example, John Ogilby in *The Entertainment of His Most Excellent Majestie, Charles II, in His Passage through the City of London to His Coronation*, described the arches erected along the king's route. The first presents Rebellion with "torn Crowns, broken Scepters, a bloody Sword." But in another of the pedestals, the one imaging the restoration of the king, monarchy is revealed but only with scepters and crowns. Beneath the restored prince, the figures of his father and grandfather, James I and Charles I, sit crowned, with orb and scepter. "*Behind the said figure* of *CHARLES the Second*," also crowned, also carrying the orb and scepter, "*is deciphered the* ROYAL OAK bearing Crowns, and Scepters."[26] Edmund Waller is representative of many Stuart poets, and while his themes are about war and conquest, he gives his readers a king who brings peace and union "without unsheathing the destructive sword." For Waller, Charles II attained the throne more in heaven's debt than the sword's.[27]

Thus, in spite of the visual presence of crown, sword, and scepter in the coronation ceremonies of the English kings from the Restoration onwards, the sword – of sovereignty, justice, conquest, or war – was less frequently found in the political literature of Defoe's time. Perhaps one expects the absence of the sword in the language of parliamentarians like Locke and Thomas Rymer, but

---

[23] And leaves it also devoid of crown and scepter; see Henry Dawbeny, *Historie & Policie Re-viewed, In The Heroick Transactions of his Most Serene Highnesse, Oliver, Late Lord Protector* (London, 1659).

[24] Cited in *Puritanism and Liberty*, 2nd ed., ed. A. S. P. Woodhouse (Chicago: University of Chicago Press, 1951), pp. 134–35. But see the following for the period's hospitality to war: James A. Freeman, *Milton and the Martial Muse: "Paradise Lost" and European Traditions of War* (Princeton: Princeton University Press, 1980), esp. pp. 16–48. An earlier but still useful work is John M. Steadman, *Milton and the Renaissance Hero* (Oxford: Oxford University Press, 1967).

[25] John Rutt, *The Diary of Thomas Burton* (1828), IV, 11, cited in Lois Schwoerer, "*No Standing Armies!*," p. 70. For a Restoration attack on Cromwell utilizing the same imagery see the closing lines of *Hells Higher Court of Justice* (1661), cited in Allardyce Nicoll, "Political Plays of the Restoration," *Modern Language Review*, 16 (1921), 229.

[26] London, 1662, pp. 13, 17, 37.

[27] "Of the Invasion and Defeat of the Turks, In the Year 1683," *The Poems of Edmund Waller*, ed. G. Thorn Drury, 2 vols. (London: G. Routledge & Sons, 1905), II, 102; cf. "A Panegyric to My Lord Protector," II, 17, 14; and "To the King," II, 37.

so pejorative had the martial symbol become that even a moderate Tory spokesman in the allegiance debate had to assert that "it is Scripture that establishes the Order and Superiourity of Kings, and therefore he holds his Crown and Scepter, by Scripture-Patent, and Divine Right."[28] Englishmen realized, as Garrison writes, that "to praise the monarch for personal heroism is potentially to subvert the monarchy as an institution . . . In short, to celebrate the monarch as a military hero would be to invite the possibility of celebrating a military hero as a monarch."[29] As the new century began, Dryden spoke for his countrymen, and not solely for the Country party, when he connected the image of the warrior-king with tyranny and usurpation; his monarch was a Nimrodian despot whose wars abroad and at home endangered England's welfare and peace.[30] In 1698 Defoe attacked the editors responsible for the publication of Edmund Ludlow's *Memoirs*; it was "the Government of a single Person [they] opposed covertly, under the person of *O.C.*"[31] Not only did he read the *Memoirs* as a republican attack on William's rule; he also understood that they implied that William, like Cromwell, had risen to the throne on the point of a sword. By the century's end, and in the elegies to William in 1702, the sword, when prominent, was a tainted metonym, and it had been disengaged from the crown and the scepter in the literature of the age.[32]

In his study of the development of responsible government in seventeenth-century England, Clayton Roberts concluded "that under William III and Queen Anne ambition for office and party passions led men to grasp at the sceptre."[33] Defoe, writing the history of his own times, concluded that the sword, displaced from the crown and the scepter, had resulted in weak and

---

[28] For Locke see *Two Tracts on Government*, p. 230, and *Two Treatises of Government*, II, xvi ("Of Conquest"); for Rymer see *A General Draught and Prospect of Government in Europe: Shewing the Antiquity, Power, Decay of Parliaments* (1681), 2nd ed. (London, 1714), p. 6. This edition is titled *Of the Power of Parliaments*. Also *A Friendly Debate Between Dr. Kingsman* (1689), p. 6. Note also the following: Philip Warwick, *A Discourse of Government* (London, 1694), p. 118 ("the scepter, and the sword, and the miter"); Jonathan Swift, "Ode To The King On His Irish Expedition" (1691), *Swift: Poetical Works*, ed. Herbert Davis (London: Oxford University Press, 1967), p. 3 ("Scepter, Crown and Ball"); and the fine reading of the title page of *Leviathan* in Margery Corbett and Ronald Lightbown, *The Comely Frontispiece: The Emblematic Title-Page in England, 1550–1660* (London: Routledge & Kegan Paul, 1979), pp. 218–30 (sword, crozier, and crown).

[29] *Dryden and the Tradition of Panegyric*, p. 115.

[30] See Michael West, "Dryden's Ambivalence as a Translator of Heroic Themes," *Huntington Library Quarterly*, 36 (1973), 347–76.

[31] *A Brief Reply to the History of Standing Armies*, p. 22. See also Blair Worden's Introduction to his edition of Edmund Ludlow, *A Voyce From the Watch Tower, Part Five: 1660–1662*, Camden, 4th ser., vol. 21 (London: Royal Historical Society, 1978).

[32] See, for example, R. Daniel, *The Dream: A Poem on the Death of His Late Majesty William III*, p. 22. Cf. Charles Davenant, "Of Private Mens Duty in the Administration of Public Affairs," *The Political and Commercial Works of . . . Charles D'Avenant*, ed. Sir Charles Whitworth, 5 vols. (London, 1771), II, 301; also IV, 297. In the language of Whigs and parliamentarians Anne was given only "the *Scepter and the British Crown*" (*The Observator*, no. 49 [7–10 Oct. 1702]).

[33] *The Growth of Responsible Government*, p. 441. See also his "The Growth of Ministerial Responsibility to Parliament in Later Stuart England," *Journal of Modern History*, 28 (1956), 233.

demoralized administrations. His life-long respect for the sword and those who bore it helps to explain his insistence, in opposition to nearly all of his contemporaries, that the revolution of 1688 had been a violent one, and that the sword in the hands of the English had brought the return of their liberty and freedom. With one voice whiggism proclaimed that the revolution under William had been "a Deliverance perfected without shedding of Blood."[34] At his death all eulogists praised the fact that "ce Prince a monté ainsi sur le Throne sans tirer l'épée."[35] Robinson's supposed namesake, Rev. Timothy Cruso, sermonized that "a *Sword not drawn*, hath obtain'd our Peace."[36] Professor Kenyon has made much of the fact that the Whigs of Defoe's generation tried to live down their earlier argument of resistance.[37] Defoe never did. He insisted all of his life that "King *James* was resisted, was fought with, was shot at."[38] He never let his Tory audience forget that their Queen and her bishop of London "*join'd in Arms against* Popery, and Arbitrary Power, *in the late King James's Reign.*"[39] He maintained his admiration for the war victories and the reign of Oliver Cromwell, for under his generalship the English flag had been carried to the far corners of the continent. "*Tho' his Government did a Tyrant resemble*' / *made* England *Great, and her Enemies tremble,*" was a refrain he quoted approvingly in the standing army debate, and he characteristically loved to tell and retell an anecdote about Cromwell as a successful commander of the English armies.[40]

As he watched at century's end the disintegration of his ideal of a Heaven-sanctioned warrior-king, Defoe moved unswervingly towards a full articulation of the royal triune. From the standing army debates of 1697–98, he had

34 Richard Kingston, *Tyranny Detected*, p. 266. Cf. John Guy, *On the Happy Accession of Their Majesties King William and Queen Mary*, p. 9.

35 J. B. Renoult, *Le Panegyrique de leurs majestez Britanniques, Guillaume Le Grand Troisieme du Nom . . .* (A. Londres, 1702), p. 36. Cf. John Piggott, *The Natural Frailty of Princes Considered . . .* (London, 1702), p. 16. White Kennett preached on the "merciful Temper" of the Revolution, "No Retaliation," "Armed Multitudes not killing, nor, I think maiming one single Person; and in our Courts of Judicature, hardly one Example made of Legal Justice" (*A Sermon Preach'd before the honourable House of Commons, at St. Margaret's Westminster, on January XXX, 1705/6* (London, 1706), p. 20).

36 *The Mighty Wonders of a Merciful Providence* (London, 1689), p. 12, also p. 14. See also *Angliae Decus & Tutamen: Or, The Glory and Safety of this Nation, Under Our Present King and Queen . . .* (London, 1691), p. 58.

37 In "The Revolution of 1688: Resistance and Contract," in *Historical Perspectives: Studies in English Thought and Society in Honour of J. H. Plumb*, ed. Neil McKendrick (London: Europa, 1975), pp. 43–69.

38 *Review*, VI, 115 (31 Dec. 1709); cf. *Review*, IV, 158 (14 Feb. 1708) and *Review*, VII, 28 (30 May 1710).

39 *Review*, VII, 79 (26 Sept. 1710); also his *Hannibal at the Gates* (London, 1712), p. 27.

40 *An Argument Shewing, That A Standing Army, With Consent of Parliament, Is not Inconsistent with a Free Government*, p. 7. See John Robert Moore, "Defoe Acquisitions at the Huntington Library," *Huntington Library Quarterly*, 28 (1964), 49–50. For Defoe's positive views on Cromwell see also *The Danger of the Protestant Religion* (1701). in *A True Collection of the Writings of the Author of The True Born English-man* (London, 1704), p. 8; for negative views see, for example, *Review*, I, 32 (24 June 1704); I, 51 (29 Aug. 1704); for contradictory views see VI, 31 (14 June 1709); and VII, 57 (5 Aug. 1710).

learned that "when Kings the Sword of Justice first lay down, / They are no Kings, though they possess the Crown."[41] Defoe's authorship of *A New Satyr on the Parliament (1701)* has been questioned, but internal evidence points to him in the distinctive Defovian cadence of stanza xxii:

> You shou'd find out some other word
> > To give the Crowns *Accepter*;
> To call him King wou'd be absurd,
> For tho' he'l seem to wear the sword,
> > 'Tis you have got the Scepter.[42]

In *Royal Religion*, affirming the sincerity and the authorship of the prayers that William III composed at his death, Defoe found it appropriate only to observe that his hero had laid "down the Scepter as a Burthen, and resign[ed] the Crown." Yet even then, as we have noted, Defoe ended his pious and pacific theme by reminding his readers that England had been blessed with "a Praying and Fighting Monarch."[43] In his private correspondence to Harley that same year, we have come to understand what the accession of a weak and gouty queen meant for him. The assumption behind the game plan to the new prime minister was that the queen, unable to wield the sword, would no longer be able to handle the complexity of politics in these times of crisis. In his publications, though, Defoe made the best of an insoluble problem.

Hymning Marlborough's victory at Blenheim, in a poem dedicated to the queen – who, it should be noted, wears no crown – Defoe expectedly divorced the civil authority from the authority of the sword, and with the queen regnant reverses as he must the pattern that has been his trademark; now " 'tis the Scepter helps the Sword to Fame."[44] His panegyrical passages to the queen end with an ambivalent stance concerning conquest, Defoe's final lines attributing to the victorious general the poetic commonplaces usually reserved for the monarch:

> *Faction* and *Parties* fly before your Name;
> *Faction* and *Parties* die beneath your Fame.
> Her Majesty, and all her People stand
> Debtors to all the Conquests you obtain'd.[45]

Throughout Queen Anne's reign Defoe was prepared to accept the

---

[41] *The True-Born Englishman*, *POAS*, VI, 291.

[42] In *POAS*, VI, 327; for attribution see p. 319.

[43] *Royal Religion*, pp. 16, 27.

[44] *A Hymn to Victory. To the Queen* (1704), in *The Second Volume of the Writings of the Author of The True-Born Englishman*, p. 121.

[45] *A Hymn to Victory*, p. 153. Note also Defoe's language in *The Dyet of Poland* (London, 1705), *POAS*, VII, 87. And when he cites the Scottish Parliament's amendment to an article of the Treaty of Union, he particularly writes that the crown, sword, and scepter are to be retained in Scotland (*The History of the Union of Great Britain* [Edinburgh, 1709], p. 474). Cf. his essay in *Applebee's Journal* (2 June 1722), in Lee, *Daniel Defoe: His Life and Recently Discovered Writings*, III, 10–11.

successful, if unnatural, demitting of the sword to Marlborough; but his writings indicate that he had already deciphered the critical problem, and thus the critical failure, of that reign. In the fall of 1710, following the debacle of the Sacheverell trial and anticipating the grab for power by the resurgent Tory-Jacobites, he returned to his political-metaphorical preoccupation:

> Princes – never part with the Royal Dignities; the Crowns of Sovereigns are too Sacred to themselves, and make too deep an Impression upon their affections, to suffer them to give them up to any Body, till they can keep them no longer.
> While then the Queen is willing to possess the Crown, willing to hold the Scepter of Britain, and Govern the People, God has in his Providence given to her Royal Charge; so long as her Majesty will keep entire her Power, so long she will preserve the Power, so long she will preserve the Foundation on which it stands. ————— *And that is the Revolution.*[46]

Later, following the accession of George I and the relative Whig stability of 1715, when he came to the defense of Harley, now Earl of Oxford, who was soon to be impeached by a vindictive Whig government for suspected mismanagement of his ministry, Defoe couched that defense in his special vocabulary. Facing a potentially disruptive Whig Junto in 1705, Harley had only schemed "to restore her Majesty to an entire Freedom of Acting; that all her Affairs should be explained to, and laid before her Majesty, that She Should no more wear the Crown without the Scepter."[47]

In January 1715, less than three months after the coronation of George I, Defoe's ecstatic voice informed his countrymen that Heaven and circumstance had conduced to make England once again the acme of political stability. A prince had arrived, much like William of old, "filled with Resolutions to make us Safe, Rich, Easy and Happy, willing to do all that lies in him to contribute to our National Felicity, and to hearken to all good Counsel for his Direction, inspir'd from Heaven with a Zeal for Religion." No longer, Defoe exults, is there "A Woman on the Throne, but a vigorous and magnanimous King; a Prince experienc'd in Government Equal to the Weight, as he is Equal to the Dignity of the Office, and as able to handle the *Scepter*, and wield the *Sword*, as he is to wear the *Crown*."[48] At the end of the month Defoe published another account of Anne's reign: *The Secret History of State Intrigues in the Management of the Scepter*. His insights have compelled one historian to dub him "the earliest of all historians of responsible government."[49] But the tract is also his most complete and most exhaustive diagnosis of the failure of monarchy in his time. It is also an explication of and a commentary on, in its secular and historical mode, the scriptural model of true monarchy that he fully articulated in his poetic elaboration

---

[46] *Review*, VII, 79 (26 Sept. 1709).
[47] *An Account of the Conduct of Robert, Earl of Oxford* (London, 1715), p. 27.
[48] *Strike While the Iron's Hot* (London, 1715), pp. 17–19.
[49] Roberts, *The Growth of Responsible Government*, p. 412.

of the First Book of Samuel in *Jure Divino* a decade earlier. In Defoe's myth all monarchies, like Saul's, spring forth, phoenix-like, favored by Fortune and Providence. Like Saul, too, Defoe's monarchs are "*born kings*," imbued with a "Spirit of Government," anointed "from Heaven," with crown on head, sword in hand, and the scepter of civil authority willingly presented by the people. Majesty, valor, and right rule maintain the delicate balance of government.[50] The failure of successive English monarchs to co-ordinate and control the full regalia of majesty led to the administrative failures since the reign of Charles I. Though each monarch had come to the throne with the regalia firmly in place, each had misunderstood the natural egoism and drive for dominion in mankind, each had loosened his grasp, and each had thus contributed to that loss of integrity due to the throne. The indolence of Charles II, Jesuitical intrigue that James II was unable to control, the ignorance of English affairs exhibited by William III, and the feminine in-capacity of Anne – for all of these reasons English monarchs had failed to protect the triunity of sovereignty and had brought on those fatal breaches of ministerial and factional usurpations. But now with the coronation ceremony reinforcing his metonymic imagination, Defoe can conclude with his vision of a new dawn, "when we see the *Sword* and the SCEPTER, put again into the same Hands with the Crown; and which adds to our Satisfaction, we see Reason to hope, they shall not be separated again, as they have been. We see the *Crown* upon the Head of a PRINCE equally qualify'd to hold the SCEPTER, and of Abilities sufficient to manage the *Sword*, and both *without Help*; and we doubt not, His Majesty will discharge Himself in all *Three* suitable to the greatest Expectation."[51]

Edward Wright titled Andrew Marvell "the poet of the garden and the sword."[52] Defoe's mythopoeia in *Jure Divino*, which he sustained throughout his journalistic career, enables us to label him "the poet of the crown, sword, and scepter." His triune symbol of true monarchy, an anachronism in his time, resolved his search for a creative synthesis between God and king, on the one hand, and sovereign and subject on the other. The Defoe we have come to understand from an *Essay Upon Projects*, for whom war was a civilizing agent conducive to beneficent change, is the Defoe of *Jure Divino*, for whom every progression to political stability and communal order is initiated by a warrior-king crowned by God and legitimated in his kingship with the gift of the scepter of civil authority. Never, in *Jure Divino* or elsewhere, does Defoe indicate that crowns are given by the people. When, in *Jure Divino*, he takes poetic license and versifies the prose of the Lord from 1 Kings 12.24, the Lord speaks to Rehoboam in the political-poetical language of Daniel Defoe:

[50] *The Secret History of State Intrigues In the Management of the Scepter, In the Late Reign* (London, 1715), pp. 14–15.
[51] *Secret History*, p. 64.
[52] *Andrew Marvell, 1621–1678: Tercentary Tributes*, ed. William H. Bagguley (1922; rpt., New York: Russell and Russell, 1965), p. 122.

> *STIR NOT A FOOT: Thy new rais'd Troops disband,*
> Says THE ETERNAL VOICE, *'Tis my Command:*
> *I gave thy Fathers first the* Hebrew *Crown,*
> *I set it up, but* 'tis your selves pull down:
> *For when to them I* Israel'*s Scepter gave,*
> *'Twas not my chosen People to inslave:* . . .
> *Draw not thy Sword, thy Brethren to destroy,*
> *The Liberty they have'*s their Right t'enjoy. (V, 26)

Throughout *Jure Divino* it is only the sword wielded for the people's freedom that is "consecrated" by Heaven (III, 28). But in his narrative history of Europe and England, Defoe never completely impugns governments of the sword. " 'Tis observed," he writes, "and 'tis the chief End of searching all these Matters in History, that in all these Cases, Conquest gave an unquestion'd Right of Government, and the Right of a King was no longer regarded in the World, than that King would maintain his Possession" (VIII, 26). Defoe is not inconsistent here, he has not forgotten his earlier vitriol directed at Nimrod; rather, in Defoe's myth, following the post-Noachic dispersal and the heavenly dispensation grafted to the martial kings of Israel, the sword alone attained a limited credibility. But alone, it is always suspect in Defoe's myth. Saxon England, with its history of bloody conquests and tribal enmities, reveals that "*The Sword and Scepter then was all but One*" (IX, 15). Finally Egbert emerged as the single victor, the unifying force of the petty principalities:

> Thus from the *Jus Divinum* of the Sword,
> The *English* Crown obey'd an *English* Lord:
> The *mighty Egbert*, strong in Arms and Law,
> The suppliant Kings in humble Posture saw,
> And all their Crowns and Scepters kept in awe. (IX, 22)

When he versifies Tyrrell's *History of England*, the usurping reigns of Edgar and William the Conqueror are once again signaled by the disrupted arrangement of the regalia:

> The *longest Sword* the *longest Scepter* brings;
> The Royal Genealogy comes down,
> And from *the Sword* advances to *the Crown*;
> The Right of Conquest's all our *Right Divine*. (X, 4)

The irony does not undermine what for Defoe is also a statement of fact: a crown hewed out by a conquering prince is not the best example of true monarchy. Those that cannot fight, of course, cannot claim any throne. But those victors can only become kings and rule morally with the free consent of their people:

> The Vict'ry he with his bright Sword obtain'd,
> But still untouch'd the *English* Crown remain'd;
> For still the *English* Nation kept their own,
> And he laid by the Sword, *to ask the Crown*. (X, 11)

In a less than perfect accommodation to monarchy gained by legitimate conquest, Defoe's prose notes realign the forced poetry as they reaffirm the
rhythm of accession; thus "to ask the crown" is to subscribe to a coronation
oath which reads, "*This Scepter, I most thankfully receive,* (a plain Acknowledgment, that 'twas the Peoples Gift)" (X, 12).

As the quotations reveal, Defoe's story of western civilization, and his patterns for monarchy when they stray from the sublime model promulgated in
the First Book of Samuel, reek of Hobbesian passions that make men wage
wars of aggrandizement and indulge in conquests that enslave. *Jure Divino,*
Defoe's "paradise lost," is a catalogue of kings who obtain their crowns
without consent, who rape, but who legitimately reign only upon a necessary
reconciliation with their subjects. Where in all these sad narratives of models
emanating from purgatory, if not from hell, can one find heaven's example,
the matter, form, and power of the true monarch?

> . . . where's the Man that thus can wear a Crown,
> With so much Sense and Justice fill the Throne;
> Deny the flattering Baits of lustful Men,
> And glittering Tyranny with Scorn contemn;
> That sees Oppression's foolish and absurd,
> And loves to make the Scepter rule the Sword; . . .
> Such, *Dear Britannia,* such thy Scepter bore,
> When *William* travers'd thy remotest Shore,
> And rul'd thee, *as ne'er wast rul'd before:* . . .
> Thy banish'd Freedom he at once restor'd,
> And guarded it with *his unconquer'd Sword.* (XI, 16)

King William III – Defoe's warrior-king, Saviour, Deliverer, "*William,* the
Glorious, Great, and Good and Kind," singled out as an "Instrument" of
God, whom He "wrought by his Hand" – remained for the next twenty-five
years, until Defoe's death in 1731, the avatar of the earthly monarch.[53]
Defoe's epic poem is his most sustained text on the origins of government and
the establishment of a nearly perfect political society benevolently
superintended by "a genius to the war." Its ideas inform his fiction of a pirate
commonwealth on an uncharted island in the Indian Ocean where the
supreme power is lodged in the hands of one *pater patriae.*[54] They inform also
the monarchy of Robinson Crusoe on an uncharted island in the mouth of the
Orinoco.

---

[53] *Mock-Mourners, POAS,* VI, 387–96; *Review,* IV, 20 (27 March 1707). Also *The Danger of the Protestant Religion Consider'd* (London, 1701), p. A2v; and Moore, *Daniel Defoe,* chapter x.
[54] See Manuel Schonhorn, "Defoe: The Literature of Politics and the Politics of Some Fictions," in *English Literature in the Age of Disguise,* ed. Maximillian E. Novak (Berkeley: University of California Press, 1977), pp. 44–48.

6

The politics of *Robinson Crusoe*

It was evident to Defoe's eighteenth-century biographers that he was the foremost political pamphleteer of the Revolution, steeped in the knowledge of his country and his time.[1] In 1766 the essayist of the *Biographia Britannica* wrote that *Robinson Crusoe* "was the delectable offspring of the teeming brain of Daniel de Foe, a writer famous in his generation for politics and poetry, especially the former."[2] Though Defoe himself admitted that "Writing upon Trade was the Whore I really doated upon," even the most conservative bibliography of his printed works would support the contention that politics was the woman he was married to.[3] And the previous chapters have maintained, if proleptically, that *The Life and Strange Surprizing Adventures of Robinson Crusoe* is a political fable that emanated from an imagination that had been actively engaged in the most intense political debates in modern English history. Yet this assertion of a significant political component to *Robinson Crusoe* should come as a surprise to the present reader, for given the scholarship of the past fifty odd years, Defoe's great fiction appears to have everything in it but politics. In 1925 Charles Whibley judged it a miracle, not that the *Adventures* were written, but "that Defoe, the politician, should have recorded them."[4] Later critics realized that "knowledge of Defoe's political journalism had opened some important windows to his art," but political considerations rarely penetrated their texts. Crusoe simply became "a kind of ruler over his strange land."[5] The "real subject of the novel," one of the most astute critics of Defoe concluded, is "of a Caribbean nabob who makes a little England in remote surroundings." Crusoe is simply "*homo domesticus*; his narrative, the epic of home-making, and housekeeping."[6] Pat Rogers "aims

---

[1] See, for example, Theophilus Cibber [Robert Shiels], *Lives of the Poets* (London, 1753), pp. 315–23.
[2] London, 1766, vol. VI, part II, Supp., p. 7.
[3] *Review*, I [IX], 106 (11 June 1713).
[4] *Robinson Crusoe*, ed. Charles Whibley (London: Constable, 1925), p. xxiv. Cf. the odd conclusion of a percipient historian: "*Robinson Crusoe* is entirely non-political." Wolfgang Michael, *England Under George I: The Quadruple Alliance*, 2 vols. (1939; rpt., New York: AMS Press, 1970), I, 44.
[5] Hunter, *The Reluctant Pilgrim*, pp. 1, 169.
[6] Pat Rogers, "Crusoe's Home," *Essays in Criticism*, 24 (1974), 390.

to provide a scholarly introduction and a stimulus to critical thought and discussion'' in a book-length introduction to *Robinson Crusoe*, but one could ask how ''an informed understanding'' can come about without a single consideration of the political issues of the time. His text and index say nothing about any political ''occasion;'' any suggestion of politics slides over immediately into economics; appendices still find it necessary, as late as 1979, to include two contemporary narratives of Alexander Selkirk, his life on and his rescue from Juan Fernandez Isle.[7] Michael Shinagel, in his Norton Critical Edition of *Robinson Crusoe*, continued that ''source hunting'' that Arthur Secord began in his pioneering study of 1924; ''Contemporary Accounts of Marooned Men'' comprise Shinagel's ''Backgrounds'' to the fiction.[8] The doyen of Defoe studies in our day discovered the ''imaginative genesis of *Robinson Crusoe*'' to be the instances of shipwrecks, storms, wild beasts, and earthquakes that were the content of Defoe's new journalism in the years immediately preceding the writing of *Robinson Crusoe*; these reports structured the fictive dream that is Defoe's memorable narrative.[9] And those who continue to catalog the contexts of his novels and factual works itemize every conceivable academic discipline but politics or the political.[10]

Before considering three significant episodes of Crusoe's adventure – his possession of the island, the coming of Friday, and the evolution of the island's political community – that reveal its political component, we might glance briefly at aspects of Crusoe's vocabulary in which is revealed, perhaps only intermittently, his sustained consciousness of his political self. Unassuming singly, when considered collectively that vocabulary reveals an imagination vibrantly afloat in regal waters.

Homer Brown has neatly remarked that *Robinson Crusoe* is ''a factualization of the metaphors of the whole tradition of spiritual autobiographies.''[11]

[7] *Robinson Crusoe*, ed. Pat Rogers (London: George Allen & Unwin, 1979), pp. ix, 74–75, 106–07.

[8] Daniel Defoe, *Robinson Crusoe*, ed. Michael Shinagel (New York: W. W. Norton, 1975), pp. 245–47. Following citations from *Robinson Crusoe* will be from this edition and will appear in the text.

[9] Maximillian E. Novak, ''Imaginary Islands and Real Beasts: The Imaginative Genesis of *Robinson Crusoe*,'' *Tennessee Studies in Literature*, 19 (1974), 57–78.

[10] See, for example, Michael White, ''Reading and Rewriting: The Production of an Economic *Robinson Crusoe*,'' *Southern Review* (Adelaide), 15 (1972), 115–42; Henry Knight Miller, ''Some Reflections on Defoe's *Moll Flanders* and the Romance Tradition,'' in *Greene Centennial Studies: Essays Presented to Donald Greene in the Centennial Year of the University of Southern California*, ed. Paul J. Korshin and Robert R. Allen (Charlottesville: University Press of Virginia, 1984), p. 72; Paula Backscheider, ''Defoe and the Geography of the Mind,'' in *The First English Novelists: Essays in Understanding*, ed. J. M. Armistead (Knoxville: University of Tennessee Press, 1985), p. 48. But for a more thoughtful approach see J. A. Downie, ''Defoe, Imperialism, and the Travel Books Reconsidered,'' *Yearbook of English Studies*, 13 (1983), 66–83; *The Elusive Defoe*, ed. Laura Ann Curtis (Totowa, NJ: Rowman and Littlefield, 1979). Richard Braverman reads the novel as an assertion of political will in support of a radical Whig perspective; see ''Crusoe's Legacy,'' *Studies in the Novel*, 18 (1986), 1–26.

[11] Homer O. Brown, ''The Displaced Self in the Novels of Daniel Defoe,'' in *Studies in Eighteenth-Century Culture*, vol. IV, ed. Harold E. Pagliaro (Madison: published for the American Society for Eighteenth-Century Studies, 1975), p. 72. The article was first published in *ELH*, 38 (1971), 562–90.

Language in that tradition is anchored in the Old and New Testaments. It is then worth observing that one of the metaphors derived from scriptural rhetoric that was associated with magistracy or monarchy was "hedge" or "fence." Hamlet's stepfather had no fear for his person, for "there's such divinity doth hedge a king, That treason can but peep to what it would, Acts little of his will."[12] At Prince Henry's death, a loss cataclysmic for England and Protestantism, Sir John Holles exclaimed: ". . . now that our hedge is broken down all passengers will pull off our grapes; our sea banks be overwhelmed and who or what shall defend us from the overflowing, all devouring, tyranny of pope and Spaniard?"[13] Significantly, the image was also one of the most common used by the puritan ministers who gave the election day sermons in New England in the last half of the seventeenth century. These speakers "frequently described the ideal magistrates as 'hedges', as 'walls', or as 'repairers of the old breach.' "[14] Robinson Crusoe's "Living-Hedge" (p. 94), his walls and his fences that surround his "Castle" and his "Country Seat" (pp. 121, 119), then, are more than just utilitarian terms.[15] In Defoe's political vocabulary the idea of monarchy generally summons up the fence image. In his *Reflections upon the Late Great Revolution*, when Defoe's persona spoke of the "Publick Person" of the king, who, because he is more exposed is thus more vulnerable as the executor of justice, he asked that "the Law and the People ought to set up a double Fence about the King's Person, and take particular care to secure him from those Hazards to which his High Place and Office may render him more liable than inferiour People."[16] Eulogizing his dead hero in *Mock Mourners*, who had given England's Constitution and England's Government its "Soul," Defoe implied that it was William who "Fenc't [it] with just Laws, [so] impregnable it stands, / And will for ever last in *Honest Hands*."[17] In 1711, in a lengthy and passionate essay on the just exercise of power, Defoe challenged the excessive praise heaped upon the Czar of Muscovy by the *Spectator*. "Had the *Czar* of *Mosco* a Spirit of true Greatness, to reject and contemn the Brutish and truly Contemptible part of a Monarch, *viz.* Tyrannizing over his People . . . and restor'd Liberty to his People, made them Masters of their own Property, and fenc'd that Property with Laws . . . Then had he been a Hero Indeed."[18]

Now it might be taken as axiomatic, as a necessary condition of factual and

---

12 *Hamlet*, IV.v.124.
13 Cited in J. W. Williamson, *The Myth of the Conqueror, Prince Henry Stuart: A Study of 17th Century Personation*, p. 178. There are some useful comments in Elkin Calhoun Wilson, *Prince Henry and English Literature* (Ithaca: Cornell University Press, 1946).
14 T. H. Breen, *The Character of the Good Ruler: A Study of Puritan Political Ideas in New England, 1630–1730* (New Haven: Yale University Press, 1970), p. 100. Breen remarks that "All of these terms were common in the sermon literature of the period" (p. 100n).
15 There are thirty-six references to "my Fence," "Hedge," or "wall" in the text.
16 *Reflections*, pp. 38–39.
17 *Mock-Mourners, POAS*, VI, 378. Defoe wrote of the protection "Fences and fortifications" afford to the Anglican Church (*Jure Divino*, Preface, p. xvii).
18 *Review*, VIII, 67 (23 August 1711). Cf. *Spectator*, no. 139 (9 August 1711).

fictional narratives, that men marooned on a desert island or even exiled in
hostile countries would busy themselves with the erecting of fences, hedges,
or walls.[19] Oddly enough, contemporary accounts of marooned men that
Defoe and his audience presumably might have been familiar with, those
genres that supposedly supervise and control the writing and the reading of
Robinson Crusoe, reveal nothing of the sort. Like Crusoe, all the central figures
of tales of voyaging, shipwreck, and utopias make themselves clothes and ink
and baskets and huts. They attempt pottery and build boats. Robert Knox
began a lucrative business knitting caps for his Ceylonese captors. Many kept
fowl. Most, like Francois Leguat, spent their time "looking after our cabins,
and cultivating our gardens." None fenced, or hedged, or walled the "three
Plantations, *viz.* my Castle, my Country Seat, which I call'd my Bower, and
my Enclosure in the Woods" (p. 130) – which none of them had – of their
"little Kingdom" the way Crusoe did (p. 108).[20]

Dickens wrote that it was curious, "that *Robinson Crusoe* should be the only
instance of an universally popular book that could make no one laugh."[21]
Humor in Defoe is a sombre dissertation exercise that could never reach the
publishing light of day. Yet Defoe's critics have found nothing but histrionics
and humor in Crusoe's fantasy of politics or in his vocabulary of rule. But can
we so facilely overlook how quickly his thoughts generally return to a rhetoric
of magistracy? His inability to turn his grindstone, "turn it and grind my
Tools too, this cost me as much Thought as a Statesman would have bestow'd
upon a grand Point of Politicks, or a Judge upon the Life and Death of a
Man" (p. 66). In the extended episode with the English mutineers it is
Crusoe, "dress'd in my new Habit, and now I was call'd Governour again,"
who tempers the harsh "Justice" of the English captain with his "Mercy,"
who "give[s] them their Lives," who "set[s] them at Liberty" (pp. 213,
214), as if Crusoe had absorbed the lesson plan his creator had provided
Robert Harley fifteen years earlier. In that memorandum the great and good
leader of a grateful people would, like Cardinal Richelieu, "Let Others have
the Mannagement of Offences, and the Distribution of Justice." The
"Peoples Darling" should be the visible dispenser of executive clemency.

At one stage in his role playing with the English captain and some captured
mutineers over plans to seize the ship, Crusoe tells us the following:

---

[19] It is a condition of medieval and Renaissance images of Eden; see John Prest, *The Garden of
Eden: The Botanic Garden and the Recreation of Paradise* (New Haven: Yale University Press, 1981);
and Roland Mushat Frye, *Milton's Imagery and the Visual Arts* (Princeton: Princeton University
Press, 1978), pp. 226, 236.

[20] See the following, all generally noted as Defoe's "sources": Henry Neville, *The Isle of Pines*
(London, 1668); Robert Knox, *A Historical Relation of the Island of Ceylon* (London, 1681); Gar-
cillaso de la Vega, *The Royal Commentaries of Peru*, trans. Sir Paul Rycaut (London, 1688);
Henry Pitman, *A Relation of the Great Sufferings and Strange Adventures of Henry Pitman* (London,
1689); Francois M. Misson, *A New Voyage to the East Indies by Francis Leguat and His Companions*
(London, 1708); *The Improvement of Human-Reason. Exhibited in the Life of Hai Ebn Yokdan*, trans.
Simon Ockley (London, 1711).

[21] Cited in John Forster, *The Life of Charles Dickens*, 3 vols. (Philadelphia, 1874). III, 135n.

When I shew'd my self to the two Hostages, it was with the Captain, who told them, I was the Person the Governour had order'd to look after them, and that it was the Governour's Pleasure they should not stir any where, but by my Direction; that if they did, they should be fetch'd into the Castle, and be lay'd in Irons; so that as we never suffer'd them to see me as Governour, so I now appear'd as another Person, and spoke of the Governour, the Garrison, the Castle, and the like, upon all Occasions.(p. 210)

Perhaps one should not be asked to take this too seriously as Defoe's rendering of the mystic fiction of the "King's Two Bodies." It was, as Ernst Kantorowicz's massive study reminds us, a viable idiom of political thought into the Restoration and a distinctive if implicit feature of English political debate over resistance to James II.[22] With sarcasm and irony, Defoe had mocked the enemies of revolution principles who attempted to rationalize their actions by distinguishing between the Stuart king's private and public political capacity. Yet only a day earlier in the episode, "the Commander of the Island," who "might hang them all there, if he pleased," who exacts quarter "as Justice requir'd," but grants "Mercy," had, with "my great Army of 50 Men," helped capture the second contingent of landed sailors, "only that I kept my self and one more out of Sight, for Reasons of State" (p. 208).[23] Crusoe's "Reasons of State" is a startling aside only if we *refuse* to acknowledge the political theme of Defoe's narrative. In Defoe's time, reason of state continued to denote the extra legal power of the sovereign; it legitimated his use of the prerogative beyond statute or fundamental law when he saw a need to preserve the commonwealth.

In Roger Manwaring's 1628 sermon, *Religion and Allegiance*, reason of state was cited to equate the king's power – in this instance, Charles I's – with the omnipotency of God. It was possibly one of the pronouncements that caused his impeachment. (It is significant that the proceedings of Manwaring's trial for sedition in 1628 were republished in 1709. Its title page proclaimed him "the Sacheverell of his Day" and the text kept alive the belief that reason of state had originated with Machiavelli and was opposed to the idea of justice.)[24] In 1690 Archbishop Sancroft, in *Modern Policies, Taken from Machiavel, Borgia, and other Choice Authors*, had cautioned his readers that "Necessity of State is a very Competent Apology for the Worst of Actions."[25] It is true that earlier, in the 1640s, Henry Parker had argued reason of state to be the counterpart of and even superior to the lawyers' justice and even the common law; it then became a justification for *de facto* sovereignty of the

---

[22] *The King's Two Bodies: A Study in Mediaeval Political Theology* (Princeton: Princeton University Press, 1957), pp. 41, 413; *A Friendly Conference Concerning the New Oath of Allegiance to K. William and Q. Mary* (London, 1689), p. 3.

[23] Douglas Hay makes some revealing comments about the mysterious and disembodied king as the dispenser of mercy; see "Property, Authority, and the Criminal Law," in *Albion's Fatal Tree*, ed. Douglas Hay *et al.* (London: Allen Lane, 1975), pp. 46–49.

[24] *The Proceedings of the Lords and Commons in the Year 1628 against Roger Manwaring D. D., the Sacheverell of his Day, for two Seditious, High Flying Sermons.*

[25] London, 1690, p. 19. First published in 1652.

parliament.[26] Nevertheless, in Defoe's time reason of state was judged an absolutist concept that permitted monarchical infringement on the "public interest;" it was an "opaque cloak for royal ambition."[27] Filmer began his *Patriarcha* somewhat ingenuously by disavowing any intention "to meddle with mysteries of the present state. Such *arcana imperii*, or cabinet councils, the vulgar may not pry into. An implicit faith is given to the meanest artificer in his own craft; how much more is it, then, due to a Prince in the profound secrets of government: the causes and ends of the greatest politic actions and motions of state dazzle the eyes and exceed the capacities of all men, save only those who are hourly versed in managing public affairs."[28] Robert Eccleshall, in his study of absolute and limited monarchy in the seventeenth century, cites the Filmer passage and concludes: "Here was the traditional idea that politics was properly a business for experts. And it was linked with the belief that God had retained effective, though oft-times inscrutable, control of public affairs."[29]

Attached, then, to monarchy, and synonymous with it, reason of state asserted that the commands of the sovereign became law by the mere supremacy of his office or position. Right is defined by what the sovereign permits. Reason of state is as absolute an embodiment as is any Hobbes absolute. The sovereign's command is supreme, irreversible, and unhampered by the scrutiny of conditions. In the Restoration and the post-Revolution years reason of state was intoned by exponents of *de facto* single rule; it was tied up with a special ruler morality.[30] Defoe was keenly aware of the uses to which the phrase could be put. On the one hand, it rationalized political expediency, being one of "different Terms which Statesmen turn so often into Fine Words to serve their Ends;" on the other, "*Reasons of State* are

[26] Henry Parker, *The Contra-Replicant, His Complaint to His Majestie* (1643), pp. 18–19, cited in M. A. Judson, "Henry Parker and the Theory of Parliamentary Sovereignty," in *Essays in History and Political Theory in Honor of C. H. McIlwain* (Cambridge, MA: Harvard University Press, 1936), 135–56.

[27] J. W. A. Gunn, *Politics and the Public Interest in the Seventeenth Century* (London: Routledge & Kegan Paul, 1969), pp. 39, 42; see also pp. 126–29.

[28] Ed. Laslett, p. 54. See Locke's comment on this passage in *Two Treatises*, I, 2 (p. 163).

[29] *Order and Reason in Politics: Theories of Absolute and Limited Monarchy in Early Modern England* (Oxford: Oxford University Press, 1978), p. 164. I have learned much about reason of state from the following: George Mosse, *Holy Pretence: A Study of Christianity and Reason of State from William Perkins to John Winthrop* (Oxford: Basil Blackwell, 1957); Ernst H. Kantorowicz, "Mysteries of State: An Absolutist Concept and Its Late Mediaeval Origins," *Harvard Theological Review* 48 (1955), 65–91; Felix Rabb, *The English Face of Machiavelli*; and Friedrich Meinecke, *Die Idee der Staatsrason in der neueren Geschicte*, trans. *Machiavellism: The Doctrine of Raison D'Etat and its Place in Modern History*, by Douglas Scott (New Haven: Yale University Press, 1957). David Norbrook has some stimulating observations about mysteries of state in the reigns of Elizabeth and James I; see his *Poetry and Politics in the English Renaissance* (London: Routledge & Kegan Paul, 1984), pp. 130, 151, 172, 198.

[30] See, for example, *A Brief Account of the Nullity of King James's Title* (London, 1689), p. 5; George Savile, Marquess of Halifax, *Some Cautions Offered to the Consideration of Those Who Are to Choose Members to Serve in the Ensuing Parliament* (1695), in *Halifax: Complete Works*, ed. J. P. Kenyon, p. 181.

principally the Great Doctrine of Self-preservation . . ."[31] But eighteen years later, when he dramatized the origin and development of political society on Crusoe's island, the concept serves as the last stone in the arch of his political imagination, in something more than a histrionic episode, in which the monarch of his island sustains his sacred and mysteriously omnipotent character. At times, like Manwaring's King, he is God's surrogate. He wars like Saul and builds his temple like Solomon. God speaks to Crusoe as he spoke to Joshua, the army leader who commanded the Israelite nation when it came to possess the chosen land. And like the psalmist's God, Crusoe too can spread his table in the wilderness for his "Subjects" who own him for their "Deliverer."[32]

Before the end of his second day on his island, Crusoe "call'd a Council, that is to say, in my Thoughts" (p. 44). Before his first year ends, "with a secret Kind of Pleasure" he thinks "that this was all my own, that I was King and Lord of all this Country indefeasibly, and had a Right of Possession; and if I could convey it, I might have it in Inheritance, as compleatly as any Lord of a Mannor in *England*" (p. 80). In the sixth year of his "Reign" he attempts "the Circumference of my little Kingdom" (p. 108). In his eleventh year remembering the psalmist's tablespread calls up the following scene by the "Lord of the whole Manor; or if I pleas'd, I might call my self King, or Emperor over the whole Country which I had Possession of. There were no Rivals. I had no Competitor, none to dispute Sovereignty or Command with me" (p. 101):

It would have made a Stoick smile to have seen, me and my little Family sit down to Dinner; there was my Majesty the Prince and Lord of the whole Island; I had the Lives of all my Subjects at my absolute Command. I could hang, draw, give Liberty, and take it away, and no Rebels among all my Subjects.   (p. 116)

Of course, this is Crusoe the king dining alone, attended by his three orders or estates of servants: Poll, his dog, and the cats. Stoics may smile, we may smile, though Crusoe does not. Years later, despite the varieties of narrative experience available to Defoe, Crusoe's self-vision and the triadic nature of his family have not changed at all:

My Island was now peopled, and I thought my self very rich in Subjects; and it was a merry Reflection which I frequently made, How like a King I look'd. First of all, the whole Country was my own meer [complete, sole] Property; so that I had an undoubted Right of Dominion. 2dly, My People were perfectly [absolutely] subjected: I was absolute Lord and Lawgiver; they all owed their Lives to me, and were ready to lay down their Lives, *if there had been Occasion of it*, for me. It was remarkable too,

---

[31] *The Original Right*, in *A True Collection*, p. 145; *The Danger of the Protestant Religion Consider'd*, p. 30.

[32] For the allusion to Solomon's temple see *Robinson Crusoe*, pp. 100, 101; and I Kings 6.1. Cf. J. A. Mazzeo, "Cromwell as Davidic King," in *Reason and the Imagination: Studies in the History of Ideas, 1600–1800*, ed. J. A. Mazzeo (New York: Columbia University Press, 1962), pp. 29–54.

we had but three Subjects, and they were of three different Religions. My Man *Friday* was a Protestant, his Father was a *Pagan* and a *Cannibal*, and the *Spaniard* was a Papist.

(p. 188)

Crusoe's triadic pattern may allude to the authority of the first kings, Adam and Noah, and the absolute authority they exercised over their three sons.[33] (Perhaps this scriptural pattern is behind the medieval notion that a commonweal had to be an union of at least three families.)[34] But it is more important to recognize that Crusoe's catalog of his estates, his three animals in the first case, a tawny Protestant and foster-son, a pagan, and a Spanish Catholic in the second, is the substance of a momentous political and constitutional issue that engaged the seventeenth century and was continued into the eighteenth.[35] It is the co-ordination controversy.

The principle of co-ordination in the legislative power became the "linchpin of the community-centered view of government."[36] The monarch, who was once different in degree from his subjects, was deposed from his lofty political eminence and leveled with the people represented in parliament. The crown was no longer distinct from the three traditional estates of the realm, the lords spiritual, the lords temporal, and the commons. "Dependent on the assumption that the community was the source of political power, the revolutionary principle was gleaned from Charles I's vastly influential Answer to the Nineteen Propositions of June 1642. Under its terms the king was no more than a single member of three co-ordinate estates of parliament," that is, only a third part of the political nation, sharing legislative authority with lords and commons, who were co-ordinate with him but in no way subordinate.[37] But that is not the language of Robinson Crusoe, who images himself to be a superior ruler, different in degree and kind from his accumulating subjects. Crusoe's enumeration is the ideology of royalism. For the royalists, their three inferior estates of the realm, like Crusoe's, could never intrude upon their monarch's indivisible power. The citadel of sovereignty was the throne. The three estates could never share that sovereignty with him. They remained completely his majesty's servants, as do all of Crusoe's remnants, who are always to be "wholly Directed and Commanded by me in every thing" (p. 199), who have "no Power without me" (p. 215), and who all "owe [their lives] to me, and acknowledge it upon all Occasions, as long as [they] liv'd" (p. 199). Crusoe's language echoes the language of those who denied that England had a mixed and limited monarchy. For the royalists as for Crusoe,

[33] Filmer, *Patriarcha*, p. 5. Locke, *Two Treatises*, II, 36 (p. 311).

[34] Gordon J. Schochet, *Patriarchalism in Political Thought* (Oxford: Basil Blackwell, 1975), p. 31. See also Don Cameron Allen, *The Legend of Noah* (Urbana: University of Illinois Press, 1949).

[35] There is a remarkable anticipation of Crusoe's triune animal schemata in the eccentric metaphor of an early twelfth-century priest; see Michael Mendle, *Dangerous Positions: Mixed Government, The Estates of the Realm, and the Making of the "Answer to the XIX Propositions"* (University, Alabama: University of Alabama Press, 1985), pp. 29–30.

[36] Weston and Greenberg, *Subjects and Sovereigns*, p. 1.

[37] *Ibid.*, p. 3.

co-ordination, equality, was an unacceptable tenet. In the University of
Oxford's highly influential *Judgment and Decree* of 1683, co-ordination is the
fourth of those "damnable Doctrines, destructive to the sacred Persons of
Princes, their State and Government, and of all Human Society." That
"damnable Doctrine" made clear that "The Sovereignty of *England* is in the
three Estates, viz King, Lords and Commons. The King has but a co-ordinate
Power, and may be over-ruled by the other Two."[38] And it should not be
forgotten that the annual prayer on the Fifth of November in the *Book of Common Prayer* offered thanksgiving to God "for the Happy Deliverance of King
James I, and the three Estates of England, from the most Traiterous and
Bloody Intended Massacre by Gunpowder."

But the University and the royalists were facing a dramatic shift in political
thought; they were the losers in the debate over an independent sovereign and
three lesser estates of the realm. Defenders of the Revolution in 1689, both
Whig and Tory, declared that the sovereignty of England resided in three
distinct and concurrent estates, the king being one.[39] Locke remarked that
"three distinct Persons" make up the supreme lawmaking power.[40] In
William's reign the king's supporters hesitated over ascribing any co-ordinate
status to him, given his old-fashioned jealousy over prerogative and status.
The evidence suggests that it was generally the Tories who denied co-
ordinate power to the parliament.[41] Professor Gunn noted the ambiguity and
circumspection in the language of estates in Anne's reign, partly
the result of the Whigs' "tendency to minimize the changes that the Revolution had wrought."[42] Yet Thomas Whincop preached an assertive Tory sermon before the Commons on 5 November 1702, "Being the Anniversary
Thanksgiving for the Happy Deliverance of King James the First, and the

[38] *The Judgment and Decree of the University of Oxford, pass'd in their Convocation, July 21, 1683*, in *State Tracts* (London, 1689), p. 154. *The Judgment* was republished in later volumes of *State Tracts*. It can be readily found in *The Stuart Constitution, 1603–1688: Documents and Commentary*, ed. J. P. Kenyon (Cambridge: Cambridge University Press, 1966), pp. 471–74. See also Filmer, *Patriarcha*, pp. 282, 299–300. That the king was a separate estate was maintained by the Tory lawyer, Sir Robert Sawyer, and the Earl of Nottingham; see Lois Schwoerer, *The Declaration of Rights*, p. 179; and Henry Horwitz, *Revolution Politicks: The Career of Daniel Finch, Second Earl of Nottingham, 1647–1730* (Cambridge: Cambridge University Press, 1968), pp. 75–76. See also *Remarks Upon the Most Eminent of our Anti-monarchical Authors and their Writings*, pp. 367, 383–89, 535. Published in 1699, the *Remarks* was written in 1684. For the royalists' denial of the concept see also Corinne C. Weston, "Concepts of Estates in Stuart Political Thought," in *Representative Institutions in Theory and Practice: Studies Presented to the International Commission for the History of Representative and Parliamentary Institutions*, XXXIX (Brussels, 1970), pp. 115–16.

[39] See, among many, the following: *A Justification of the Whole Proceedings of Their Majesties King William and Queen Mary* . . . (London, 1698), pp. 11, 27; Charles Blount, *The Proceedings* (London, 1689), p. 11; Thomas Long, *A Full Answer to All the Popular Objections* . . . (London, 1689), p. 8; Samuel Masters, *The Case of Allegiance in our Present Circumstances*, pp. 10–11; *A Friendly Debate*, pp. 20–21.

[40] *Two Treatises*, II, 19 (p. 426).

[41] See Philip Warwick, *A Discourse of Government* (London, 1694), p. 10.

[42] J. A. W. Gunn, *Beyond Liberty and Property: The Process of Self-Recognition in Eighteenth-Century Political Thought*, p. 125.

Three Estates of the Realm, from the Gunpowder-Treason Plot."[43] And the
most prominent attack on Locke and his schemes of government published in
Anne's reign insisted that sovereignty resided solely in the king. The three
estates remained servants of his majesty; "he is independent over them, they
all dependent on him."[44] For Leslie and Milbourne the *anti*-co-ordination
tenet was one of the supreme props of their divine right-royalist platform.[45]

Defoe contended with the co-ordination principle in the first year of the
Review's publication. In December 1704, the Scandal Club, Mr. Review's at
times facetious, at times morally somber, arbiter of culture and mores, was
asked the following question: "*Who, or what are the three States that compose or con-
stitute the Government of* England"? Defoe's politic answer indicated that he
knew the controversy; he quotes Coke, Selden, and Grotius. But he chose to
answer the query with a quotation from the Duke of Ormond, "found in the
Second Vol. of *Milton*'s Works," to the effect that "*the three Estates,* [are] *of
King, Lords, and Commons, whereof in all Ages, Parliaments have consisted,*" and he
concluded: "Now if these are not the Three Estates, than [sic] was my Lord
Duke of *Ormond* very much mistaken, but however this proves, that the
Notion of the King, Lords and Commons making the Three Estates, is not
a Phanatick, but a Loyal Cavalier Principle, believ'd in an Army, and by a
Nobleman, who all People allow, to be intirely in the Interest of the Royal
Family, and fully bent, to the Pulling down Rebellion and all Anarchichal
Principles; and this is as much as I desire to Claim from the Quotation. . ."[46]
Defoe continued to assert this balance among the three estates throughout Anne's reign.[47] Ten years later, though, in 1719, after retrospectively
assessing the failures of political stability, the dispersal of sovereign power,
and the decline of kingly authority, we discover him aligned, once again,
with conservative Tory-royalist antecedents and contemporaries. Like Leslie
and the most fervent monarchists, in his dramatization of an emerging
political society Defoe has embraced a position that secures the power
of the monarch. Crusoe's vocabulary of magistracy denies the possibility
that a parliament or a legislature can numerically dominate the king.
It refutes the arguments of the Whigs and parliamentarians of his age.
His political ideology, fictively reconsidered, remains antithetic to a

---

[43] London, 1702.
[44] *An Essay Upon Government*, p. 63.
[45] Leslie, *Rehearsals*, nos. 3, 36, 49; in the last-mentioned, Leslie quotes from James Harrington's *Oceana* to show that the idea of co-ordinate powers was found wanting by one of the
leading Whig political theorists. See Leslie's *Cassandra, Numb. 1* (1704), pp. 10–17, and his *The
Constitution, Laws, and Government of England, Vindicated* (London, 1710), pp. 7–8. For the ex-
tremist *jure divino* apologist Luke Milbourne, see his *The People Not the Original of Civil Power*
(London, 1707), p. 9. Leslie's ultra-royalist position was attacked in the Whig *A Letter Occasioned
by the Second Part of the New Association* (London, 1704), p. 16.
[46] *Review*, I. *A Supplement to the Advice from the Scandal Club*. December [1704], Numb. 4, pp.
13–14.
[47] *Jure Divino*, p. v; *The Case of the Dissenters in Carolina*, pp. 22–23; *Queries to the New Hereditary
Right-Men* (London, 1710), pp. 10–11.

community-centered one and runs counter to traditional Whig orthodoxy.

As we have seen, Defoe's language of contract and covenant discovered in the *Reflections Upon the Late Great Revolution* was generally maintained in his political mythmaking of the origins of government that he published in Anne's reign. Despite asides to the contrary, Defoe's covenantal structure is hierarchical; that is, it is solely between the sovereign and his subjects. There is scarcely a mention of the radical notion of contract founded on natural rights and universal consent. For Defoe, as for Bolingbroke, "there is no initial coming together of all to form a political community;"[48] king and community exist as a natural and God-given phenomenon – though, as I have suggested, in his most instinctive voice Defoe's God-designated king is almost the creator of his community. Rather than initiating a political society, contracts are subsequent to and derived from an anterior condition that presupposes prince and people as a fact in time, and "there is a Mutual Compact, Tacit or Express, between a Prince and Subjects."[49]

Hardly anyone in Defoe's time denied that "God approved of rulers, called them to office, and endowed them with the sanction of His authority."[50] But post-Revolution political philosophy affirmed that God's will was realized through the consent of the people. God's power passed to the king through the medium of popular choice or a popular covenant. However the process, popular contracts established government and placed rulers in charge of it. Defoe's political language harks back to an earlier mode, in which covenants are initiated between the deity and his chosen kings. Divine approbation is thus given to the reigning monarch. It permits him to perform a godly service with godly assistance. During his whole political career, Defoe reaffirmed the covenantal importance of the ruler's role. He denied the reiterated language of appointment and election, for his prince was singled out to contract directly with the creator, a process that seems deliberately contrived to dignify his monarch and distinguish him from the masses. Defoe's myth of origins, rather than affirming that political activity resides in the whole populace, glorifies executive authority.

Returning to the *Adventures*, we find it difficult to take too seriously the political implications of Crusoe's actions with his subjected family of animal servants and of Friday. Just as Crusoe was God's subject, they were his; and like God over him, Crusoe "had an undoubted Right [by Conquest] to govern and dispose of [them] absolutely as he thought fit" (p. 123). But parrots, dogs, cats, goats and a slave, all of whom, in one way or another worshipped him and his gun, are no fit citizens of any commonwealth. Yet the distinctive web of political relationships involving Crusoe and his animals, and then Crusoe and Friday, undergoes no modification with the advent of

---

[48] Kramnick, *Bolingbroke and his Circle*, p. 99.
[49] *Queries to the New Hereditary Right-Men*, p. 10.
[50] *Puritan Political Ideas, 1558–1794*, p. xxiii.

either the Spaniard or of the English sea captain and his crew. For just as Crusoe's dominion over the animal and cannibal world had been absolute, just as Friday, setting his head beneath Crusoe's foot "made all the Signs to me of Subjection, Servitude, and Submission imaginable" (p. 161), so too do all the civilized and Christian additions to Crusoe's domain. His dominion over his new family, his "new Subjects" (p. 188), remains absolute, for they too "all owed their Lives to me, and were ready to lay down their Lives, *if there had been Occasion of it*, for me" (p. 188). Of the English, too, Crusoe demands that they "should be wholly Directed and Commanded by me in every thing." No matter who is recruited, all must promise, upon being taken into his service, to solemnly engage to live and die with the *Generalissimo*, the King, the *Commander*, the Governor of the island (pp. 207, 209).[51]

Crusoe's rhetoric of absolutism and submission, of kingly authority and subject obedience, places the right and might of sovereignty in the office of the monarch. Significantly, the implied contract that immediately follows suggests no lessening of his absolute authority:

Well, says I, *my Conditions are but two.*

1. That while you stay on this Island with me, you will not pretend to any Authority here; and if I put Arms into your Hands, you will upon all Occasions give them up to me, and do no prejudice to me or mine, upon this Island, and in the mean time be govern'd by my Orders.

2. That if the Ship is, or may be recover'd, you will carry me and my Man to *England* Passage free.

He gave me all the Assurances that the Invention and Faith of Man could devise, that he would comply with these most reasonable Demands, and besides would owe his Life to me, and acknowledge it upon all Occasions, as long as he liv'd. (p. 199)

Crusoe's legitimacy here, and the obligation, political or otherwise, consented to by his subjects, can be construed in many ways. Like a theocratic king, "sent directly from Heaven" (p. 198), or like a conqueror, or a fatherly prince, Crusoe expects dutiful and submissive compliance from his men. Whatever society develops on Crusoe's island, it surely is not one that "began from a Voluntary Union and mutual Agreement of Men, freely acting in the Choice of the Governors, and Forms of Government," as Locke and the transmitters of Lockean principles were proclaiming in the eighteenth century.[52] The political component of Crusoe's condition-making activity, comprised of a sovereign monarch and a grateful and dependent community, resembles that of the constitutional monarchists. For Clarendon and others,

---

[51] Thus I cannot accept Rousseau's reading that "Robinson Crusoe was [sovereign] of his island, as long as he was its only inhabitant; and this empire had the advantage that the monarch, safe on his throne, had no rebellions, wars, or conspirators to fear." *The Social Contract*, trans. and ed. G. D. H. Cole (London: Dent & Sons, 1913), p. 8. Note also that Prince William of Orange had been named "generalissimo by sea and land" by James II; see Stephen Baxter, *William III and the Defence of European Liberty, 1650–1702*, p. 245.

[52] *Vox Populi, Vox Dei* (London, 1709), p. 11.

the power of the monarch was original and absolute, yet there could be "voluntary abatements" of that power.[53] He could limit his power by self-imposed restraints, or he could prescribe a formal diminution of that power which, once accepted, could only with great difficulty be rejected or altered. Even Filmer, while seeming to reject without qualification any will in the community or any initiative in its enactment of legislation, admitted that the monarch could respond "to supplication from the people in Parliament."[54] His later dogmatic defenders asserted that the rights of the people came "from the Grace and Bounty of Princes."[55]

It was the Whig writer who realized the danger of grounding the liberties of the subject on the whim of the sovereign. Rights extracted from a somewhat recalcitrant monarch afforded small security for perpetual peace and union; hence the essentiality of an active community in Whig doctrine, its faith in some sort of original contract entered into by free individuals agreeing "upon certain terms of Union and Society."[56] And if a king assumed command via conquest it was the voluntary consent of an unintimidated community that legitimated the conqueror's right to rule. But it was the resolute Tory who diminished the force of the popular will by arguing that a king only voluntarily "limits his right of Conquest, by referring himself wholly to his People."[57]

The rhythm of societal evolution that Defoe dramatizes in *Robinson Crusoe* also makes the concessions of a monarch the basis for law. His more traditional views of politics and society appear to have taken a conservative turn as the Revolution slipped further into the past and as what can be called "a Whig version of the Constitution" hardened in the reigns of Anne and George I. His views about sovereignty and the rights of the people that he propagandized for various English and British ministries appear to be alien to his instinctive preferences, revealed in his fascination for a warrior-king and his memorandum to Harley that offers a program for a unitary sovereign. "Give us good men and they will make us good Laws," Harrington wrote, "is the maxim of a demagogue, and is exceedingly fallible. But give us good orders and they will make us good men, is the maxim of a legislator, and the most infallible in politics."[58] In Harrington we hear a "modern" voice that reinforces our belief that the best political society is made by law and not by man. Law transforms men and transforms society. *Robinson Crusoe* recalls an older view of politics that believed that "where many rule there is no

---

[53] Cited in Robert Eccleshall, "Richard Hooker and the Peculiarities of the English," *History of Political Thought*, 2 (1981), 108. Cf. Lewes Sharpe, *The Church of England's Doctrine of Non-Resistance Justified and Vindicated* (London, 1691), pp. 36–37.

[54] *Patriarcha*, pp. 82–83; also p. 119.

[55] Edmund Bohun, *A Defence of Sir Robert Filmer* (London, 1684), p. 5; also p. 11.

[56] *Cato's Letters*, no. 33 (17 June 1721). Cf. no. 59 (30 Dec. 1721).

[57] *A Friendly Conference Concerning the New Oath of Allegiance*, p. 5.

[58] *Oceana* (London, 1747), pp. 75–76, cited in Gunn, *Politics and the Public Interest*, p. 116.

order.''[59] The state is ordered for the best when it is instituted and maintained by a warrior-statesman. Law originated in some single will and such a will was the possessor of sovereignty. That sovereignty possessed by Defoe's monarch belongs to him as an innate right; it is prior to the state, the people, or any contractual obligation. His crown is God's crown, secured in combat. Violence is the condition of human society, to be quelled by a warrior-prince. For Crusoe is always in his island kingdom with ''a naked Sword by my Side, two Pistols in my Belt, and a Gun upon each Shoulder'' (p. 197). His custom is to go nowhere without his arms (p. 194). To the end of his reign he is in complete control of all the ordnance of his army. (Arms, not work, might be the most frequent motif in his narrative.) For Defoe it is not the mild law of nature but the violent law of arms that is the foundation of kingship and rule. Political society originates, not from the ''free resolve of free men,''[60] but in violence. The society in Crusoe's island affirms that truth; it does not create any precedent. It is the warrior-king and not the community who is the soul animating the body politic. If one were to ask what must be asked of all political theorists, ''what is the ultimate guarantee of law and government, what insures the capability and efficiency of the state, what was its origin,''[61] Defoe's answer is not society, not the gregarious instincts of man, but the will of the heroic individual.

Crusoe, then, is no simple Austen country squire bent on improving his estate; he is, as we finally see, a monarch whose vision of self and society remains in many ways antithetic to the principles of Whig, Lockean, and contractualist political thought that was dominant in Defoe's time. From the scholarship that has explored the spiritual autobiographical tradition, we have learned much that helps us to understand the providentially directed deliverance of Defoe's hero. His salvation is at the disposition of the Deity. His new private self is legitimated by divine providence. Yet our preoccupation with the personal dimension of that tradition has permitted us to overlook its equal, if not greater, national dimension. For example, the first words that Crusoe reads upon opening his Bible in his illness are from Psalms 50.15: *"Call on me in the Day of Trouble, and I will deliver, and thou shalt glorify me"* (p. 75) – which is echoed later when he panics over the naked footprint of a savage (p. 124). The Psalmist's insights, it should be noted, were favorite texts of those who wished to sermonize on national emergencies and national deliverances. Rev. John Moore, preaching from these texts in two sermons before Queen Mary in 1690, observed: "How frequently hath the inter-

---

[59] Quoted in David Little, *Religion, Order, and Law: A Study in Pre-Revolutionary England* (New York: Harper & Row, 1969), p. 143.

[60] Sidney, *Discourses Concerning Government* (London: 1763), II, 5 (p. 76). Defoe's Captain Singleton, by "the Law of Arms," justifies war, prisoners, servants, and slaves (*Captain Singleton*, ed. Shiv K. Kumar (London: Oxford University Press, 1969), p. 54.

[61] Frank I. Herriott, *Sir William Temple on the Origin and Nature of Government* (Philadelphia, 1893), p. 34.

position of the Divine Power been clearly manifest in the Rise and Declension of Kingdoms, and in the surprizing Periods which have been put to mighty Empires." Like Crusoe, Moore also believed that God gave national punishments for national offenses. "Histories of all Countries furnish us with instances of this kind; and we may read abundantly of the mysterious variety of the working of Providence in the quick turns, and amazing changes which did happen to the Kingdoms of *Judah* and *Israel*." In the present, too, "the Growth and Fall of Nations and Kingdoms, comes from the Lord."[62]

Throughout William's reign, countless sermons on the Fifth of November stressed the national contexts of God's "particular and special Providence." Rev. William Dawes, in his sermon preached before the King on 5 November 1696, returned to "the strange, surprizing and unusual" events of that day. Deliverances of this special kind have to be ascribed to God's account, "who has the Management and Superintendency of all Accidents, and therefore can Connect and Range them together in such an useful order."[63] Rev. Stephen Charnock's "Discourse on the Fifth of November," collected with other discourses on the existence and attributes of God, and on Divine Providence, spoke of England's "memorable Deliverance" on this day of thanksgiving.[64] Here and elsewhere, English divines stressed the secret hints, the confirmations in Scripture, the voice of the Lord in the shakings of the earth, that signify great alterations not in the personal but in the political state of affairs.[65] Crusoe's reign, too, in addition to his salvation, is at the disposition of the Deity. God has given Crusoe not only the keys to his conscience but also the keys to his kingdom. In his Adamic sense of self, he exhibits early in his narrative his Adamic inheritance from God: ". . . I was remov'd from all the Wickedness of the World here. I had neither the *Lust of Flesh, the Lust of the Eye, or the Pride of Life*. I had nothing to covet; for I had all that I was now capable of enjoying: I was Lord of the whole Manor; or if I pleas'd, I might call my self King, or Emperor over the whole Country which I had Possession of. There were no Rivals. I had no Competitor, none to dispute Sovereignty or Command with me" (p. 101). Following his conversion, Crusoe appears to be a king by God's immediate designation, his reign certified by the deity.

Rather than "the fallen Adam," whom the Calvinists believed was "politically helpless," Crusoe resembles more Pufendorf's "first man [who]

---

62 *Of the Wisdom and Goodness of Providence* (London, 1690), pp. 15, 16, 19. Cf. also Moore's *A Sermon Preach'd before the King at St. James's, April 16, 1696. Being a Day of Publick Thanksgiving for the Discovery of a Horrid Design to Assassinate His Majesty's Person* (London, 1696), also on Psalm 50.15.

63 *A Sermon Preach'd Before the King at White-Hall, Novemb. 5. 1696*, 2nd ed. (London, 1696), pp. 7, 8, 13.

64 *Works, The Second Edition Corrected*, 2 vols. (London, 1699), II, 588.

65 Of the presence of Providence in earthquakes see Robert Fleming, *A Discourse of Earthquakes* (London, 1693); and J. D. R., *The Earth twice shaken wonderfully* (London, 1694).

received his authority over all things."[66] That authority, that embryonic political power, so resolutely affirmed throughout his reign on his island, is further guaranteed by his subduing of the land.[67] That Defoe perhaps knew the moral and legal justifications for Crusoe's title to full property rights on his island may not be as important as the fact that the principles of sovereignty enunciated in *Jure Divino* and dramatized now in *Robinson Crusoe* dispute an essential tenet of Whig thought. Crusoe obviously rules his world because the world's his own. The inner logic and rhythm of Defoe's biblical and imperial vision compels Crusoe to roam, to explore, to plant, and to subdue all of the island. But that inner logic and the results therefrom are at odds with the language of Tyrrell, Locke, and other liberal political writers of his day. Tyrrell's *Patriarcha non Monarcha*, published in 1681, has been called "a *First Treatise*," that is, a "Lockean" response nine years earlier than Locke's to Filmer's *Patriarcha*. The principle of dominion and possession laid down by Tyrrell became the dominant Whig line of orthodoxy thereafter: ". . . no man in the state of nature, hath a right to more land or territory than he can well manure for the necessities of himself and Family; that is, can reduce into actual possession, otherwise a man that first sets his foot on an uninhabited island, would have an absolute right to the whole, even though it were a Thousand miles long, or to all the Territory he could discover with his Eyes, so that no man could make use of one foot of land, in that Island but by his

---

[66] Walzer, *The Revolution of the Saints*, p. 37; Samuel Pufendorf, *Elementorum jurisprudentiae universalis libro duo*, trans. William A. Oldfather (Oxford: Clarendon, 1931), II, 36. The passage reads:

It was, therefore, by title of occupation alone, if you remove from consideration the concession on the part of God, that the first man received his authority over all things, and he needed no further title, because there existed no one whose right could stand in his way. And he acquired dominion over all things none the less because he was unable by an act to take possession of all things, and apply them to his own use. For it is sufficient that, while he took possession physically of some portion of things, he had included others in his intent, and was going to take possession of them also when need of them arose; just as he who has entered merely one apartment of a palace, has occupied the whole, and, in the case of things which, as a whole, have devolved upon some one, he who has taken hold of some portions only, is adjudged to have taken possession of them one and all.

For Pufendorf and Defoe see Maximillian E. Novak, *Defoe and the Nature of Man* (Oxford: Oxford University Press, 1963).

[67] For this interesting historical-legal background to Crusoe's tenure, which has yet to be investigated, see Wilcomb E. Washburn, "The Moral and Legal Justification for Dispossessing the Indians," *Seventeenth-Century America: Essays in Colonial History*, ed. James Morton Smith (Chapel Hill: University of North Carolina Press, 1959), pp. 15–32; Fred M. Kinney, "Christianity and Indian Lands," *Ethnohistory*, 7 (1960), 44–60; and Francis Jennings, *The Invasion of America: Indians, Colonization, and the Cant of Conquest* (Chapel Hill: University of North Carolina Press, 1975).

permission.''[68] The essence of this ''labor theory of value'' was echoed, of course, by Locke. Plagiarized by the anonymous author of *Political Aphorisms*, it propounded the new liberal principles of political economy into the eighteenth century: ''If the Possession of the whole Earth was in one Person, yet he would have no Power over the Life or Liberty of another, or over that which another gets by his own Industry, for Propriety in Land gives no Man Authority over another.''[69] But the writer of *Jure Divino*, who believed that the man who was ''*Landlord of the Isle* . . . *must be King*, because he own'd the Soil'' (V, 3), is the creator of Crusoe, who is validated in his high office by all the signs of Heaven but whose right to dominion is a condition of his right of possession.[70] Lord of the soil, Crusoe is, *ipso facto*, lord of the manor of his whole kingdom. If there is a kind of ''Lockean'' component to Defoe's political thought in *Robinson Crusoe*, it is Locke in his younger and more authoritarian stage, who wrote that ''this much is certain, that, if the magistrate is born to command, and if he possesses the throne and the sceptre by divine institution and by the distinction of his character and nature, then it is beyond dispute that he is the sole ruler of the land and its inhabitants without contract or condition and that he may do whatever is not forbidden by God, to whom alone he is subjected and from whom alone he received his title to live and to rule.''[71]

If John Locke had been alive to read Crusoe's life and adventures in 1719 and had been asked to reflect on a political reading of Crusoe's narrative, he might have responded by repeating his comment about Filmer's *Patriarcha*, that ''he takes great care there should be Monarchs in the world, but very little that there should be People.''[72] Crusoe is an Adam and no Adam, firing ''the first Gun that had been fir'd there since the Creation of the World'' (p. 44). He has been singled out and saved by God, without whom he would only be another loathed man of great ambition who ''are frequently represented dreaming of the Powers they envy invading them, and of their conquering them, which it is not unlikely, is acted, and injected, by the

---

68 *Patriarcha non Monarcha* (London, 1681), p. 114 (mispaged; this is the second p. 114). Laslett remarks that the section was ''a *First Treatise*'' (Locke, *Two Treatises*, p. 60).

69 *Political Aphorisms*, p. 29.

70 Cf. Defoe, *Party-Tyranny*, pp. 3, 5. There is another remarkable instance of Defoe appropriating without irony the language of his hereditary right, *jure divino*, enemy. In 1705, coming to Filmer's defense, the anonymous writer of *An Essay upon Government* observed: ''Mr. *Lock* objects against the Divine Grant, *Gen.* 1. 28, because no Grant conveys right to what the words of it do not express; but there is no express mention of *Adam's* posterity, and therefore he had no Dominion granted him over them. *A.* It is contain'd in the words of the Grant, *Be fruitful, and multiply, and replenish*, and (then) *subdue*; i.e. exercise Dominion'' (p. 32). The following year, in his *Fourth Essay at Removing National Prejudices* Defoe construed the same text as ''that is, Govern it'' (p. 28). For both authors a verb of conquest and oppression becomes a verb of magistracy and governance.

71 *Two Tracts*, ed. Abrams, p. 23. Note here Locke's crown/sceptre construction, the absence once again of the sword.

72 *Two Treatises*, I, iv (p. 182).

Devil, to prompt their Ambition.''[73] It is time, then, to ask, how does Defoe people Crusoe's world? How does Friday appear, how do Crusoe's subjects multiply, to replenish his earth? A Defoe reader in 1719 who then knew the typology of his fictions could easily anticipate the story's subsequent action. For Crusoe, younger son that he is, conforms to Defoe's incessant fairy tale of younger brothers, and will, eventually, attain success by force of arms. Like Captain Bob Singleton and Colonel Jack, Crusoe's prowess in combat will reveal growth to manhood.[74] Crusoe is also the predecessor of Captain Misson, ''a younger Brother of a good Family.'' Separated from his plantation investments, singled out by God on a desert island, we can say of the former what Defoe wrote of the latter: ''our Rover had but little Hopes of other Fortune than what he could carve out for himself with his Sword.'' Both are ''of a roving Temper . . . and chose the Sea as a Life which abounds with more Variety, and would afford [them] an Opportunity to gratify [their] Curiosity.'' The later rover, we recall, ''took up the Sword'' to become the mythic leader of an island utopia. Misson ''. . . had Eyes impartial, and allowed nothing but Merit to distinguish between Man and Man; and instead of being a Burthen to the People by his luxurious Life, he was by his Care for, and Protection of them, a real Father, and in every Thing acted with the equal and impartial Justice of a Parent.''[75]

Of greater interest beyond these speculations of the prototypical monarch who emerges from the fused portraits of Generalissimo-Governor Crusoe and Captain-Lord Conservator Misson, is Defoe's introduction of Friday. One recent critic, attempting to minimize any sign of aesthetic coherence or conscious artistry in Defoe's fictions, discovered him to be constrained by convention and responding to the narrative strategies of the voyage and pirate tales. Thus the relationship between Crusoe and Friday ''lies not in the elusive psychology of Crusoe, but in the conventional form of the fiction.'' Limited in resources and fixed by the expectations of his audience, Crusoe's creator can do nothing but introduce a second-rate subordinate character. ''The typology from which he draws his fiction casts natives as either ferocious heathens or simple savages, and in order to establish *rapport* with his audience, Defoe has to work within the limits of his typology.''[76] But the critical issue is not the nature of native sons but the social relations that develop in the factual and fictional narratives of men marooned on desert islands. There is not one that Defoe's readers were familiar with that provided the marooned sailor with a ferocious heathen or simple savage. George Pine,

[73] *Jure Divino*, VII, 11.
[74] For Defoe's preoccupation with younger brothers and martial valor see *Review*, V, 101 (18 Nov. 1708); V, 102 (20 Nov. 1708); *The Compleat English Gentleman*, ed. Karl Bulbring (London, 1890), p. 43. Colonel Jack is also a younger brother among orphans.
[75] *A General History of the Pyrates*, ed. Manuel Schonhorn (London: Dent, 1972), pp. 383, 390, 392–93.
[76] Ian A. Bell, *Defoe's Fiction* (Totowa, NJ: Barnes and Noble, 1985), p. 104.

saved along with three women of different social classes, much like Adam invigorates an island in the South Seas. Huguenot colonizers do much the same in the Indian Ocean. Peter Serrano's story, which Locke read and Defoe might have seen, was one of shipwreck in the Caribbean. After three solitary years his island isolation ends with the appearance of another castaway with whom he lives in peace for four years. Henry Pitman, like Defoe, was a participant in Monmouth's rebellion, but was captured and transported to Barbados. He escaped to the Isle of Tortuga, where he and several other Europeans, rejecting a pirate career, endured for three months. No tale that has been unearthed as a possible source of or background to Crusoe's adventures provided Defoe's reader – or Defoe – with any counterpart to Friday.[77] And when Defoe and his contemporaries indulged in debates about the state of nature or the origins of government and imagined an island domain in which the political polemics would be dramatized, that island scene became populated, not by a single man nor by a single man and his cannibal servant, but by a commonwealth of equals. As Tutchin and many others observed, these men in a state of nature, before laws, "were govern'd by the Laws of Nature by which there was no distinction of Persons, the Dominions of Nature were upon a level, no one could claim Preheminence over the Rest."[78]

It is essential, then, to see that Defoe has created distinctions of persons, and that Crusoe from the very beginning of his island experience does "claim Preheminence over the Rest" who set foot in his kingdom. In spite of all his yearning for "the Society of my Fellow-Creatures" or "the Conversation of one of my Fellow-Christians" (p. 147), with the arrival of Friday, a servant, a savage, a subject, the island's population doubles. Friday is a captive; his relationship is defined by power, dominion, rather than service. And whatever Crusoe's abiding faith in "secret Hints" or "secret Intimations of Providence" (p. 137), it is clear that in this one case Crusoe does not depend upon his "Dream" to get "a Savage into my Possession" (p. 157). Crusoe's world, not Crusoe's dream, carries incitements to violence. It is Defoe, not Providence, who legitimates a war of conquest and deaths. For Defoe's "Dream" is a pacific one; but Defoe's myth of political authority is initially and always reinforced by human accretions that are gotten through war. These repetitive and repeated sequences enable Crusoe to acquire virtually absolute power over the life of the native who has lost the power to control his own. Friday "made all the Signs to me of Subjection, Servitude, and Submission imaginable, to let me know, how he would serve me as long as he liv'd" (p. 161). Earlier, God's authority – and Crusoe's tobacco – had saved Crusoe for governance; God's authority – and Crusoe's "Guns" and

[77] See footnote 20 above. For Locke's keen interest in de la Vega see *Two Treatises*, I, vi (p. 200); II, ii (p. 295).
[78] John Tutchin, *First Volume of Observators* (London, 1703), pp. 1–4 ("A Vindication of the Observator").

"my Sword, which hung naked in a Belt by my side" (p. 159) – now account
for the dominion that the lord of the manor exercises over his conquered
subject-slave. It is the beginning of Crusoe's "commonwealth by acquisi-
tion." His sovereign power is substantiated "by Warre [wherein he] sub-
dueth his enemies to his will, giving them their lives on that condition."[79] If
Crusoe then began as an Adamic monarch, with full and unlimited personal
ownership of all the property on his island, his dominion now includes even
the power of life and death over his accumulating family.

While Defoe's myth of the nature and sources of political power echoes
much of Filmer's arguments for society's origins drawn from the book of
Genesis, Defoe divorces himself from Filmer's royalist and patriarchalist
tenets in one very significant way. In fact, Robinson Crusoe can be read as a
refutation of indefeasible hereditary right; as such, it became one of the important proof texts of the revolutionary debate that was transferred to the col-
onies in the later part of the century.[80] For Crusoe, in the terminology that
Defoe and his critics like to use, is a father and no father; that is, his patriarchal power, in a distinction that Defoe continued to make till the end of his
life, derives from institution and education, not from biology.

His power is not a fatherly power but a political power. Thus we find that
Defoe has here aligned himself with those political commentators of his age,
men like Tyrrell, Sidney, and Locke, for example, for whom the distinction
between paternal and political power was categorical.[81] Crusoe's relationship
with Friday, dominant though it is, becomes a dramatic illustration of the
contention that fatherhood is not grounded on generation but is "acquired by
[the] performance of that nobler part of their Duty . . . the trouble and care
. . . in Education."[82] Such "is the true original of Paternal Authority, or
Filial Subjection." Preoccupied like Filmer and many other political writers
of the seventeenth century with the origins of political society, Defoe was still
unwilling to concede, as Locke did, that in the first ages of the world the father
was indeed monarch.[83] Rather, Defoe seems to insist on the non-filial, arti-
ficial origins of government. He thus casts up, not an Englishman, or a European, or even a white man, but a very tawny heathen, thus reinforcing the
distinction between the island's sovereign and his first subject.

[79] Thomas Hobbes, Leviathan, ed. C. B. Macpherson (Penguin, 1976), p. 228. Most of Jure
Divino, as we have seen, ratifies with history Hobbes's belief that "Covenants without the
Sword, are but Words" (p. 223).
[80] See the stimulating analysis of the uses to which the American colonists put Robinson Crusoe in
Jay Fliegelman, Prodigals and Pilgrims: The American Revolution Against Patriarchal Authority,
1750–1800 (Cambridge: Cambridge University Press, 1983).
[81] The Speech of Algernon Sidney, Esquire before his Execution, in State Tracts (London, 1692), p. 269;
Sidney, Discourses Concerning Government (London, 1698), p. 250. Locke, Two Treatises, II, i
(p. 286).
[82] Tyrrell, Patriarcha non Monarcha, pp. 16–17, 21, 45–46.
[83] Two Treatises, II, viii (pp. 358–361). For Filmer's views see Patriarcha, p. 57. For Hobbes's
denial of generation as the foundation for power see Gordon J. Schochet, "Thomas Hobbes
on the Family and the State of Nature," Political Science Quarterly, 82 (1967), 427–45.

Many of Defoe's readers have noted that Friday's discovery of his father serves, on the level of narrative, the purpose of conflict resolution that began with Crusoe's flight from *his* father. That is, the reconciliation of the native son and father recapitulates but resolves that initial disruption of English son and English father. An earlier disjunctive sequence is thus concluded harmoniously, if only at the psychic level. But it also is worth noting that on the political level it asserts the benign paternalism of Crusoe which is now seen to be distinct and different from the patriarchal. Crusoe is fatherly, not the father, even though Friday's "very Affections were ty'd to me, like those of a Child to a Father" (p. 163). Defoe's political imagination makes clear that Crusoe's developing political empire is not coterminous with the natural family. In the first commonwealth, Defoe seems to be saying, the father was not the monarch. Undermining the literalizing imagination of eighteenth-century Filmerites, Defoe is thus able to embrace the distinction between paternal power and political power upon which Revolutionary Whig argument was founded, and at the same time is able to legitimate Crusoe's sovereign power since not only has it been gained by lawful conquest but also by his "performance of that nobler part of [a parent's] Duty . . . the trouble and care . . . in Education." And finally, it could be noted that, by losing his putative son to his real father, Crusoe is once again alone, absent children, like his predecessor, model, and alter ego, William III, able to be a true *pater patriae* to his kingdom, a monarch free of familial and dynastic corruption. "Fate seems to make it look like Nature's Law . . . That where consummate Vertue, Shall remain, / The Last of every Line shall be the Man."[84]

That Daniel Defoe was a strong supporter all his life of England's constitutional monarchy and her mixed government, and particularly, of William III and the Revolution of 1689, cannot be denied. And it has not been the design of this essay to prove Defoe a closet adherent of *jure divino* monarchy. But we can expect that there were many Englishmen who "albeit illogically, acquiesced in the Revolution but still hankered after some kind of divine sanction for government."[85] Daniel Defoe is a writer as complex and as contradictory as any we can read in English literature, and thus there are many Defoes. And there is one Defoe for whom "modern" or "Lockean" political paradigms have been misleading Procrustean formulas. They have obscured some distinctly idiomatic aspects of Defoe's political Revolutionary and Hanoverian Whiggism. H. T. Dickinson concluded that "an essential aspect of Whiggism was its suspicion of the executive."[86] The progress of Defoe's political thought reveals that he saw English liberty endangered by the grasping power of the new parliamentary interests. He grew to understand that

---

[84] *Jure Divino*, XII, 12.

[85] From a private communication to me by Professor W. A. Speck, drawn from one of his published essays.

[86] See *The Whig Ascendancy, Colloquies on Hanoverian England*, ed. John Cannon (London: Edward Arnold, 1981), p. 55.

England's deliverance by William and his Protestant hero's reign had not settled the dangerous and incipiently destructive struggle for political domination that is the history of his Stuart century. Post-Revolution shibboleths of limited monarchy, king-in-parliament, balance of power, and co-ordinate government – these Defoe understood as smokescreens that were meant to obscure the growing domination of parliaments. He anticipated the self-conscious theme of the later eighteenth century, what was to be called "legal tyranny;" that is, the enslavement of the people by the very patriots who were the people's representatives, a tyranny established by law, authorized by consent, and fathered by the electors of the people.[87] He believed, whether instinctively or ideologically, that to restore the balance was to reassert the strength and independence of the king. To the very end of his life Defoe's king remained the equipoise of England's balanced constitution and the linchpin of a stable political society.

Defoe's *Of Royall Educacion*, composed in 1728, three years before his death, is one of two lengthy unfinished tracts in which he formularized ideals of conduct for the early modern world. Unlike the other, *The Compleat English Gentleman*, it dictates the education of princes. The tract is vintage Defoe. As in the *Essay Upon Projects*, he continues to assign his monarch functions of considerable importance, as A. E. Levett recognized almost sixty years ago.[88] The visionary retrospection of the sixty-eight year old political propagandist who had been born in the reign of Charles II and had lived to see the coronation of George II, and who had lived through more than one sort of revolution, is an echo to the fervent admiration the twenty-eight year old had accorded William III.[89] He is contemptuous still of William, the Norman, a "meer soldier," who brought his army to England to rule his subjects with a rod of iron.[90] The tract is studded with negative examples of military reigns when English princes, instead of the book in their hands, put helmets on their heads, only to become "*crown'd asses*" (p. 29). But his faith remains unshaken in the availability of leaders singled out by God, "design'd for eminent stations, exalted glory, and inimitable accions" (p. 2). There are still "souls of differing glory and furnish'd by Nature with infinitely greater capascityes then some others may be, tho' all issuing from the same hand, emitting divine powers and influences to them" (p. 2). As he thought in 1689, so he thinks now: "We read of this more particularly in Scripture, and that in severall instances, especially of kings and leaders of armyes and others, such as were destined to great actions, as of Joshua, of Saul, of David, or

---

[87] See Gunn, *Beyond Liberty and Property*, pp. 7–42.
[88] "Defoe," in *The Social and Political Ideas of Some English Thinkers of the Augustan Age*, ed. F. J. C. Hearnshaw (London: Harrap, 1928), p. 162.
[89] See Peter G. M. Dickson, *The Financial Revolution in England: A Study in the Development of Public Credit, 1688–1756* (London: Macmillan, 1967); and Dudley Bahlman, *The Moral Revolution of 1688* (New Haven: Yale University Press, 1957).
[90] *Of Royall Educacion*, p. 6. Further citations will be noted in the text.

Solomon, of Elisha, and others. 'Tis said of Saul that God gave him another spirit'' (p. 3). His ideals, in the past and now, had always been those of an extraordinary political genius both "in the Camp [and] in the Cabinet." From Scripture he now inferred "that the souls of princes, men of nobility in birth and blood, especially such as the divine prescience has, as above, design'd and determin'd for great employment and glorious accions in life, and as are, *or are to be*, plac'd in high stations, are often times furnish'd thus in an extraordinary manner from a superior hand with powers suitable to, and capable of, the great things they are to do and the great figure they are to make in the world" (p. 3). "Men of the sword" (p. 16) coming to crowns via the sword, remain only "crown'd asses," tyrants and destroyers of their people. The great kings prove to be fathers and guides to their people. Such was Henry V, who understood "the duty and office of a king, who ought to be the father, protector, and vigilant defender, as well as the governor and monarch of his people and kingdom" (p. 32). "Nature fitted him for the field, learning fitted him for the throne" (p. 33).

Clifford Leech has remarked that "a dramatist returning to a group of characters already handled, taking up their story after a marked pause or an original terminal point, is frequently led to consider his subject more shrewdly."[91] With the last of Defoe's many voices in our mind, we can return to *The Farther Adventures of Robinson Crusoe* for Crusoe's last comment on his island adventure. He perhaps knew better than any of us what kind of polity he had established and what kind of king he was. After sending supplies to his tenants and Portuguese wives for his Spanish subjects, Crusoe writes:

> I have now done with my island, and all manner of discourse about it; and whoever reads the rest of my memorandums, would do well to turn his thoughts entirely from it. . .
> I was possessed with a wandering spirit, scorned all advantages; I pleased myself with being the patron of those people I placed there, and doing for them in a kind of haughty majestic way, like an old patriarchal monarch; providing for them, as if I had been father of the whole family, as well as of the plantation. But I never so much as pretended to plant in the name of any government or nation, or to acknowledge any prince, or to call my people subjects to any one nation more than another; nay, I never so much as gave the place a name, but left it as I found it, belonging to no man, and the people under no discipline or government but my own, who, though I had influence over them as father and benefactor, had no authority or power to act or command one way or other, farther than voluntary consent moved them to comply.[92]

---

[91] "The Two-Part Play; Marlowe and the Early Shakespeare," *Shakespeare Jahrbuch*, 94 (1958), 92. I owe this citation to my colleague, Professor Jack Brown.

[92] *The Farther Adventures*, in *The Works of Daniel Defoe*, vol. 2, ed. G. H. Maynadier (New York: Jensen Society, 1907), p. 185. Further citations will be noted in the text. For Defoe's final judgments on the Czar of Moscow, which would help to interpret Crusoe's Russian experience, see *The Compleat English Gentleman*, pp. 35–38. Defoe describes the Czar in language that echoes the fulsome language of *Of Royall Educacion*: he is a younger brother, "genius lent by Heaven" (p. 36), a complete union of "body and soul" (p. 36), and "a hero" (p. 37).

Many years later, stalled in his wanderings and forced to winter in Tobolsk, Siberia, Crusoe's thoughts suddenly return to "my beloved island" (p. 302). Tobolsk, "being the country where the state criminals of Muscovy . . . are all banished, this city was full of noblemen, princes, gentlemen, colonels, and, in short, all degrees of the nobility, gentry, soldiery, and courtiers of Muscovy" (p. 303). Crusoe meets a banished minister of state of the Czar. He is a strange figure, exiled from the court, living in a prison, who rejects Crusoe's offer of deliverance despite his claim earlier that "nothing that I know of in this world would move me to deliver myself from this state of banishment, except these two; first, the enjoyment of my relations; and, secondly, a little warmer climate" (p. 306). Recognizing, then, that the minister's "true felicity" (p. 304) bears an uncanny and disturbing resemblance to the "true Felicity" of Crusoe's father, and with full consciousness of the ambiguity and uncertainty in Defoe's portrait of this isolatto, we read the following dialogue when talk of Crusoe's "particular case began" (p. 303):

He had been telling me abundance of fine things of the greatness, the magnificence, the dominions, and the absolute power of the Emperor of the Russians. I interrupted him, and told him I was a greater and more powerful prince than ever the Czar of Muscovy was, though my dominions were not so large, or my people so many. The Russian grandee looked a little surprised, and fixing his eyes steadily upon me, began to wonder what I meant.

I told him his wonder would cease when I had explained myself. First, I told him I had the absolute disposal of the lives and fortunes of all my subjects; that notwithstanding my absolute power, I had not one person disaffected to my government or to my person in all my dominions. He shook his head at that, and said, there indeed I outdid the Czar of Muscovy. I told him that all the lands in my kingdom were my own, and all my subjects were not only my tenants, but tenants at will; that they would all fight for me to the last drop; and that never tyrant, for such I acknowledged myself to be, was ever so universally beloved, and yet so horribly feared, by his subjects.

After amusing them with these riddles in government for a while, I opened the case, and told them the story at large of my living in the island, and how I managed both myself and the people there that were under me, just as I have since minuted it down.
(p. 304)

Select bibliography

This is a select bibliography that includes the most significant of Defoe's works, works by his contemporaries bearing importantly on the subject of the study, and secondary works of pertinence and insight. Contemporary tracts, pamphlets, sermons, and works by Defoe and others, cited in the text and the notes, are indicated in the Index below. Unless otherwise noted, the place of publication of Defoe's works is London.

Defoe's Works

An Apology for the Army. In a short Essay on Fortitude, Etc. 1715
The Case of the Protestant Dissenters in Carolina. 1706
The Character of the Late Dr. Samuel Annesley. 1697
A Complete History of the Late Revolution. 1691
An Essay Upon Projects. 1697
Jure Divino. A Satyr in Twelve Books. 1706
The Letters of Daniel Defoe, ed. George H. Healey. Oxford: Clarendon Press, 1955
The Life and Strange Surprizing Adventures of Robinson Crusoe. 1719
The Original Power of the Collective Body of the People of England, Examined and Reasserted. 1702 (1701)
The Present State of the Parties in Great Britain. 1712
Reflections upon the Late Great Revolution. 1689
The Secret History of State Intrigues in the Management of the Scepter. 1715

Other Works

Ashcraft, Richard. *Revolutionary Politics and Locke's "Two Treatises of Government."* Princeton: Princeton University Press, 1986
Ashcraft, Richard and M. M. Goldsmith. "Locke, Revolution Principles, and the Formation of Whig Ideology." *Historical Journal,* 26 (1983), 786–800
Baxter, Stephen. *William III and the Defense of European Liberty, 1650–1702.* New York: Harcourt, Brace and World, 1966
Breen, T. H. *The Character of the Good Ruler: A Study of Puritan Political Ideas in New England, 1630–1730.* New Haven: Yale University Press, 1970
Daly, James. *Sir Robert Filmer and English Political Thought.* Toronto: University of Toronto Press, 1979
A Defence of Liberty Against Tyrants. A Translation of the Vindiciae Contra Tyrannos by Junius Brutus. Introduction Harold J. Laski, 1924; Gloucester, MA: Peter Smith, 1963

Dickinson, H. T. *Liberty and Property: Political Ideology in Eighteenth-Century Britain.* London: Weidenfeld and Nicolson, 1977

Earle, Peter. *The World of Defoe.* London: Weidenfeld and Nicolson, 1976

Eccleshall, Robert. *Order and Reason in Politics: Theories of Absolute and Limited Monarchy in Early Modern England.* Oxford: Oxford University Press, 1978

An Essay Upon Government. Wherein the Republican Schemes Reviv'd by Mr. Lock, Dr. Blackal, etc. are Fairly Consider'd and Refuted. London, 1705

Filmer, Robert. *Patriarcha and Other Political Works.* Ed. Peter Laslett. Oxford: Basil Blackwell, 1949

Goldie, Mark. "The Revolution of 1689 and the Structure of Political Argument. An Essay and an Annotated Bibliography of Pamphlets on the Allegiance Controversy." *Bulletin of Research in the Humanities,* 83 (1980), 473–564

Gough, J. W. *Fundamental Law in English Constitutional History.* Oxford: Clarendon Press, 1955

Gunn, J. A. W. *Beyond Liberty and Property: The Process of Self-Recognition in Eighteenth-Century Political Thought.* Kingston: McGill-Queen's University Press, 1983

Horwitz, Henry. *Parliament, Policy, and Politics in the Reign of William III.* Manchester: Manchester University Press, 1977

Kantorowicz, Ernst H. *The King's Two Bodies: A Study in Mediaeval Political Theology.* Princeton: Princeton University Press, 1957

Kenyon, J. P. "The Revolution of 1688: Resistance and Contract," in *Historical Perspectives: Studies in English Thought and Society in Honour of J. H. Plumb.* Ed. Neil McKendrick. London: Europa, 1975

Revolution Principles: The Politics of Party, 1689–1720. Cambridge: Cambridge University Press, 1977

Leslie, Charles. *The New Association Part II.* London, 1703

The Rehearsal. Four Volumes. London, 1708–9

Locke, John. *Two Tracts on Government.* Ed. Philip Abrams. London: Cambridge University Press, 1967

Two Treatises of Government. Ed. Peter Laslett. 2nd ed. London: Cambridge University Press, 1967

Mackworth, Humphrey. *A Vindication of the Rights of the Commons of England.* London, 1701

Pocock, J. G. A. *The Ancient Constitution and the Feudal Law.* Cambridge: Cambridge University Press, 1957

Political Aphorisms: Or, The True Maxims of Government Displayed. The 3rd Edition. London, 1691

Rabb, Felix. *The English Face of Machiavelli: A Changing Interpretation, 1500–1700.* London: Routledge and Kegan Paul, 1965

Sidney, Algernon. *Discourses Concerning Government. The Third Edition.* London, 1751

Skinner, Quentin. *The Foundations of Modern Political Thought.* 2 vols. Cambridge: Cambridge University Press, 1978

The Source of Our Present Fears Discover'd. London, 1703

Stephens, Edward. *The True English Government.* London, 1689

Tierney, Brian. *Religion, Law, and the Growth of Constitutional Thought, 1150–1650.* New York: Cambridge University Press, 1982

Toon, Peter, ed., *Puritans, The Millennium, and the Future of Israel.* Cambridge: Cambridge University Press, 1970

Tutchin, John. *The First Volume of Observators.* London, 1703

Tyrrell, James. *Bibliotheca Politica: or, An Enquiry Into the Antient Constitution of the English Government*. London, 1718
   Patriarcha non Monarcha. London, 1681
Weston, Corinne C. and Janelle R. Greenberg. *Subjects and Sovereigns: The Grand Controversy over Legal Sovereignty in Stuart England*. Cambridge: Cambridge University Press, 1981

Index